Migration in Perspectives

Migration in Perspectives

Towards Theology of Migration from the Margins

Edited by
Songram Basumatary

Gurukul Lutheran Theological College & Research Institute

United Evangelical Lutheran Churches in India

Christian World Imprints

First Published in 2018 by

Gurukul Publications
Gurukul Lutheran Theological College & Research Institute
in collaboration with and initiative of Rev. Dr. A. G. Augustine Jeyakumar, the Executive Secretary of
United Evangelical Lutheran Churches in India
94/95 Purasawalkam High Road, Kilpauk, Chennai-600010
gltc.principal@gmail.com
www.gltc.edu
Phone: +91 44 42651072

&

Christian World Imprints
Christian Publishing & Books from India
H-12 Bali Nagar, New Delhi-110015
info@christianworldimprints.com
www.ChristianWorldImprints.com
Phone: +91 11 25465925

ISBN: 978-93-5148-323-6 (HB)
ISBN: 978-93-5148-324-3 (PB)

Cover Design: Designed by Rev. Jeevaraj Anthony. The picture depicts the plight of migrants/refugees/displaced especially the women and children due to war/natural calamities.

Printed in India

Contents

III
TOWARDS THEOLOGY OF MIGRATION

Foreword

I am very much delighted to write few lines of introductory words about this volume of Gurukul Publication on a pertinent issue the world is facing today.

One of the serious issues the globalized world, society and people encountering today is the problem of migration. The landless farmers of Indian villages, mostly belonging to Dalit, Tribal and Adivasi communities who are deprived of all the basic rights in the society, are moving to metropolitan cities for livelihood and security in life. Migration of semi-skilled and unskilled people are growing at an alarmingly fast rate in the metropolitan cities. They are mostly absorbed as labour force in unorganised sectors with heavy workload, tremendous competition, poor pay, worst sanitation and insecurity, especially the women and children who undergo various kinds of misuse, abuse and physical violence.

In fact, the Constitution of India under Article 19 guarantees the fundamental rights to the citizen. The fundamental right includes the right to every citizen to travel, reside and carry out any trade, profession or business in any part of the country. However, in reality it is all opposite. The migrants are forced to work for long hours and live in a very pathetic conditions even without knowing what all constitutional rights they have. Even it is sad enough, no one seems worried about these poor migrants and their human rights.

The little historical creed that we find in the book of Deuteronomy reminds us with the verse "My father was a wandering Aramean" clearly elucidates how the Jewish people were asked to teach their children about their fore parents history in the Egypt as migrant slaves. Also this creed as reminiscence assures them that God walked with them, lived with them, suffered with them and finally delivered them with outstretched arms from the slavish migrant life they experienced in Egypt by providing them a land flowing with milk and honey. This creed also affirms that God is a faithful migrating God with the people who are suffering by migration. As a called out community how do we understand migration and its effects in today's globalized world? Does the church in her mission agenda have any space for the people who suffer by migration?

As the Lutheran communion in India predominantly consists of Dalits, Tribals and Aidvasis, the Gurukul Lutheran Theological College and Research Institute, the theological wing of the United Evangelical Lutheran Churches in India has a great responsibility in sensitizing the churches towards this serious issue. This indeed prompted the Gurukul Summer Institute to come out with a significant publication on this issue. The Gurukul Summer Institute used to be a powerful contributor to the theological enterprises. With a bold theological vision and a commitment to empower the downtrodden, the Gurukul Summer Institute publications always motivated the theological and ministerial fraternity to carry forward the legacy of Jesus's compassionate ministry towards the people at the margins. However, unfortunately it was not active for about two decades.

Thankfully, considering the importance and the significant contribution of the Gurukul Summer Institute to the theological and ministerial fields, the Gurukul has taken a painstaking effort to revive it. After a great struggle and the untiring efforts from the managements and the faculty, the Institute came back to life through this volume. I believe that this book - "*Migration in Perspectives*" would certainly challenge the readers to see the seriousness of the issue of migration and inspire them to think of possible strategies for practical action.

I believe that this publication would sensitize the readers and inspire them to work for the betterment of the poor migrants. I wish Gurukul should produce more theological input to recall local congregation and the society at large. May the Holy Spirit guide the readers to discern the living realities of the poor migrant workers in the society and motivate them to commit themselves for the emancipation of the suffering migrants.

With this note, I take this opportunity to thank the editor and convenor of the Gurukul Summer Institute, Rev. Dr. Songram Basumatary for shouldering great responsibility in bringing out this book with great passion and hard work. Also thanks to all the contributors of this book for their academic credibility. I also record our gratitude to the Christian World Imprints, New Delhi for publishing this book as a co-publisher and we are looking forward their continuous support to publish our Summer Institute publications in the future.

May God bless all of us!

In God's Mission,

Rev. Dr. A. G. Augustine Jeyakumar
Executive Secretary UELCI & LWF National Committee of India

04.10.2018

Introduction

Globally and locally, migration has become an inconceivable complex phenomenon in our times today. The surge of migration in general, and the inflow of refugees and migrant workers from one place to the other in particular, are increasing in alarming proportion. There are varieties of migration such as trans-nation, trans-state and trans-region taking place due to various factors. Some of the key factors of migration are political unrest, economic insecurity, ethnic tension, religious persecution and natural calamities. It is estimated that over three percent of the global population are migrants today. And it is predictable that the political and demographic forces, globalization and environmental degradation, economic distress and unemployment, ethnic and socio-religious tensions will lead to increase the population of migrants in drastic manner in the coming days. It is realised in our times that such trend of migration has affected each and every country of the globe, each and every states of those countries, each and every communities of every region, and every individuals of all communities.

If we look at locally too, there are migration of every kinds everywhere. In India in particular, the village to city or rural to urban migration is alarmingly increasing due to various push and pull factors like education, job opportunities, livelihood, comfort and security of life etc. Many of the migrants are forced to move out from their respective places and regions predominantly by socio-economic push factors in India.

Since migration takes place predominately due to economic factors, there are many tensions that emerges between the migrants and the natives of the host nation or region. Perhaps, there is always perceived mutual threats between the two. While the natives or claimed as "people of the land" attempt to use political power to overcome their fears of economic defeat and cultural subordination to the migrants, if they are better educated, more highly skilled and more enterprising; the migrants claim for equal access to opportunities, equal treatment at per with the natives and protection by the state. In responding such issues, the state often take biased position and approach due to which the migrants mostly become susceptible to various injustices, discriminations and even human rights violations.

Such phenomenon of migration is seen and addressed in many ways by different organisations and institutions around the world. First and foremost, it is seen as mere territorial, political and economic ***issues***. Approach of addressing the situation also is from the perspective of the natives and the dominants. Looking at the issue and addressing it from the perspective of vulnerability is very little or even absent in many of the discourses on migration. Perhaps, humanitarian approach and response to the issue of refugees or migrants are always charity-centred. Their life situations and experiences are mere site of pity, charity or social service.

Therefore, what is necessary against such trend in addressing the issue of migration is a concerted effort to look at it as a challenge to humanity and human community as a whole, rather than mere political and economic challenges. One needs to look at it not as an external territorial issue, but an internal issues facing peoples and communities of various societies. One of the most worrisome serious concerns is the plight of migrants who are strangers in their own Mother Land because of abject economic systems and the indifferent political culture and polity. If we see the situation of migrant workers, especially in Indian villages, towns and cities alike; they are mere object of economy. The utter poverty and unemployment push them out from their native places for survival and the utter exploitative trends of globalised market economy pull them inn to work like machines for economic growth.

This raises numerous questions on the approach taken to address the issue of migration: Is migration in itself an issue? What concerns are talked about around the issue of migration? Is it mere demographic or regional concern? Is it cultural and religious concern? Is it mere economic and political issue? If it is so, of whom? Migrants or the states? Is it not the issue of humanity, human identity, dignity and human rights? Ultimately, is it not a theological concern?

Perhaps, two options or possibilities of looking at the whole phenomenon of migration is at the fore. Since migration is a universal phenomenon, the first option is theorizing or theologizing it conceptually. Secondly, since migration today is a complex phenomenon of human society with question of life and death issues, the option is to address it practically. While following the first option, the challenge is how best we can construct theories and theologies that would serve as an epistemological tools for the second option. Conversely, while following the second option, the challenge is what are the best practical strategies or steps we can take to address the issue of migration that would help both the migrant people/community and the host people/community.

Perhaps, the first option seems easy and possible that anyone can do. But when it comes to the question of relevance to the complex plethora of migration, it appears mere abstract concept and notion as well as too hypothetical and mystical speculation. For example, the recent times' theological exploration on migration have come up with beautiful theological expressions and claims such as "Migrant God" or "God is the primordial migrant" or "Biblical God is a migrant God" or "Christian God is God of the Migrants", "Migrant Jesus" or "Jesus the Migrant", "Salvation History is a Migration History" or "No Migration no Salvation", "No Migration no Mission", "History of Christianity is a Migration History" or "No migration no Church" so on and so forth. What all these mean to the practical reality of issues around migration in our times? In fact, possible answer people may give would be either "it means lot" or "it means nothing!"

Coming back to the second option, we got lot of challenges. As noted above, different institutions and organizations have approached and addressed the issue differently. Among many, two umbrella approach undertaken worldwide are Diplomatic and Humanitarian. While solution to the issue according to first approach, which is political in nature, is diplomatically sought between country to country, people to people and community to community; the second approach predominantly go for practical action in meeting the immediate basic human needs as well as human right issues. As it is already expressed, these approaches have their limitations.

Now the question is what is the link between the first option and the second? Here lies the challenge of connectivity. The conclusion here is that without practical action mere concept and knowledge has no meaning, and without sound conceptual framework and epistemological tools the mere practical action has no relevance or sustainable impact.

Hence, how Theo-intelligentsia and Church are to look at and address the issue of migration in terms of epistemology and functionality becomes a challenging task. It is an established fact here that migration is a complex phenomenon. Hence, reflecting migration theologically and proposing a theology of migration for practical action is all the more a challenging task. However, considering the reality of migration and its wide and depth impact on all realms of nation and peoples' lives, we cannot any longer treat migration as stepchild or putting it at the margins of our theological reflections. Rather it must be at the centre of theological thinking and reflection. Both the dogmatic or systematic theology as well as contextual theologies need to move to the sites of the reality of migration so far neglected.

With strong affirmation on the necessity of reflecting migration from the perspective of every dominant theological disciplines, this volume therefore tries to reflect in line with dominant theological disciplines as well as reflections from the perspective of margins. Notwithstanding the critical aspects raised above, indeed migration is a running stream in the Bible, Christian mission, History of Church and so on. Perhaps the salvation history in the Bible is a "migration-bearing", a story of wandering people of God. From Genesis to Revelation, we could see stories of migration, and thus, the core theme of theology and the Church – the issue of migration.

Considering all the ambiguities and the prospects mentioned above, this volume of Gurukul Publication, which is the outcome of Gurukul Summer Institute 2018, tries to venture into the depth of the phenomenon of migration in diverse perspectives. Threading through the ambiguous views and approaches, attempt is made to explore and highlight the positive dimensions in migration as well as challenges therein. The basic hypothetical question that runs through the volume is, whether migration is a blessing or a curse for both migrants and the hosts! Though mix or even ambiguous answers are evident in various articles, one fact remains clear that the issue of migration is not a mere human concern, but it is a divine concern.

The first two articles on the go are general overviews on the phenomenon and issue of migration. The article by ***Bernard D' Sami*** on "Labour Migration in India: Issues and Concerns" which was initially presented as Key Note address in the Gurukul Summer Institute-2018 is a kind of ground breaking epistemological tools in terms of concept, notion and different categories of migration. The second article of the first set – "Manipulation of Migrant Labour Flow and Capital Accumulation by Free Market Economy" is a critical look at whole issues of migration from the perspective of market economy. By diagnosing the manipulative nature of Free Market Economy, the author, ***Livingstone Arphutaraj*** brings out very clearly that the migrant labourers are mere commodity of market economy system. The economic boons brought by free market economy are all at the cost of migrant labourers' lives and to serve only the few section of people who are affluent. Therefore, the author calls for a challenge to transform the 'free market culture' into a 'fair market culture' by upholding the values that stand against injustice, inequality and exploitation in order that the migrant labourers too find a life worth living.

The second set of articles in the volume is reading migration from multi-faceted perspectives. The first article in the set is from an Old Testament Perspective. The article – "Migration Motif in the Ancestral Narratives" by ***Nagaiyasamy N.S. Samuel*** brings out a clear fact that the migration is not a modern phenomenon. While explicating the inherent migration motif in the ancestral narratives, the author comes out with a conclusion that the ancestors moved from one place to another place not for the commercial purposes, nor to the cities to settle permanently, but under the guidance of the divine, travelled from place to place until Yahweh assured them the promise of the child(ren) and the land.

Yet another Old Testament article – "Justice for the *Ger* (*rg*) in the OT Traditions against the Exilic Context" by ***S. Jaganathan*** deals with the issue of Justice in relation to the reality of migration. By explicating the concept of *Ger* in the OT Traditions, the author brings out a quite strong conclusion that the very migration experience of the people of God during exilic period served as an instrument to re-form and stabilize their identity and restore and revivify their Jewish heritage. Disputable the conclusion may be, but the fact seems to be true that in the context of dehumanizing situations, a sense of self-worth, self-assertion or self-affirmation of ones' identity and human dignity are pre-requisites of freedom and liberation.

The third article from the Biblical Perspective is "Strangers and Aliens in 1 Peter: Towards Constructing a Symbiotic Community" in which the author, ***K. Balakrishnan*** explores into the depth of first epistle of Peter with detail backgrounds and scholarly discussions on the concepts and challenges of "Strangers and Aliens", and then envisages and proposes for Church as an *oikos* community which is characterised by reconciliation, brotherhood/sisterhood and embracive fellowship. He strongly put forward challenges to the Church to be a place of hospitality, healing and wholeness. The Church being an *oikos* of God she cannot, but become an agent of transformation and restoration of the broken people and broken world!

The fourth perspectival article – "Challenges from the Migrants to the Church-in-Mission" presents an important Missiological challenge that 'diaspora mission', 'reverse mission' and 'intercultural mission' are some of the challenges from migrants to the church-in-mission. By exploring on how missiologists have attempted to address the complex and yet fluid situation of 'migration', the author, ***K. David Udayakumar*** also makes a strong practical challenge that the church-in-mission should be prepared to meet both the physical as well as spiritual need of the people, and at the same time be bold enough to address injustices and violence done to the migrant people.

The fifth perspectival article – "Is God still the Refuge for Refugees: An Interfaith Perspective?" is an exploration of the understanding of migration in various religious traditions, particularly in Christianity, Hinduism and Islam. By highlighting inseparable connection between religion and migration, the author of the article, ***J.M.P. Thomas Birla*** envisions that the inter-faith relations can make people of all religious walks realize that God alone owns the entire creation and the whole human race are the members of one family. The author calls for an openness of hearts and minds among the people to see God in and among migrants and refugees in order to find answer to the question, "Is God still the refuge for refuges?" The article is beautifully concluded with a challenging theological note that it is not whether God is refuge for refugee, but whether God Himself/Herself is refugee in the religious camps!

The sixth article on the row – "Immigrants or Inhabitants: A Search for Identity from the Margin" looks at migration from the perspective of the margins, particularly from Dalits and Adivasi contexts, where the author, ***Anthony Jeevaraj*** takes the discourse on a different footage. While answering the question of whether Dalits and Adivasi are migrants or natives, the author with historical evidences bring out a fact clear that as a result of migration of powerful Aryans, the original inhabitants of India, the Dalits and Adivasis have become migrants and refugees in their own lands leading to undergo experiences of identity crisis, injustice, oppression and discriminations in all spheres of life for generations.

The seventh perspectival article is "Migration in Gender Perspective" by ***W.S. Annie***. Here the whole phenomenon and issue of migration is read from the perspective of gender and author makes attempt to feminise the whole phenomenon and issues of migration, particularly from the vulnerable women's perspective. The author challengingly brings out the reality of the migrant-ness of women throughout their life and the dehumanizing experiences of women as migrants. Women are first of all migrants in their own homes and society. They are not permanent member or resident in their family and village or town. Once they are married they migrate to husband's house or family. Therefore, with various case narratives and few theological models like Trinitarian sharing, the author challenges and envisages an embracive and inclusive community where everyone are at home.

The eighth and the final article of the second set is looking at migration from yet another perspective from the margins, particularly from the geographical location known as "Seven Sisters", the North East India. The author of the article, ***Walotemjen*** elaborately highlights the intricacy of migration and why and how the migrants from the region in other Indian states and cities are vulnerable to injustice and different kinds of discriminations and exploitations. The author is of the opinion that the migrants from the region, particularly working in various companies, hospitality and beauty industries undergo such experiences just because of racial differences or distinctiveness as they by no means in appearance look similar to other Indians.

The third set of the volume is a proposal towards constructing theology of Migration that contains two enlightening articles. The first is – "Migration: Exploring a We Communion Theology" by ***Daniel Kirubaraj*** in which the author after analysing the phenomenon and issues of Migration and Migrants, and the interface between Migration and Theology, Migration and Suffering, Migration and Communication, proposes an insightful theology called – "We Communion." The second on the set and the final article of the volume – "Discerning the Signs of the Times: Towards Theology of Migration" is the climax of the volume where the author ***N.G. Prasuna***, considering the signs of the times in relation to migration, engages in a serious theological reflection. Focussing on the concept and issue of identity crisis, the author explores some hermeneutical tools towards constructing a Theology of Migration and calls the church to understand the significance of migration and provide space for migrants to deal with their identity crisis and to connect themselves to God and to God's community.

Though the contents of the articles in this volume may be just a beginning to see the issues around migration theologically in multi-dimensional perspectives, it is hoped and believed that this volume in small way would offer some conceptual tools and epistemological resource to the wider academic world about the huge challenge of theological reflection ahead, and the practical action awaited from the policy makers, civil society and the Church as a whole.

With this concluding note, I, as convenor of the Gurukul Summer Insitute-2018 and the editor of the volume, congratulate and thank all the contributors of this volume of Gurukul Publication. I also extend my sincere gratitude to the responsible governing officials of the Gurukul Lutheran Theological College & Research Institute, particularly the Executive Secretary of UELCI, Rev. Dr. A.G. Augustine Jeyakumar and then Principal of the College Rev. Dr. K. David Udayakumar for entrusting me the humble responsibility of looking after the Summer Institute and all the encouragement and support offered. Last, but not the least, a heartfelt thanks to all the organizing committee members, participants and the respondents of the articles. Let the blessings received by the readers of this volume be their portion!

Songram Basumatary
Editor

October, 2018

I

OVERVIEW ON PHENOMENON OF MIGRATION

1

Labour Migration in India
Issues and Concerns

Bernard D' Sami

Migrants: International and Inter-State Migrants

India has both the categories. People from India go out to other countries to work at the same time people from northern and eastern states from India are descending on the Southern States as migrant workers. It is estimated that around 12 million Indians work with Indian passports which means they are in the destination country for work and they are expected to return back once when they complete their contract period. Most of the Indians go to Gulf region to work, it is estimated that there are 6 million Indians working in the Gulf region besides Singapore, Malaysia and other South East Asian countries. Kerala and Tamil Nadu have long been known for sending workers to the above countries. Now the trend is changing the new states that are opening up for labour migration to Gulf countries are UP, Rajasthan and Bihar. Large numbers of workers are leaving from these states for wages as low as Rs. 10,000 to 15, 000 per month. Tamil Nadu and Kerala continue to have a big stock of its labour in the Gulf and in the South East Asian countries.

Migrant Workers: Definition

A country's population is altered by fertility, mortality, and migration. Of these three factors, migration is the most difficult to measure. In India, the two major sources of information on migration are the reports provided by the National Sample Survey Organisation (NSSO) and the census of India's migration tables. It is the NSSO that is responsible for recording internal migration. The census of India defines migrants as '*one whose place of birth (PoB) is different from his or her place of enumeration*'. The PoB is the main criterion used to distinguish a migrant from a non-migrant. Since 1971, however, the census of India included place of residence (PoLR) as another criterion to the definition of migrant. The

PoLR states a migrant is *'a person whose last residence is different from the place where he or she is enumerated'*. A 'return migrant', on the other hand, is identified as a person who has returned to his or her place of origin. But while NSSO uses the concept of native place and usual place of residence (UPR) as criteria for defining a migrant worker, it has neglected to take into account the movement of labour from India to other countries. The above two sources are relating to internal migration within the country taking various factors into consideration.[1] There is no way to get an exact number of Indians migrated to other countries for work. The data provided are from the MOIA (Ministry of Overseas Indian Affairs) through the Protector of Emigrant (PoE) offices in India.

Current Scenario

In 2015, the number of international migrants' worldwide – people residing in a country other than their country of birth – was the highest ever recorded, having reached 244 million (from 232 million in 2013). As a share of the world population, however, international migration has remained fairly constant over the past decades, at around 3%. While female migrants constitute only 48% of the international migrant stock worldwide and 42% in Asia, women make up the majority of international migrants in Europe (52.4%) and North America (51.2%).[2]

UN High Level Dialogue on International Migration and Development took place between 3-4 October 2013 at the UN in New York. This is the second UN HLD which brought various stake holders involved in migration for discussion. *It has been estimated that half of the world's 214 million international migrants are migrant workers* (Martin 2010) *of whom a rising proportion is women.* The feminization of labour migration has occurred over the last few decades. In Asia, Philippines and Indonesia are major labour export countries and majority of them are women.

Labour Migration

During 2012, 747,041 workers emigrated from India after obtaining emigration clearance. There are seventeen countries for which ECR (Emigration Check Required) is mandatory. Those who fall under the category of ECR are mostly the labour migrants who are unskilled or semi-skilled. States of Uttar Pradesh, Kerala, Andhra Pradesh, Bihar, Tamil Nadu, Rajasthan and Punjab were the leading sending States in order of the numbers who emigrated from these States. The pattern of migration has dramatically changed in the last five years. It used to be Kerala and Tamil Nadu at the top of the list of migrants who moved out

---

1 Migration in India: Data sources by Gayathri Balagopal, *Review of Development and Change,* vol. IV, no. 2 (July-December, 1999).

2 International Organization of Migrants (IOM) Report 2015.

of India for work. Now it is from UP, Bihar, Rajasthan and Punjab from where a large number of migrant workers are going to Gulf countries.

Remittances

India gets the highest amount of remittances 70 billion US$ from abroad by overtaking countries which are known for getting huge remittances like Mexico and China. India's remittance mainly comes from the gulf region which means it is the ordinary workers who go out of India and faithfully send the money back home. It is shocking to note that the remittances are next to exports in foreign exchange earnings. Our remittances are more than the ODA (Overseas Development Assistance) to India by other industrialized countries.

The US and the Paris based Financial Action task force on 'Money Laundering' are depriving the very countries most need remittances by imposing blanket sanctions against governments and financial intermediaries suspected of funding terrorist organizations. As part of their effort to monitor suspicious transactions, western countries are compelling institutions that transfer money abroad to install expensive new compliance technologies that poor sending countries cannot afford.[3]

Migration and Trade

Various studies have been presented on the huge economic gains for the host countries mostly developing countries in promoting this temporary movement of natural persons (TMNP or Mode 4). Poverty will increase in the sending countries by the liberalization of the flow of low-skilled workers in Mode 4 agreements. Human dimensions in such migratory or cross-border movements of people are largely ignored. When migrant workers move to another country, they will often been entering a significant different social, cultural, and work environment without any of the traditional (family or community based) support systems that they are accustomed to in their home countries. The social and economic impact of the movement of migrant workers, who in general tend to belong to prime working and child bearing and self-rearing age sectors of the sending countries' population and who also tend to possess physical and or intellectual skills most needed by their home countries' economies are often overlooked or underappreciated by such economic assessments of the benefits of GATS Mode 4 liberalization.[4]

It is the poor who are forced to migrate from the source to destination. Hence, their inherent vulnerability and socio-economic marginalization make extremely high the risk of gross human rights, health and labour violations occurring in

3 Devesh Kapur and John Micheal, Migrants New Payoff by in Foreign Policy, Nov-Dec, 2003.

4 "Migration and Trade: A Report from Cancun," a background paper prepared by Genevieve Gencianos of Migrant Rights International collaboration with the National Network for Immigrant and Refugee Rights.

such a 'mechanized trading system of labour utilization' that is inherent in the WTO system. Since GATS Mode 4 movements of people are strictly temporary, the receiving country has no obligation to accord to the worker social security and other rights that may be entitled to a person who decide to migrate.[5]

Issues relating to out-migration and out-migrants

Push Factors such as inadequate employment opportunities, poor living conditions, little or no education, conflict, environment disaster, structural adjustments policies, violation of fundamental and human rights, discrimination based on caste, religion and gender and family breakdown are major causes for the migrant workers to leave the country. These are the main reaons for migrants to move out of the country and this has to be addressed by the sending country.

Regulate the labour migrants by establishing a central Man Power Corporation to protect the interest of the migrant workers. (along the lines of overseas Manpower Corporation in some of the states who regulate the skilled/ professional's migration) Action to be taken or erring agents who cheat the migrant workers left and right. Many migrant workers suffer financial loss due to the cost involved in migration (agents collect huge money) The Protector of Emigrants (PoE's) offices deal only with the Emigration Clearance Required (ECR) category of migrant workers which is very small with the volume of migrants workers who go out of India for work.

Migration is more than four decades old in Asia. The lessons learnt are enormous. Top priority has to be given to both the sending and receiving countries to regulate the migrant labour recruitment industry. There are multiple layers of agents in the sending countries. It is a well-known fact that migrant workers have to spend huge money; so they sell their land and other assets in order to go abroad. This recruitment industry is outsourced to private travel agents who fleece the migrant workers by getting exorbitant money. There are many workers who are smuggled and trafficked out of the country for 3 D jobs (dirty, dangerous and difficult condition of jobs).

Bilateral Agreements are singed with receiving countries to address such issues. Thailand has instituted agreements with Cambodia, Lao PDR and Myanmar to introduce procedures for employment and return of workers and to apply national labour laws to protect migrant workers' rights. India too has signed many bilateral agreements which perhaps needs to be revisited and wages component has to be revised every year and protection mechanisms have to be monitored and improved.

One good example model for the protection of the interest of migrant workers is which is to be replicated in other states is the **model of Kerala,** - Non-Resident Kerala Affairs (NORKA). State of Kerala has made it as a department. This department has introduced several programmes for the returnee migrants.

5 Ibid.

Many social welfare measures are undertaken to protect the migrant workers and their families

To amend existing laws and initiate new laws to ensure that they contain penal sanctions for anyone who engages in the *trafficking of human beings* or who violates the human rights of migrants. Government must activate its enforcement and administrative structure on a broad front to reduce trafficking and smuggling of migrants.

Standard Labour Contracts must be in place. The right of the women to work and travel is affected by the age restriction (30 years) in the context of feminization of migration women should be allowed to take up work and government to provide separate MoU's with countries which require domestic workers on the lines developed by UNIFEM. In 2003, the Jordanian Ministry of labour endorsed a standard working contract for non-Jordanian domestic workers defining rights and responsibilities for the migrants and employers.

Another concern is of *Undocumented workers*. The undocumented workers are arrested in countries like Singapore, Malaysia and in the gulf countries and they are sent to detention centres where they experience caning, one-time food, sexual abuse so on and so forth. The sending countries through their diplomatic and necessary steps to get them back to the country. For example, the Legislation in the Philippines includes a comprehensive definition of irregular migration that includes rights violation against migrant workers and also includes trafficking as aggravating circumstances in illegal recruitment meriting serious penalties.

In order to reduce the vulnerability of migrant workers *Pre-Migration* and *Pre-departure* programmes have to be introduced by the government as well as by the civil society organizations. India should sign the international convention on protection of the rights of migrant workers and their families. The convention will protect migrant workers in the host countries as well their families in our country.

Inter-State Migrants

Nature of Migration

Migration in India is primarily of two types: (a) Long-term migration, resulting in the relocation of an *individual* or household and (b) Short-term or seasonal/ circular migration, involving back and forth movement between a source and destination. Estimates of short-term migrants vary from 15 million (NSSO 2007–2008) to 100 million.[6] Yet, macro surveys such as the Census fail to adequately capture flows of short-term migrants and do not record secondary reasons for migration.

6 Deshingkar and Akter, *Migration and Human Development in India*, UNDP Human Development Reports, 2009.

Economic Survey of India 2017

In the five years ended 2016, an average of nine million people migrated between states every year for either education or work, according to Economic Survey 2016-17. That's almost double the inter-state migration recorded in 2001-2011 and captured by Census 2011. The survey reveals that states like Delhi, Maharashtra, Tamil Nadu, and Gujarat attract large numbers of migrants from the Hindi-speaking states of Uttar Pradesh, Bihar, and Madhya Pradesh. According to the survey, internal migration rates have dipped in Maharashtra and surged in Tamil Nadu and Kerala, reflecting the growing pull factor of southern states in India's migration dynamics. Language does not seem to be a demonstrable barrier to the flow of people—a trend reflected in the southern states attracting people from the North. Inter-state migration was almost four times that of migration within states, reinforcing the perception that language is ceasing to be a deciding factor in migration. Out-migration rate or the rate at which people have moved out is increased in Madhya Pradesh, Bihar and Uttar Pradesh and dipped in Assam. The survey reinforces the fact that the less affluent states have more out-migrants and the most affluent states are the largest recipients of migrants.

Push Factors:

- Agriculture failure – land is no more productive and the climate change resulting in excessive rain or drought results in the failure of agriculture and this result in distress migration.
- The lands owned by the scheduled tribes are less productive because of the primitive ways of farming. When their production is less, agriculture is not any more profitable. So, people from tribal lands are migrating in large number to the cities.
- As the states in which the tribal's live are rich in mineral resources. In the name of development such as mining, Dams, industries and wild-life sanctuaries (Chhattisgarh, Jharkhand, Santal areas of West Bengal, MP) and other projects for private players displaces them in large number. As IDP's they become inter-state migrants.
- Industrial growth is some states Orissa, Bihar, eastern UP, parts of Bengal, Telengana, Chhattisgarh and Jharkhand are far below the industrial growth in other states.
- Lack of job opportunities, poverty, conflicts based on caste and religion are a major push factor.
- The red-corridor; where people are either caught with the security forces or Maoists try to leave for secure future with their children.
- Low human development indicators such as lack of educational facilities for children, no or poor medical facilities, transport, water facilities – all reduce the quality of life or standard of life.
- Natural disasters – floods, earthquake and drought.

- Feudal system and bonded labour still prevailing in some parts of the central, northern and eastern India also has resulted in Inter-state migration. One can also see an element of bondage in the inter-state migration.

The Pull Factors:

- Expectation of higher wages and the hope of providing education for the children/siblings.
- Family migration for better wages and to escape feudal bondage system and low wages as agricultural workers.
- A greater social and economic security.
- Absence of gun/bomb culture makes them to come to South as peaceful areas.
- Political, religious and social freedom.
- Possibility for sending children to school
- The freedom to move single or as family.

Who Migrates?

Women constitute an overwhelming majority of migrants, 70.7 percent of internal migrants as per Census 2001, and 80 per cent of total internal migrants as per NSSO (2007-08). About 30 percent of internal migrants in India belong to the youth category in the 15-29 years age group. *Child migrants* are estimated at approximately 15 million. Furthermore, several studies have pointed out that migration is not always permanent and seasonal and circular migration is widespread, especially among the socio-economically deprived groups, such as the Scheduled Castes (SCs), Scheduled Tribes (STs) and Other Backward Castes (OBCs), who are asset-poor and face resource and livelihood deficits.

The 2011 census also indicates sex differentials in the inter-state migrants. Males dominate in the rural to urban migration accounting for 47%. It is single male migration largely. Rural to rural migration where the females are more compared to males. 38% of women are migrating from rural to rural areas.[7]

The Pattern of Migration

The pattern of migration differs from state to state and sector to sector. Those involved in agriculture move to the cities to work in construction work, their wages are low and they work for more hours. They usually migrate as family and the whole family resides in the construction premises. Vulnerability of children is greater in such conditions. Those who migrate to work in the manufacturing side learn skills and their wages are better than the construction work. Here the

7 Aijaz Ahmad, "An Analysis of Internal Migration Types in India in Purview of its Social and Economic Impacts," *EPRA International Journal of Economic and Business Review*, vol. 4, no. 1 (January 2016): 162.

migration is more a single male migration. They all live together in rental houses and cook and eat together.

Problems Faced by Internal Migrants

The constraints faced by migrants are many - lack of formal residency rights; lack of identity proof; lack of political representation; inadequate housing; food insecurity, inadequate access to public health, low-paid, insecure or hazardous work; extreme vulnerability of women and children to trafficking and sex exploitation; exclusion from state-provided services such as health and education and discrimination based on ethnicity, religion, class or gender. Limited access to state-provided services such as health and education; extreme vulnerability of women and children migrants to trafficking and sex exploitation.[8]

Conclusion

Our country was able to get out of the economic crisis in the 90's as well as in the last five years due to the good Forex position (Foreign exchange reserve) and this is exactly the contribution of the migrant workers. It is they who provide the much needed oxygen to our economy. These are the workers who go out of the country as an individual. It is single male/female migration which makes their families vulnerable back home. Increasingly governments are for the remittances and not for protecting the migrant workers in the destination country and their families in the sending country. The social cost of migration is families getting separated, children grow without the care and concern of the father, women headed households are numerous. Problems faced by the spouses in the absence of their husbands in enormous within the family and in the community. While huge money comes to our country in the form of remittances their welfare goes for a toss.

8 UNESCO/ UN-HABITAT, 2012; and UNESCO Internal Migration in India Initiative 2013.

2

Free Market Economy and Labour Migration
The Dynamics of Manipulation and Exploitation

Livingstone Arputharaj

The shocking photo of the dead body of three year old Alan Kurdi on the shores of Mediterranean Sea woke up many people around the world to see the horrific realities of refugees. It also brought to light the merciless fences and walls of the high economic nations which once were built by sweat and blood of migrants. On the one hand, affluent nations desperately want millions of migrant labour force to build their sports stadiums and tall structures in scorching fatal heat, and on the other hand, there is resounding slogans like 'build the wall' to keep migrants away 'to protect the economy'. Such hypocritical standpoints clearly depict the exploitative and inhuman nature of our planet's socio-economic structures that ladle out to the rich from the plates of the poor. Of course, the economic gains brought by migration both to the host region and that of the origin cannot be dismissed. Nevertheless, the ever expanding economic inequalities where the wealth of three richest people on the planet is more than the combined GDP of 48 poorest countries[1] forces us to question the credibility of the economic structures that claim progress and growth. One must be critical of the fact that the socio-political and economic dynamics in the age of Free Market Economy[2] serves the interest of the dominant ones and thereby widening the disparities between rich and the poor.

1 The combined wealth of Microsoft's Bill Gates, Walmarts' Walton family, and the Sultan of Brunei is reported to be more than the combine GDP of 48 poorest countries of the world housing 600 million people. Satvinder Singh Juss, *International Migration and Global Justice* (Aldershot: Ashgate Publishing Limited, 2006), viii.

2 Market Economy denotes the process of production wherein the entrepreneur analyses the demand, availability of raw materials, labour and engages in business activity. Market thus refers to this process wherein business interactions between the sellers and the buyers take place. Steven Kates, *Free Market Economic: An Introduction for General Reader* (Cheltenham: Edward Elgar, 2014), 18.

It is important to note that the majority of migrant population migrate for economic reasons and work as labour force. And as the Free Market Economy play a vital role in accelerating mobility of human beings, it also makes millions of migrant labourers readily available in the global market.[3] Here the questions arise as to why do the Free Market that has *laissez faire*[4] as its core principle demands unrestricted flow of capital and trade across borders but at the same time restricts migrant labour? Is not migration of labour force manipulated to facilitate accumulation of wealth? Why do governments fail to respond to the indifference shown towards migrant work force in terms of wages, security and basic living conditions? It is a reality that hundreds of migrant dead bodies return to the home countries in highly suspicious circumstances. Such reality of migrant labour force demands for a critical outlook at the very structures of the Free Market economy which exploit them. Towards this end, this article makes an effort to critically analyse the role of Free Market Economy in labour force migration especially those pertaining to the unorganised sectors under the label 'unskilled' labourers. While doing this, a brief history of migration through economic lens and contemporary phenomenon of migration is presented with few conceptual and theoretical notes as tool to understand the issue addressed.

Brief History of Migration through Economic Lens

Migration is not a new phenomenon. It is perhaps an integral part of the evolutionary process of living beings, particularly the human species.[5] The ancient history is filled with narratives of exodus from one place to another for diverse reasons. There were mass exodus to find suitable places of habitation, to escape famines, political and religious oppression, droughts and also to do trade and business. The history of nomadic people and their patterns of life was nothing, but the history of migration. The expansion of Greek and Roman Colonies were primarily based on migration. Their Empires' prosperity was based on trade and economic interactions. Even in the medieval age migration was an important factor in settlements across the globe especially the west. There were free movement of traders across countries.[6]

In recent history, the Fifteenth to Seventeenth Centuries marked as the era of colonisation, saw millions of labourers forced to migrate to build and establish settlements in the new world of America. It is estimated that around 15 million slaves left Africa prior to 1850 to work in the mines and plantations owned

3 Eliot Dikinson, *Globalisation & Migration. A World in Motion* (Lanham: Rowman & Littlefield, 2017), 5.

4 Laissez faire is a French word which means 'leave alone' referring to a market where there is no external interference of restrictions. Kenneth S. Friedman, *Myths of the Free Market* (New York: Algora Publishing, 2003), 2.

5 Dennis C. Canterbury, *Capital Accumulation and Migration* (Leiden: Brill Publications, 2012), 1.

6 Jonathan W. Moses, *International Migration...*, 38.

by Europeans.[7] Due to anti-slavery movements and the consequent abolition of slavery colonialism resorted to indentured labour where they were made to sign contracts for five years and were given wages, housing and free transport. A large number of indentured labourers were from Asia and were transported between the colonies. However, their poor living conditions and wages along with criminalisation by laws made indentured labour yet another variation of slavery.[8]

The late Nineteenth Century and early Twentieth Century witnessed the advancement of industrial revolution and ideologies of liberalism began to spread across nations. It is not just the technological advancement that propelled industrial revolution rather it is the cheap labour force from Asia and Africa played a prime role in keeping the momentum of industrial revolution across the globe.[9] However, liberal trade encouraged free flow of capital and products but ironically restricted migrant labour like never before. Stringent policies and regulations were imposed to restrict people entering their nations based on their colour, skill, skin and nationality. These restrictions got even severe with the outbreak of World Wars. World had to grapple with the refugee crisis due to these wars which gave rise to the UN Refuge Convention in 1951 recognising the right of an individual to cross boundaries and to seek protection.[10] The Twenty First Century world is witnessing migration in an unprecedented proportion and increase in migrant population at large scale and thereby making issue of migration more complex than ever before.

Such phenomenon of migration has become a matter of concern in our times. The history reveals that the drive to migrate for survival is something that is deeply imbibed in human behaviour and is a phenomenon as old as humanity. The human migration since primitive times was owing to the combination of many reasons. Among those reasons, search for survival and improvement in the living conditions are the basic ones. The migration of ancient people therefore is seen as search for fundamental needs and the hospitality extended towards benign strangers as a must virtue.[11]

The complexity of migration in our times has gone to the extent that even defining and comprehending its nuances and dynamics has become very difficult. Of course, the human migration in common can be defined as changing residence, whether temporary or permanent, from one geographical location to another with varying distance of travel undertaken. For the very Latin word *migra* for

---

7 Jonathan W. Moses, *International Migration* ..., 43-44.

8 Robin Cohen, *Migration and its Enemies. Global Capital, Migrant Labour and the Nation-State* (Aldershot: Ashgate Publishing Limited, 2009), 20.

9 Nalin Kumar Mohapatra, "Migration and its Impact on Security of Central Asia," *India Quarterly* 69/2 (June, 2013): 134.

10 Jonathan W. Moses, *International Migration*..., 50-54.

11 Jonathan W. Moses, *International Migration: Globalization's Last Frontier* (Bangkok: White Lotus Co. Ltd, 2006), 39.

migration means 'to move from one place to another.'[12] However, among spatial demographic migration, it also involves crossing of economic, administrative and community boundaries.[13] It is perhaps an economic and social process as well which not only occurs as a result of but also results in socio economic, political and cultural changes. Due to this reason, and more so, the nexus between migration and free market economy with its highly interconnected structures, the issue of migration has become all the more complex phenomenon than ever before. Therefore, a serious scrutiny in understanding and evaluating the socio-economic dynamics of migration becomes an inescapable necessity.

Taxonomy of Migration: Patterns and Particulars

Migration patterns have been analysed by many based on the factors that drive individual's decisions, socio-political conditions, boundaries that they cross and the migrant's compliance to the policies and regulations of host nations.

The major classification of migration is into two viz. *forced and voluntary migration*. Forced migration is understood as the migration done in circumstances where an individual is forced to flee due to persecution, war, violence or natural disasters. Voluntary is often understood as the migration done by an individual with economic motives without any external pressures like that of the former. According to Alexander Betts forced migration can be defined as "the movement that takes place under significant structural constraint that results from an existential threat."[14] People are forced to leave their homes and their places of origin due to several factors such as war, conflicts, violence, natural and human made disasters and so on. According to UN report, every minute 20 people are displaced forcibly from home.[15] However, this dichotomy doesn't hold very strong as many of the "voluntary" migrations are covertly driven by the dominant structures.[16]

The prime category of forced migrants is *refugees*. With regard to refugees, the 1951 UN convention has clearly defined the status of being a refugee and the rights of a refugee. According to it any individual who migrates,

> owing to well-founded fear of being persecuted for reasons of race, religion, nationality, membership of a particular social group or political opinion, is outside the country of his nationality and is unable or, owing to such fear, is unwilling to avail himself of the protection of

---

12 Eliot Dikinson, *Globalisation & Migration*..., 5.

13 Rong Ma, *Population and Society in Contemporary Tibet* (Aberdeen: Hong Kong University Press, 2011), 97.

14 Alexander Betts, *Forced Migration and Global Politics*..., 5.

15 United Nations High Commissioner of Refugees, *Figures at a Glance (2018)*, http://www.unhcr.org/figures-at-a-glance.html (accessed on 24 March, 2018).

16 Alexander Betts, *Forced Migration and Global Politics* (Chichester: Wiley Blackwell, 2009), 5.

> that country; or who, not having a nationality and being outside the country of his former habitual residence as a result of such events, is unable or, owing to such fear, is unwilling to return to it.[17]

Refugees are considered as the visible victims of human right abuses and hence the convention grants them rights in their hosting nations. An individual under the above condition, in the process of claiming to be recognised as a refugee is referred to as an 'asylum seeker'.[18] Refugee numbers are increasing at an alarming rate due to various factors mostly pertaining to political unrest and violence. According to report, by the end 2016, the refugee population was 22.5 million which is the highest on record. Asylum seekers were around 2.8 million.[19]

The other major classification is that of *internal and international migration* based on the boundaries crossed. Internal migration is understood as the movement of people within a geographical boundary unrestrained by any legal constraints usually within one's country of origin. On the other hand, movement across borders that requires crossing country borders is termed as international migration. According to research internal migration especially rural to urban constitutes more than 70% of the migration and the rest is across national boundaries.[20] The fact sheet released by IOM's Global Migration Data Analysis Centre during 2015 states over a billion people in our world are migrants out of which 244 million are international migrants and 740 million constitute internal migrants.[21] In spite of this dichotomy, it becomes more important to view them together to see the dynamics and nexus of the dominant socio-political and economic structures. Bandana Purkayasatha and many others propose the necessity to engage in a holistic approach in understanding and analysing migration beyond nation-state categories. In subcontinents like that of India, the internal and international migrant experiences are cognate and identical. Migration of any form should be seen as enmeshed within the structures and processes on which their experiences are built.[22] This article sees the effects of free market economy alike in cases of both internal and international migrants amidst their varied experiences.

The third major distinction one can find is 'legal' and 'illegal' migrants. The usage of the term 'illegal' to label migrants is highly criticised for its derogatory

17 UN General Assembly, *Convention Relating to the Status of Refugees. Treaty Series, vol. 189* (28 July 1951), 153.

18 United Nations High Commissioner of Refugees, *The State of the World's Refugees: A Humanitarian Agenda*, 1997.

19 International Organisation for Migration, *World Migration Report 2018*, Geneva: IOM, 2017.

20 Soundarya Iyer, "Circular Migration and Localised Urban Migration in Rural India," *Environment and Urbanization ASIA* 8/1(March, 2017): 105.

21 IOM Global Migration Data Analysis Center, *2015 Global Migration Trends Fact Sheet* (Berlin: IOM, 2017), 5.

22 Bandana Purkayastha, "Migration, Migrants and Human Security", *Current Sociology Monograph* 66/2 (November, 2017): 173.

nature. Hence, the term irregular is considered to be more appropriate in referring to those who have crossed national boundaries without proper documentation or with false documents. The former ones are those who abide by the migration rules and possess valid documents that permit their stay in the host country.[23]

Theories of Migration: An Overview

In order to analyse the complex issue of migration, it is necessary to have an overview on some of the theories of migration as framework. The migration theories can be broadly classified into two: micro and macro. The micro or humanist approaches have their base on the assumption that the decision of the individual along with the family units plays a key role in migration.[24] The macro or determinist approaches have their base on the assumption that it is the socio-political and economic structures that play a major role in driving individual decisions to migrate.[25]

Ernest Ravenstein, one of the pioneers in migration studies proposed several 'Laws of Migration' to predict various factors in migration.[26] According to him, the volume of migration and distance migrated are inversely related and factors like age, gender, caste, social status play a major role in determining individual's mobility.[27] Building on Ravenstein theory, Lee played leading role in giving shape to the 'push-pull' paradigm in migration studies. According to it, unfavourable conditions in a region push people to migrate and while favourable conditions in a region pulls people in. The neo classical economic theories of migration have their base in this approach.[28]

Neo classical economic theory claims that migration is influenced by the supply and demand of labour. The relative differences in income along with scarcity or surplus of labour propel the decision of migration.[29] And it assumes that the self-regulative labour market winds down migration as these inequalities get balanced. However, according to Rajarshi, such self-regulation will take place only

---

23 Khalid Koser, *International Migration. A Very Short Introduction* (Oxford: Oxford University Press, 2007), 17.

24 Charles W. Stahl, "Theories of International Labour Migration: An Overview," *Asian and Pacific Migration Journal* 4/2-3 (June, 1995): 212.

25 Charles W. Stahl, "Theories of International Labour Migration: An Overview,"..., 213.

26 Rajarshi Majumder, "Workers on the Move: Migrated Labour in Post Reform India," Munich Personal RePec Archive, 2012, 3, https://mpra.ub.uni-muenchen.de/id/eprint/44765 (accessed on 25 March, 2018).

27 Rajarshi Majumder, "Workers on the Move..., 3.

28 Peter Kivisto and Thomas Faist, *Beyond a Border: The Causes and Consequences of Contemporary Migration* (London: Pine Forge Press, 2010), 34.

29 Rajarshi Majumder, "Workers on the Move..., 3.

if the individual has an objective freedom which is impossible to achieve.[30] These theories see the end result of migration as always beneficial and growth oriented.

The *historical structural theory*, on the other hand, sees migration as a result of inequalities perpetuated by global capitalistic forces. It is based on the notion that there is unequal distribution of economic and political power as well as unequal access to resources between the developed and developing nations. The neo liberal system functions in such a way to reinforce such inequalities. As Hein points out, they see market forces as creating ever widening inequalities, forcing dislocation and displacements thereby forcing people to migrate. For them, the individual decision to migrate is conditioned by the structural forces. The Marxian economic theorists and other structural functionalist see migration from this perspective.[31]

Migration systems theory tries to combine the macro, micro and meso level factors to give a more inclusive perspective on migration. They recognise social networks, businesses and family connections that act at the meso level influencing individual decisions. Thus, it tries to take a balanced position taking into account the individual's autonomy in making decisions as well as the structural influences and other intermediate factors of influence.[32]

This article adapts the historical structural approach in delineating the macroeconomic structures that influences the migrant labour flow, thereby tries to bring out the plight of migrants and the role played by market forces in utilising migration as a tool for capital accumulation.

A Critical look at Labour, Migration and Market Economy

As it is noted above, the goal of any migration in general is to attain a better standard of life, with peaceful and safe living conditions. The major driving forces of migration both internal and international, therefore, is search for better employment opportunities and survival means.[33] This in a globalised world mostly refers to economic well-being. So, migration of labour is not merely an individual's choice. It is the underlying currents of market economy that covertly stream the labour flow. In fact, the coercive market not only functions under the pretext of creating a borderless free world but also creates a labour pool for the capital owners which in the process increases accumulation of wealth by few rich individuals. This is how unequally the 62 richest individuals of our planet possess

30 Peter Kivisto and Thomas Faist, *Beyond a Border...*, 37.

31 Hein De Hass, "Migration and Development: A Theoretical Perspective," *International Migration Review* 44/1 (Mar-May, 2010), 233-234.

32 Tisha M. Rajendra, *Migrants and Citizens: Justice and Responsibility in the Ethics of Immigration.* Kindle Edition (Michigan: Wm. B. Eerdmans Publishing Co., 2017), Chapter 2.

33 International Labour Organisation, "Mainstreaming of Migration in Development Policy and Integrating Migration in the Post-2015 UN Development Agenda," 2, http://www.ilo.org/wcmsp5/groups/public/---ed_protect/---protrav/---migrant/documents/genericdocument/wcms_220084.pdf (accessed on 20 March, 2018).

wealth that is equivalent to half of world's population. According to Oxfam report, the wealth of these individuals has increased 45% in the last five years whereas the wealth of the bottom half of world's population has seen a fall of 38% during same period of time.[34] Even in India, the 1% richest people acquire 73% of the total wealth that was generated during the year 2017 whereas the 50% poorest people have just 1% of it.[35] Such inequalities speak out loud the injustice perpetuated by the economic system. This is how with its principles and tactics the market economy creates economic disparities and exploits the migrant populations particularly the labour force.

Free Market Economy: Philosophies and Principles

The Free Market Economy is characterised by the foundational philosophies and principles of individual freedom, self-interest, profit maximisation and competition. Free Market Economy is one in which there is little or no interference or restrictions on the economic decisions made by the individuals or groups. The entrepreneur is free to make decisions on what to produce, how much to produce, what price to fix based on one's own analysis of the market. Free market economy thus claims to be democratic in nature as it provides the individual the freedom to act independently without any external pressure.[36]

Secondly, since the Free Market Economy is highly individualistic in nature, it promotes individual interests and autonomy. Perhaps, the self-interest is the motivator of the economic system. In Andrew Schotter's words it is self-love and self-interests takes priority over humanity and benevolence in a Free Market.[37] Here even anything that hinders the individual interests in the pretext of collective good is seen as inhibitors of the market.

Thirdly, the ultimate goal of Free Market Economy is profit maximisation which is achieved by increasing the demand and increasing consumption. This behaviour is the driving force of Free Market System.[38] Often such manipulation of consumer behaviour is done in ways that are unethical and unjust. As a result, it creates a vicious cycle of exploitation and manipulation as well as takes toll on

---

34 Oxfam, "An Economy for the 1%", https://www.oxfam.org/sites/www.oxfam.org/files/file_attachments/bp210-economy-one-percent-tax-havens-180116-summ-en_0.pdf (accessed on 20 March, 2018).

35 Oxfam, "Richest 1 percent bagged 73 percent of wealth created last year - poorest half of India got 1 percent, says Oxfam India," https://www.oxfamindia.org/pressrelease/2093 (accessed on 10 September, 2018).

36 Sharon Beder, *Free Market Missionaries: The Corporate Manipulation of Community Values* (London: Earth Scan, 2006), 7.

37 Andrew Schotter, *Free Market Economy: A Critical Appraisal* (New York: MacMillan Education, 1985), 2.

38 Bert van de Ven and Ronald Jeurissen, "Corporate Social Responsibility and Strategy" in *Ethics and Business,* edited by Ronald Jeurissen (Assen: Royal Van Gorcum, 2007), 93.

resources. Moreover, wealth gets accumulated in the hands of the few who control the market system and the consumers.[39]

Fourthly and finally, in order to maximise the profit, the entrepreneurs compete with one another and make their economic decisions. As selfishness is celebrated, it is not the government and state policies that check their fairness, it is the prevailing competition of interests that acts as a check.[40] This uninhibited competition is the invisible force that regulates the market where anyone who sells a product for high price will run the risk of losing consumers to another who sells the same product for a lower price. In the same way, one who pays lower wages will have to risk the workers to those who are willing to pay more.

In fact, the Free Market System boasts itself to be efficient self-regulating model.[41] For example, Adam Smith the father of modern economics and the proponent of *laissez-faire* economic policies, for example, in his book, *Wealth of the Nation* opines that when individuals act on self-interest trying to work for their own gain and profit, it eventually lead to the growth of the society as a whole. Thus, if everyone is given the freedom to act on their own in deciding the trade rules, eventually it results in the profit of all and maintain equilibrium.[42] The presence of competition is considered to guarantee a fair and just trade that offers fair and equal opportunities to everyone. Since, the fairness of the market is claimed to be monitored by the competition, even the government and state regulations and policies are deemed unnecessary.

However, in spite of all its ambitious claims of maintaining economic equilibrium and fair practices, the real life implications of Free Market Economy seems to be contradictory. Free Market Economy is far from providing equal opportunities and creating economic equilibrium. It has provided an unjust platform for competition where the rich mercilessly exploit the poor and monopolise the market. Once the market is monopolised or oligopolised[43] there is literally no check for the economic behaviours in the Free Market resulting in a highly unjust economic system. In the name of profit making, it offers free access to plunder human and natural resources. Since profit maximisation by any means is the ultimate goal in Free Market Economy, human greed becomes the

39 Livingstone Arputharaj, "Care against Commodification in the Context of Free Market Economy. Reflecting on Pastoral Care with the Spirit of Reformation," in *Transforming Reformation. Reformation in Perspectives*, edited by Songram Basumatary (Chennai: Gurukul, UELCI & CWI, 2017), 74-75.

40 Andrew Schotter, *Free Market Economy…*, 14.

41 Sharon Beder, *Free Market Missionaries…*, 7.

42 As cited by Sharon Beder, *Free Market Missionaries…*, 6-7.

43 Oligopoly is defined as a state where the market is dominated by a few sellers or producers. In such case they may tend to collude to control the market thereby prevent other competitions. See, https://en.oxforddictionaries.com/definition/oligopoly, accessed on 10 September, 2018.

foundation of this system.[44] According to Polanyi, such a market cannot survive a moment without exploiting human and natural resources of our planet.[45] Instead of creating economic equilibrium, the Free Market in due course has led to accumulation of wealth in the hands of very few rich individuals. The nations faithfully adapting Free Market Economic policies have seen new billionaires emerging while millions of their citizens are still living in abject poverty.[46] To its worst, the Market principles have replaced human values and dignity. They have conditioned the vast majority to understand life in terms of unquestionable autonomy, unrestricted consumption, power and ever increasing profit. One of the worst affected groups of people by Free Market Economy at present is the migrant labourers or workers.

Free Market in Creating and Manipulating Migrant Labourers

The economic reforms imposed on developing countries in the name of globalisation, liberalisation, privatisation are key factors in creating labour force. One of the worst affected groups of people with this reform are the farmers and the people who runs small scale industries. The adverse effects of privatisation and opening up of borders for Foreign Direct Investments have made people economically unsustainable, jobless and finally force people to work as labourers.[47] For example, the sudden withdrawal of subsidies and exposure to unfair competition platforms, the small and marginal farmers are unable to survive with their usual farming practices. They are forced and lured to go for cash crop farming by buying genetically modified seeds from MNCs.[48] In the end, the farmers and the small scale producers were trapped to sell their produce in a much cheaper rate. Thus, many were forced to give up their production and migrate to urban regions or other countries in search of employment for survival and some even end their lives due to the huge debts incurred in the process.

44 Sharon Beder, *Free Market Missionaries…*, 7.

45 Karl Polanyi, *The Great Transformation. The Political and Economic Origins of our Times* (Boston: Beacon Press, 2001), 68f.

46 Mexico after adapting neo liberal economic policies has seen the emergence of billionaires but experienced a sharp decline in wages and a 30% reduction of the purchasing power of families. Kenneth S. Friedman, *Myths of The Free Market* (New York: Algora Publishing, 2003), 16.

47 Nandan Kumar and R. B. Bhagat, "Interaction between Migration and Development: A Study of income and Workforce Diversification in Rural Bihar," *Environment and Urbanization ASIA* 8/1 (March, 2017): 123.

48 The 1988 seed policy imposed by WTO took away the rights of the farmer over the seeds which are natural common resource. They became the property of Private giants like Monsanto who claimed their rights over the seeds by patenting. These patents prevented seed saving by farmers and thereby forced them to buy every year from the private companies. They had put high prices of these seeds which the farmers were forced to buy yet the yields were not as claimed resulting in severe debts forcing many to commit suicide. Refer, *"The Privatisation of Seeds,"* https://en.reset.org/knowledge/privatisation-seeds, accessed on 10 September 2018

The similar case is with many of the small scale industries who were forced to shut down unable to compete in the market. Mexico faced a similar situation where it was not able to protect its agriculture industry since it was not equipped to compete with US market. The grain dumping at cheaper prices from US crippled the corn farmers who were forced to switch to other crops. Even that didn't help them rather plunged them into debts there by forcing them to sell their lands and become migrant labourers.[49] This is what Marx's analysis is. A labour class is formed by separating peasants from their land thereby leaving them with the option to sell their labour in the market.[50] The successful dilution of people's attachments to land, profession, close knit kinship structures, neighbourhood etc., reduces the supporting structures of people and make them prone to be dependent on the market[51] and making their living by selling their labour.

From the perspective of the receiving countries, the migrant workers are perhaps very essential for their economic sustenance and progress. For without migrant labourers, most of the developed countries where there is population decline, ageing of the population and disinterest of natives to engage in labour work face serious economic pressure.[52] The gulf countries rich in oil resources like Kuwait, Qatar, Bahrain and others succinct example of this where even migrant population is more than the native ones.[53] The plantations in the countries like US historically have been dependent on migrant labourers. Mostly the jobs pertaining to agriculture, plantations, heavy industry, construction and domestic works come under the category of unorganised sector that requires unskilled labour force. Therefore, in order to sustain the growth and progress, the migrant workers are in dire need in those countries and such jobs are taken largely by migrants even without having no proper migration documents.[54]

Nevertheless, it is important to note the irony that on the one hand, the inflow of migrant population is encouraged to sustain their economies, but on the other hand, they press hard on migration control to restrict the inflow. Such an iron hand control, according to Teresa Hayter, is what keeps the immigrants in a state of insecurity and dependency turning them into a malleable, vulnerable and 'super exploitable' labour force.[55] The case is similar with regard to internal migration. The recent census clearly shows that internal migration within India

---

49 David Bacon, *Illegal People. How Globalisation Creates Migration And Criminalises Immigrants* (Boston: Beacon Press, 2008), 62.

50 Robin Cohen, *Migration and its Enemies…*, 13.

51 Karl Polanyi, *The Great Transformation…*

52 Teresa Hayter, "Open Borders: The Case Against Immigration Controls," in *The Cultures of Economic Migrations. International Perspectives*, edited by Suman Gupta and Tope Omoniyi (Aldershot: Ashgate Publishing Limited, 2007), 21.

53 Human Right watch, *I Already Bought You* (Chicago: Human Rights Watch, 2014), 2.

54 Khalid Koser, *International Migration* .., 33.

55 Teresa Hayter, "Open Borders: The Case Against Immigration Controls,"…, 22.

primarily happens as a move from less affluent states to more affluent states. It also shows that there is a rise in labour mobility and states like Uttar Pradesh and Bihar accounts for almost half of the migration.[56] They form the major part of unorganised sector supplying much required cheap unskilled and semi-skilled labour force to the urban regions of northern and southern states.[57] In fact, they immensely contribute to the development of those states. Yet, they are discriminated and treated inhumanely in their work places. They work in hazardous environment with little or no safety. They are paid half the wages of the native state employee for the same amount of work. They are paid half the wages of the native state employee for the same amount of work.[58] Their desperate needs of survival is exploited by the affluent ones.

In addition to this, in the pretext of national interest and development, rural regions are subject to exploitation to feed and sustain urban growth. Dams, mines, hydro water projects are erected in rural regions resulting in displacement of huge indigenous population. Most of these are executed by private sectors. Alexander Betts point out that US and European based MNC's have been given contracts for the developmental projects and displacement of the people. Urbanisation and industrialisation are seen as aspects of success and are enforced at the cost farming and the well-being of rural population. For example, in the name of expanding 12 cities, the state government of Gujarat since 2012, has tried to engulf 800 villages where farming was the major source of income.[59] The cry of millions of villagers who protest against such unjust developmental projects is 'Leave us alone.' The displaced people form the unskilled labour pool for the urban industrial units and domestic needs. The forced economic backwardness of rural areas due to non-availability of jobs feed the urban areas with domestic workers and cheap labour. The statement of Persis Ginwalla, an activist of the farmers' advocacy group, "Industries and urban centres need disposable low-wage workers, and those displaced from their villages provide for just that..." says it all.[60] According to UN report, more than half of the world's population lives in urban regions. Nearly half of the world's population live in 500 cities of the world out of which nearly

---

56 Ministry of Finance, "Economic Survey 2016-17," (January, 2017), 264-277.

57 Shreesh Chaudary, "Why Biharis are Despised," https://www.thehindu.com/todays-paper/tp-features/tp-openpage/Why-Biharis-are-despised/article15410123.ece (accessed on 17 September, 2018).

58 The pay difference of a native contract teachers as that of the Bihar contract teacher was almost double. This is an example of the existing migrant wage discrimination. See, https://www.hindustantimes.com/india-news/bihar-contract-teachers-entitled-to-salary-at-par-with-their-regular-colleagues-rules-patna-hc/story-MHy2NPiA8FV6ampWGh52iJ.html (accessed on 10 September, 2018).

59 Raksha Kumar, "Leave us alone; India's Villagers rebel against Urbanisation," *The Guardian* https://www.theguardian.com/cities/2018/feb/12/india-villagers-rebel-urbanisation-gujarat (accessed on 30 August, 2018).

60 Ibid.

one third of the population live in substandard conditions in slums surrounding them.[61] It is been observed by Stanislaus and Jose that the growth rate of slums in India is four times greater than that of the city growth.[62] Often along with the adults, children and youth also migrate in search of better living conditions for their survival. Often children from poverty stricken families end up in working as mechanics in car garages, selling flowers, newspapers, picking rags or working at a road side restaurant in urban regions. Studies show that globally 369 million children live in the streets of urban cities and 79 million in India.[63]

Commodification, Criminalisation and Exploitation of Migrant Labourers

To be a migrant labourer that too under the category of an "unskilled" labour makes an individual more prone to exploitation. Adding to it, if the label of being "illegal" is appended the individual is all the more victimised and criminalised. Denial of basic human rights and dignity has become part and parcel of majority of the migrants both internal and international. They rarely get to experience life with equal rights and dignity as that of natives.

The market operates on the ideology where everything is measured monetarily i.e. on profit that it makes or expense that it incurs. In line with this, labour market is valued on the basis of money it incurs to run the production, and nothing else. Capital owners in the race to maximise profit need just about the labour force that is super exploitable, cheap and surplus. Migrant labourers thus in the market world is reduced to nothing more than a commodity. In order to maximise the profits, their human dignity and wellbeing is completely ignored.[64] Their human worth is measured in terms of mere monitory returns.

Commodification inevitably results in exploitation and dehumanisation. It subjects the human life to serious physical, psychological and moral distress which applies to natural resources as well.[65] It costs psycho social toll on the individuals as well as society as a whole. Farther, it not only dehumanises a particular individual labourer and or a group, but have a great impact on the harmonious existence of human beings and nature itself.

---

61 "World's population increasingly urban with more than half living in urban areas," *United Nations*, http://www.un.org/en/development/desa/news/population/world-urbanization-prospects-2014.html (accessed on 11 March, 2018).

62 Stanislaus L. and Jose Joseph, "Introduction," in *Migration and Mission in India*, edited by L. Stanislaus and Jose Joseph (Pune: Ishvani Kendra/ISPCK, 2007), vii.

63 Meena Mathur, "Socialisation of Street Children in India: A Socio-Economic Profile," *Psychology and Developing Societies* 21/2 (November, 2009), 300.

64 Wajihah Hamid, "Migrant Workers in Asia Face Unexpected Challenges," (December, 2015), https://www.fairobserver.com/region/central_south_asia/migrant-workers-in-asia-face-unexpected-challenges-31011/, accessed on 10 September, 2018.

65 Karl Polanyi, *The Great Transformation…*, 72-73.

Often increase in crimes and terrorist activities are connected with migrants especially those who come under the label of 'illegal migrants.' They are blamed for the increasing crime rate, poverty, decline of morality, safety and security. This creates negative stereotypes against migrants leading to discrimination and violence both from public as well as security agents of the host nation.[66] They are viewed by the natives as a threat to their employment opportunities and even to the integrity of their culture and identity.[67] Often they are seen as parasites living on the taxes of natives and stealing away their job opportunities resulting in hostility and anger against them. However, studies have shown that migrants commit fewer crimes than natives as well as they contribute more to the host than the benefits that they receive.[68] Such xenophobic and racist ideologies are even perpetuated by the market forces in many occasions while on the other hand they exploit them to the core for building their empires.

Whether it is internal or international migrant labourers, they are exploited to the core every way. They are employed for lower wages and are made to work long hours. Their living places and conditions are extremely poor and deplorable without any access to basic needs like water and electricity. To cite and example, one of the residents of a colony by name Babita Devi, in her interview to Rashmika Majumdar expresses, "Sometimes, a family of five or six will need to share a tin shack which is not enough for even two people. We left our village to earn a living here. The money comes, but surviving here is also very difficult." Such is the pathetic status of migrant labourer's living condition.[69] They are deprived of many privileges that a native enjoys. The rights of the land seldom offer protection to the migrant labourers. Any resistance or demand for rights expressed by a migrant labourer will result in loss of employment opportunity. Even many of the migrants who work in organised sectors have no social security, and employment status is highly unstable.[70]

The vulnerability of migrant domestic workers in Gulf countries is another example of the violations of the basic human rights. The migrant population

---

66 Patrick A. Taran and Eduardo Geronimi, "Globalization, Labour and Migration: Protection is Paramount," *Perspectives of Labour Migration*, Working Paper, Geneva: International Labour Office, 2011, http://www.ilo.org/wcmsp5/groups/public/---ed_protect/---protrav/---migrant/documents/publication/wcms_232365.pdf, accessed on 21 March, 2018.

67 United Nations, "Human rights of all migrants, social inclusion, cohesion and all forms of discrimination, including racism, xenophobia and intolerance," *Refugees and Migrants*, Issue Brief 1, 2. https://refugeesmigrants.un.org/file/5497/download?token=nGUeHb3p (accessed on 14 March, 2018).

68 United Nations, "Human rights of all migrants, social inclusion…, 3.

69 Rashmika Majumdar, "Migrant Labourers: stuck in a web of contractors, builders, lack of unions, welfare schemes," *Tholizhalar Koodam*, http://tnlabour.in/migrant-workers/3680 (accessed on 10 September, 2018).

70 Deepak K. Mishra, *Internal Migration in Contemporary India-An Overview of Issues and Concerns. Kindle Edition* (New Delhi: Sage Publications, 2016), First Chapter.

constitutes a whopping 88.5% of the UAE population and are under the iron fist of their employers lacking basic policies to safeguard them from abuse and exploitation.[71] In Qatar, around two million migrant workers do the extremely hazardous manual jobs. Nearly 800,000 workers from the poor Asian countries work on huge construction projects. It is reported that every year hundreds of migrant workers die due to the working conditions.[72] Bangladesh alone is reported to receive 3154 bodies just between January to November 2017. Many of the victims are young. The number is believed to be even higher as many workers are buried abroad.[73]

While many countries have agreed upon and adapted free market trade policies it is shocking that not even a quarter of UN member states have agreed upon the rights to protect migrant workers especially the developed nations.[74] The reality is governments these days rarely interfere or check the economic ethics of capital owners. Often it is the law of the market that over powers the government. The representatives of government have become mere executers of the demands of the market. What is even more shocking is that the capitalists themselves become the highest decision making authorities. This domination of Free Market economic ambassadors has resulted in the failure of governments appropriately responding to the discriminations faced by migrant labour forces.

Responding to the Realities: A Reflection

Human migration in search of better living is something that is perennial and at the same time essential for economic growth and development. It brings about changes in the way we understand society, culture, politics and economics. The advancement in science and technology and communications has taken human growth and progress to heights. However, if these developments are at the cost of depleting natural resources then one has to be pessimistic about the developments it brings. If these advancements serve the interest of a few, to accumulate wealth and allow the others to feed on the bread crumbs that fall from their table, then one should question the structure that supports their existence. Migration as such is a necessary phenomenon but manipulating and exploiting human labour and resources cannot be left unchallenged.

---

71 Human Right watch, *I Already Bought You…*, 2.

72 "Thousands of Qatar world cup workers subjected to life threatening heat," *The Guardian*, https://www.theguardian.com/football/2017/sep/27/thousands-qatar-world-cup-workers-life-threatening-heat, accessed on 2 April, 2018.

73 Afros Jahan Chaity, "Migrant workers' dreams end in body bags," *Dhaka Tribune*, http://www.dhakatribune.com/opinion/special/2017/12/18/migrant-workers-death/ (accessed on 2 April, 2018).

74 Oxfam, "An Economy for the 1%", https://www.oxfam.org/sites/www.oxfam.org/files/file_attachments/bp210-economy-one-percent-tax-havens-180116-summ-en_0.pdf (accessed on 20 March, 2018).

The trends of free market economy and the plight of migrant labourers demands a serious reflection as there are lot of flaws in the growth and development models. It is important to challenge such trends in order to uphold the values of justice and preferential option for those who struggle. A quest for freedom and self-interest, even though is integral to human behaviour, it is important to challenge them when it is exercised in a manner that disrupts the well-being of others. In this, the Faith community has great role in responding to migrants issue through theological discourses as well as engagement in advocating migrant rights and lobbying with the state and national governments.

Reflecting theologically, perhaps the very idea of incarnation as the migration of God and looking Jesus as a migrant may help to understand and address the struggles and aspirations of migrants. Jesus is someone who migrated the borders of tradition, religion and gender, and became a victim of the structural powers. He understood the struggle and pain of all those who failed to fit into the borders set by tradition, religion and gender. He challenged the socio-economic and religious structures that manipulated and set borders for their profit and comfort. He condemned deceptive portrayal of religious salvation and economic exploitation. Suffering and death of Jesus on the cross ultimately is a symbol of resistance against the manipulative forces in the society and a source of liberation. It is a voice that demands justice and a sign of hope and solidarity. The Church as faith community therefore is called to engage in the prophetic ministry not only to articulate the migrant issues theologically but to identify, challenge and resist the deceptive economic structures that manipulate migrant labour flow. She must play active political and prophetical role in standing for the rights of the marginalised. In fact, not only she raise voice against all the forces of individualism or self-interest, profit maximisation and unjust completions, but needs to raise above all these in order that the reign of God becomes reality in our society.

Besides the gospel call, the some of the good social values that are upheld by our society such as community interests always taking priority over individual's interest, relationship bonds should be imbibed as moral strength to address the issue in migration. For struggles of the migrants call for an immediate response not only from within the economic and political structures, but also from all walks of people and institution. And more so from the confessing community.

Conclusion

An economic system that claims to offer equal opportunities to everyone should also be able to justify the platform in which these opportunities are made available. A system that operates with self-interest is prone to be more dominant and inconsiderate to the needs of those who in many ways are not equipped to compete. Such a system results in increasing polarities based on class, race and ethnic diversities. It begins to define intelligence, ability and more importantly one's fitness to survive in this planet. Free market economy very much seems to take the world in this course. Realities of migrants and the way in which labour flow is manipulated make this nature of the market more explicit. It is therefore high time that values that stand against injustice, inequality and exploitation are hailed and embraced so that the free market culture is transformed into a fair market culture where all migrant labourers too have life worth living.

II

MIGRATION IN PERSPECTIVES

3

Migration Motif in the Ancestral Narratives

Nagaiyasamy N.S. Samuel

The Hebrews Scripture or the Old Testament contains several themes, motifs, literary style, etc. that are concentrated by the Biblical scholarships. However, many scholars in their pursuit, do not concentrate much on these areas in Pentateuch. The reason could be of its complexity and remoteness from the modern reader. One among such neglected Pentateuchal scholarship is that of Migration Motif in the Ancestral Narratives.

It is fascinating to see that the ancestral narratives are all narratives of migration. The narratives begins with the call of Abraham who lived in Ur of Mesopotamia probably during late Second Millennium BCE. During this period many people moved from place to place for various reasons due various social, economic, cultural and political reasons. While discussing on the migration motif of Ancestors[1] the Biblical scholars wrestle with the questions such as "who were these Ancestors?" Were these Ancestors nomads? What type of the nomads were the Ancestors? What was their business? What was their living-style? What was their economical status? How do they contact/connect with the divine? Was their migration voluntary or forced, or of the divine guidance? This article is an attempt to answer these questions through the *historical critical tools* and the *reader response methodology* along with identifications of some of the issues that are inherent in the ancestral narratives.

The Context of the Ancestral Narratives

The Ancestral narratives generally might have emerged from the composite nature of the sources. The personalities who appear in these narratives are in fact less accessible to the modern reader. The ancestral tradition emerged from the life of the Ancestors who were called by God to leave their own land and to go to the place where God shows to them. The Ancestral history has been arranged in

1 This article attempts to use the inclusive language. At the same time most of the materials referred herein used as the Patriarchs were retained as it is.

three main, more or less clearly defined, parts: the stories of Abraham, Isaac, Jacob and Joseph. The story of Jacob is clearly divided into three parts, corresponding to three stages in his life: the account of his relations with his immediate family especially with his brother Esau, is bisected by the story of Jacob's journeys and his relations with his uncle Laban (Chs. 28-31).[2]

Any literary work basically needs to have base in the scripture. In this pursuit, the Ancestral narrative can be traced back in four sources as per the Biblical scholarship, such as, the Yahwistic (J) sources, the Elohistic (E) source, Priestly (P) source,[3] and Deuteronomic (D) Source. The questions of the context of the Ancestors were set at all levels. Since the ancestral narratives were made part of the Genesis and of the Pentateuch, the concern here is which of their place in ancient history the exact context.[4] The Patriarchal stories are family stories, with almost mention of no people or events which would find their way into the sort of written records which have survived from the Middle East.[5]

The Relationship of Archaeology to Israelite History

The archaeological evidence of the Israelite history is the theoretical importance of the material from the early Second Millennium BCE. For questions of early Israelite origins has long been recognised, especially after the Mari texts provided such abundant data.[6] But the Nineteenth-Century biblical criticism had abandoned that of reconstructing a historical, social and cultural milieu of the Second Millennium BCE in which early Israelite origins could be understood.[7]

The influx of Amorites into Palestine is hypothesized on the basis of (1) archaeological remains from late third and early Second Millennium Palestine which at least cultural changes in that region, including some cultural features derived from Syria and (2) texts from Egypt which contain references to nomadic Asiatics who might be identified with the Amorites.[8] Support for the northern Mesopotamian origin of the Ancestors of Israel is often cited in the fact that

---

2 R.N. Whybray, *Introduction to the Pentateuch* (Grand Rapids, Michigan: Wm. B. Eerdmanns Publishing Company, 1995), 52.

3 R. D. Vaux, *The Early History of Israel to the Exodus and Covenant of Sinai*, trans. by David Smith (Philadelphia: The Westminster Press, 1978), 161.

4 J. Goldingay, "The Patriarchs in Scripture and History," in *Essays on the Patriarchal Narratives*, edited by A.R. Millard & D.J. Wiseman (England: InterVarsity Press, 1980), 46.

5 G. W. Ramsey, *The Quest for the Historical Israel: Reconstructing Israel's Early History* (London: SCM Press Ltd., 1982), 28.

6 J. H. Hayes and J.M. Miller, *Israelite and Judean History: Old Testament Library* (London: SCM Press Ltd., 1984), 112.

7 Hayes and Miller, *Israelite and Judean History...*, 71-72.

8 Ramsey, *The Quest for the Historical Israel...*, 37.

several of the relatives of Abraham possess names identical with known cities in that region: Terah, Nahor, Haran, and Serug.[9]

The Amorite Migration Theory

The story of Abraham's migration from Ur to Haran (Gen. 11:31) has been located by some historians in the context of this Amorite infiltration which contributed to the downfall of the Ur III Kingdom (dated c. 2060-1950 BCE) in Mesopotamia.[10] The movement of the Hebrew Patriarchs from Mesopotamia and Syria to Canaan, reported in Genesis 12,[11] has been reckoned by many Old Testament scholars to be plausible and historically likely when placed in the context of the movements of the 'Amorites', who are believed to have been active throughout the Near East at the end of the 3rd Millennium BCE and the beginning of the 2nd Millennium BCE.[12]

Many scholars who doubt the historicity of the migration from Ur to Haran nevertheless are prepared to argue that the story of the migration from Haran to Canaan is historically grounded in one or another movement of Amorites into Palestine (and Egypt) just before or just after 2000 BCE.[13] We read of invasions of 'barbarians' into the lands of the Fertile Crescent about 2000 BC., particularly into northern Syria and Mesopotamia. The Babylonians called[14] the new invaders as *Amurru* - that is, '*Westerners*' or '*Amorites*' - in the Mesopotamian sources, gradually gained the ascendancy in the settled portions of both Syria-Canaan and Mesopotamia, so that in the early Second Millennium they took the leadership in the reestablishment of Urban centres.[15] The Aramaeans, to whom Laban was related, are thought to have been an Amorite people (Gen. 31:20). The Israelites, too, acknowledged their Aramaean origin in the confession, 'A wandering Aramaean was my father' (Dt. 26:5). It is of interest that Haran is known to have been an Amorite state shortly after 2000 BC.[16]

The Ancestors and Sources

Two sources understand that Abraham migrated to Canaan from an area around Haran in northern Mesopotamia, called Aram-naharaim (Aram between the

---

9 N. K. Gottwald, *The Hebrew Bible: A Socio-Literary Introduction*. (Philadelphia: Fortress Press, 1987), 168-169.

10 Ramsey, *The Quest for the Historical Israel...*, 37.

11 Gen. 24; 28-33.

12 Ramsey, *The Quest for the Historical Israel...*, 36.

13 Ramsey, *The Quest for the Historical Israel...*, 37.

14 Pfeiffer, *Old Testament History...*, 42.

15 P.K.M. Carter, Jr., *The Patriarchal Age*, in *Ancient Israel, A Short History from Abraham to the Roman Destruction of the Temple,* Ed., By Shanks, H., 1998, p.7.

16 Pfeiffer, *Old Testament History...*, 55.

Rivers) by J and Paddan-aram (the Field of Aram) by P.[17] Abraham's migration[18] from Ur would have provided a link between the story of the Tower of Babel and the 'scattering of the peoples over the whole face of the earth,' that is, in Lower Mesopotamia (Gen. 11:1-9) on the one hand and the story of Abraham which begins in Upper Mesopotamia (Gen. 12:1-5) on the other. But Gen. 11:1-9 and Gen. 12:1-4 a belong to the Yahwistic tradition and Gen. 11:28-30, which states that Abraham's family was present at Ur, also belongs to this tradition. The migration from Ur therefore forms part of the ancient Pentateuchal tradition and what is more, it is mentioned again in Gen. 15:7. It could not therefore have been invented when these traditions were being edited, for Ur was at that time completely forgotten.[19] The priestly editors stressed that the Patriarchs had been strangers who had settled in Canaan (Gen. 17:8; 23:4; 36:7; 38:1).[20] The Priestly source (and may be J) adds that, prior to coming to Haran, Abraham had lived in southern Mesopotamia at Ur.[21]

According to the Yahwistic account (11:28), Abram's brother Haran[22] died in the presence of their father Terah in their nature land, *`ur kasedim.* According to the priestly tradition (Gen. 11:31), Terah, Abram, Sarai and Lot left *`ur kasedim* to go to the land of Canaan, but they settled in Haran. In the Yahwistic-Elohistic(?) account of the covenant, Yahweh says to Abram: "I am Yahweh who brought you out of *`ur kasedim* to make you heir to this land." (Gen. 15:7). The Hebrew version is always *`ur kasedim* and Greek version is *'the land of Chaldeans.'* It has been suggested that the primitive version was 'Ur in the land of Chaldeans' and that this form was abbreviated differently in Hebrew and in Greek.[23] The positioning of the cycles and saga chains so that Abraham, Isaac, Jacob and Jacob's twelve sons represent four successive generations in a single family provides the axis for the entire narrative complex.[24] The specific connection of the first homeland to Abraham with places in Mesopotamia, however, belongs more to the framework of the traditions than to the contents of the sagas.[25]

17 Gottwald, *The Hebrew Bible...*, 168-169.

18 The migration from Ur took Abraham and his father to Haran, a northern Mesopotamian City on the Bilikh River about sixty miles from its entrance into the Euphrates. The word Haran means 'road' and the city was located on an important Caravan route connecting Nineveh and Babylon with Damascus, Tyre, and Egypt. (Pfeiffer, *Old Testament History...*, 55).

19 Vaux, *The Early History of Israel...*, 188.

20 Vaux, *The Early History of Israel...*, 167.

21 Gottwald, *The Hebrew Bible...*, 168-169.

22 Haran, like Ur, was devoted to the lordship of the Moon God. People from Ur would feel at home there, and the temptation was great to forego the uncertain journey into Canaan. Terah, Abraham's father, got no further than Haran, but Abraham himself moved on to Canaan. (Pfeiffer, *Old Testament History...*, 55).

23 Vaux, *The Early History of Israel...*, 187.

24 Gottwald, *The Hebrew Bible...*, 155.

25 Gottwald, *The Hebrew Bible...*, 168-169.

To literary arguments used to distinguish the sources, Hayes and Millers quotes Wellhausen added historical correlation. For example, King Josiah's reform in the Seventh Century confined sacrifice to the temple at Jerusalem. Previously, there were a number of legitimate cultic sites. Thus there was a historical development from sacrifice at numerous locations at a time.[26] The link of Abraham with Haran has been significant in various reconstructions of patriarchal history including Albright's view of Abraham as a Caravan and the thesis of the patriarchs as part of a movement of Amorites, and also the connection of the patriarchs with a moon cult.[27]

Who were the Nomads?

The true Bedouin - *'man of the desert'* raises Camels as they can live for several days without drinking or eating, can cover very long distances and carry very heavy loads. With Camel, people can live in places which would otherwise be inaccessible and uninhabitable. The Camel-raising Bedouins derive all that is essential in their life from the animals-milk, for example, hair for his clothes, skin for is tents and occasionally meat, though this is exceptional. The Bedouins are, however, of necessity a *'great'* nomad, because they have to travel with their flock to pasture land that is still green and to the rare sources of water in the desert. Their contact with people living settled lives are very limited. They buy things they need in towns situated at the edge of the steeple and are from time to time in touch with small populations of the oases and little desert towns or villages, since they have to pay a 'brotherhood tax' in the form of dates or grain.[28]

What type of Nomads were the Ancestors?

Travellers between Southern Mesopotamia and Palestine did not journey through the desert but took the longer route around the Fertile Crescent. Abraham with Terah, his father set out along the familiar road northward from Ur.[29] Several scholars have proposed that the mode of life depicted in the patriarchal stories be classified as a dimorphic society in which herdsmen and farmers achieve a symbiosis. This sort of society is represented in the seminomadic population reflected in the Mari texts of Eighteenth Century BCE.[30]

In Genesis, the Ancestors are depicted as nomadic herdsmen. They live in tents; they raise sheep and goats; and dig wells; they move from one camp to another with their flocks.[31] Their great migrations are from Upper Mesopotamia to Canaan, from Canaan into Egypt and then from Upper Mesopotamia to Canaan,

26 Hayes and Miller, *Israelite and Judean History...*, 124.

27 Hayes and Miller, *Israelite and Judean History...*, 130.

28 Vaux, *The Early History of Israel...*, 222.

29 Pfeiffer, *Old Testament History...*, 53.

30 Ramsey, *The Quest for the Historical Israel...*, 36.

31 Gen. 12:8, 13:3, 18; 18:1-10; 24:67; 31:25, 33, 34; 30:32-43; 21:30; 26:15-22; 12:9, 13:3.

from Canaan to Egypt and then from Egypt back to Canaan. Inside Canaan itself, they went from Shechem to Bethel, Hebron, Beersheba and the Negeb. They observe the unwritten law of the desert, preserving blood relations (24:3-4; 28:1-2), keep the law of hospitality (18:1-8; 19:28-32) and take collective revenge (34:25-31).[32] Certain features which are often regarded as exclusive nomadic such as tents, tribal structures, asses, flocks and herds - are now known to have been characteristic of other modes of life in the Ancient Near East as well.[33]

The knowledge from the biblical text shows that the biblical Ancestors had their own herds, cattle. The domestication of camels for their livelihood in the desert was not practice of the Ancestors. This way of life was unknown during the patriarchal period. It did not really begin to develop fully until the beginning of the modern era, and was first practised in northern Arabia. Other authors, however, believe that the Camel was domesticated at a much earlier date. On the other hand, there is no evidence before the end of the Second Millennium of the breeding and keeping of cattle or small livestock and of the use of the Camel for Caravans and war.[34] There is an ample of evidence that the patriarchs had the possession of Camel.[35] At the same time, the other possibilities in the patriarchal narratives were that there is no mention of Camels in any of the other patriarchal stories.[36]

De Vaux concludes that it is probable that the reference to Camels in Genesis reflects the situation prevailing at the time when the traditions became established, not the life of the people during the patriarchal period. What is more, even if we accept that the patriarchs may have possessed a number of Camels, this does not necessarily mean that they were *'great'* nomads. It would, moreover be entirely wrong to think of the patriarchs of Israel as Bedouin Sheiks.[37]

The Ancestors were not Caravan Traders

The Patriarchs have been described as breeders of donkeys and leaders of Caravans, in other words, as 'donkey nomads.' It has been suggested for example, that the name 'Hebrew' like the name Habiru/'Apiru, really meant *'dusty'* or *'socially alienated'* and denoted the donkey drovers who followed their animals[38] and they appear in many parts of the Near East during patriarchal times[39] including the later than the ancestral age. In this context, it has been pointed out that the places where the patriarchs broke their journey were all on caravan trails. Unlike the

32 Vaux, *The Early History of Israel...*, 221.

33 Ramsey, *The Quest for the Historical Israel...*, 35.

34 Vaux, *The Early History of Israel...*, 223.

35 Gen. 12:16; 30:43; 24:1ff.: 31:34; 24:10; 37:25; 31:17; 32:16.

36 Vaux, *The Early History of Israel...*, 224.

37 Vaux, *The Early History of Israel...*, 225.

38 The leaders of Camel caravans walked ahead of their beasts.

39 Pfeiffer, *Old Testament History...*, 45.

Camel, the donkey does not provide man with food or clothing, its flesh is not eaten, it yields little milk and its hair cannot be woven. The donkey-breading nomads much have had sheep or goats. Otherwise, they must either have been hunters or leaders of caravans or else have practised certain minor industries.[40] Caravans were generally very large and almost always escorted by guards to protect them.

In Genesis, donkeys are mentioned as part of the patriarchs' flocks or herds[41] always show that they were used as mounts or as beasts of burden. This is, of course, fully in accordance with the needs of people who keep small livestock and does not in any way imply that the Ancestors went in for trading. There is not a single biblical text which suggests that they were donkey-drovers who led Caravans. The routes which they followed might have been the same as the established caravan trails, but this was no doubt because the needs of both groups of people were the same - pasture and spring. On the other hand, there is no evidence that they broke their journey in Canaan at points along the Caravan trail between Syria and Egypt. During the patriarchal period, Caravans must have travelled, as they did later, through Damascus, Meggiddo and Gaza on their way into Egypt.[42]

Inspite of this, however, R.D. Vaux have insisted that the patriarchs were in fact traders. One argument put forward in favour of this theory is that the verb סָחַר (*saḥar*) in Gen. 10, 21 and 42:34 means 'to trade,' 'to travel', 'to go round' so that these three texts show that Jacob's sons were about to settle, first Shechem and secondly, in Egypt and to trade there. The verb, R.D. Vaux argue that was certainly understood in this sense in the early versions and participle of the verb means 'merchants' in classical Hebrew and in Gen. 23: 16 and 37:28.[43]

We may add here that the social situation of the patriarchal was not in any way similar to that of the merchants of Ugarit during the fourteenth and thirteenth centuries BCE or to that of the Babylonian Merchants at the beginning of the Second Millennium. As far as the verb סָחַר (*saḥar*) is concerned, its basic meaning it *'to travel'* or to *'go around,'* which is also the meaning of the same root is Akkadian and in Aramaic, for example in the Qumran Genesis Apocryphal. This basic meaning of '*to move about*' is perfectly acceptable in the three texts of Genesis quoted above as well as in the two other cases in which the verb is used in a finite form in the rest of the Old Testament.[44] The meaning of the participle in Hebrew and in Phoenician is clearly a derivative, since travelling merchants were known everywhere in the Ancient Near East.[45] We may therefore conclude that

40 Vaux, *The Early History of Israel...*, 225-226.

41 Gen. 12:16; 24:35; 30:43; 32:6, 16.

42 Vaux, *The Early History of Israel...*, 225-228.

43 Vaux, *The Early History of Israel...*, 228.

44 Jer. 14:18; Ps. 38:11.

45 The present scholarship call it as the Ancient West Asia.

the Ancestors were no 'great' nomads who raised Camels, nor were they donkey drovers who led caravans or merchants.[46] In the Ancestral narrative, Abraham keeps travelling, never settling in one place for very long. Isaac and Jacob continue this pattern. The patriarchs sound like tent-dwelling nomads. They hand their flocks from place to place to secure the best pasturage and water supply.[47]

The Vulnerable Life of the Ancestors

The biblical narration long supposed, therefore, that a chief factor in the urban collapse was an invasion-or at least a massive immigration - of nomadic people from the desert fringes of the region.[48] Abraham journeyed through the Fertile Crescent and had contacts with its people. His descendants Isaac, Jacob and Joseph likewise moved from Canaan northward to Paddan-aram and south-ward to Egypt. The culture of the patriarchs is described as semi-nomadic, but it was touched by some of the most advanced civilizations the world has ever seen.[49] In this process of movement, the Ancestors face life challenges such as threat of life, their wives were taken by the other people and then returned them, they dig well, but it was taken by the native people, their goods were stolen. The patriarchs, then, followed a way of life which was transitional, half way between a nomadic life and a settled one. It is moreover, very probable that the various stages in this evolutionary process from a nomadic to a settled way of life where compressed in the patriarchal tradition.[50]

In Genesis, whenever the Ancestors possessions are listed, their livestock, that is to say that their sheep and goats, are always mentioned and what is more with one exception, these animals are mentioned first. The raising of sheep and goats is, of course, dependent on certain geographical and climatic conditions. It is, after all, not possible to keep small livestock in the desert, but it is possible to do so in country-bordering the desert, where the animals can graze and find water more easily. The sheep-breeding tribes of today move their flocks much less than the Camel-keeping tribes move their beasts from one pasture to another.[51]

Abraham's first trip was a long one, from Ur to the land of Canaan. The reference to the temporary stop in Haran confirms over assumption that Abraham took the traditional route between these two locations by travelling up the

46 Vaux, *The Early History of Israel…*, 228-229.

47 I. Provan and V.P. Long and III Longman, *A Biblical History of Israel* (Louisville: Westminster John Knox Press,, 2003), 118.

48 P. Kyle Mc Carter, Jr., "The Patriarchal Age," in *Ancient Israel, A Short History from Abraham to the Roman Destruction of the Temple,* edited by Hershal Shanks (Biblical Archaeology Society, 1988), 7.

49 Pfeiffer, *Old Testament History…*, 40.

50 Vaux, *The Early History of Israel…*, 231.

51 Vaux, *The Early History of Israel…*, 229.

Euphrates and then descending into Canaan from the north.[52] It is interesting to note that the places where the patriarchs halted on their journey, Haran, Shechem, Bethel, Hebron and Beersheba are situated within this zone. These sheep-breeding tribes living on the fringe of the desert are often in touch with the towns and with people whose main industry is agriculture, with the result that they naturally tend towards a settled way of life. They add cattle to their flocks and these larger, less mobile animals restrict their movements. They acquire land and begin to cultivate it. They build huts of mud and branches or even stone houses. In the winter and spring, part of each tribe will set up tents in the grazing land where the flocks are, but the rest of the year, these flocks are entrusted to shepherds.[53] The obstacles to situating the Ancestors of Israel have often been obscured by the assumption that references to their movements and manner of life indicate that the Ancestors were pastoral nomads.[54]

Quite apart from the question of the vocabulary used, however, the patriarchal mode of habitation is described in Genesis in a way which is to some extent similar to that of the Mari texts. The patriarchs, for example, set up their encampments, which could also be called *nawum* (to sleep, to take rest), in the neighbourhood of existing urban centres. Abraham pitched his tents between Bethel and Ai (Gen. 12:8). He left this site and returned to it (Gen. 13:3). Leaving it again, he established his camp at Mamre near Hebron (Gen. 13:18), where he was to be buried. He also lived as a nomad in the Negeb (Gen. 20:1). Jacob camped near Shechem (Gen. 33:14) and later at Mamre (Gen. 35:23), but he moved his flocks from there to Shechem and Dothan (Gen. 37:12, 17). The Patriarch concluded treaties with city dwellers - Abraham, for instance, with Abimelech (Gen. 20:15) and with the people of Hebron (Gen. 23), Isaac with Abimelech (Gen. 26:30), and Jacob with the people of Shechem (Gen. 33:19, 34).[55]

What is more, the biblical tradition made a clear distinction between the way of life led by the patriarchs and that followed by other groups of nomads. Isaac, for example, is contrasted in Genesis with Ishmael (Gen. 16:12; 25:16-18) and Jacob with Esau.[56] The patriarchal way of life is shown to be quite different from that of the Midianites or the Amalekites, with whom the Israelites came into contact later in their history.[57] We may therefore conclude that the Ancestors were originally shepherds or goatherds and that they entered Canaan and lived on the fringe of cultivated land, and in contact with settled people, they too began to

52 Provan, *A Biblical History of Israel...*, 118.

53 Vaux, *The Early History of Israel...*, 230.

54 Gottwald, *The Hebrew Bible...*, 172.

55 Vaux, *The Early History of Israel...*, 232.

56 Vaux, *The Early History of Israel...*, 232. (cf. Gen. 25:27; 27:39).

57 Vaux, *The Early History of Israel...*, 233.

lead a settled life.[58] These tribes are not unsettled people who invade the settled areas; rather they live in the shadow of the settled area during the dry season and journey out during the wet period when grazing land and water become scarce.[59]

In fact, the movements of the Ancestors are largely explained as historically caused migrations for strife with outsiders, securing wives, escaping famine, and the like, rather than due to the regular seasonal movements of pastoral nomads. The references to the Ancestors' forms of wealth include not only the flocks of sheep and goats typical of (though not exclusive to) pastoral nomads at the time, but also herds of cattle, wealth in metal, and cultivated land which suggest either sedentary farming and animal husbandry or commercial enterprise.[60]

The Ancestors and Divine Revelation

The historical movements of the patriarchs' link closely to their reaction to the divine promise.[61] Often the patriarchal narrative mentions the fact of revelations with no clue as to the means by which it is accomplished. Gen. 12:1 explains that the Lord said to Abraham, go from your country and your kindred and your father's house, it has not described whether God spoke in a dream, a vision, an audible voice or a theophany.[62] The term theophany is frequently used in describing visible appearances of God to man. The Gen. 17:1 reads that the Lord 'appeared' to Abram, changed his name to Abraham, promised the land of Canaan as an inheritance to his descendants and established circumcision as the sign of the covenant. He further declared that Sarai, whose name was changed to Sarah, would bear a son who would become Abraham's heir.[63]

In Gen. 12:1-3, they are not simply juxtaposed. Everything that is promised is contingent on Abraham's obeying the command to leave his old world behind him and go to[64] the land he will be shown. The land, therefore, has logical priority in that everything else depends on the promise that he and his descendants will

58 Vaux, *The Early History of Israel...*, 233.

59 Provan, *A Biblical History of Israel...*, 118.

60 N.K. Gottwald, *The Hebrew Bible...*, 172.

61 Provan, *A Biblical History of Israel...*, 109.

62 Pfeiffer, *Old Testament History...*, 106. The fact, rather than the means of revelation is stressed.

63 Pfeiffer, *Old Testament History...*, 107.

64 The juxtaposition of command ('go to the land') and promise suggests that the commitment to make Abraham a great nation and a blessing to humanity is contingent on occupation of the land, that this is what first must be done. Hence Abraham's perambulations from one sanctuary to another: from Shechem (12:6-7) to Bethel (12:8; 13:3-4), then Mamre (13:8) and later, Beersheba (21:32; 22:19). These apparently random movements are explained by the command to walk the length and breadth of the land in anticipation of possessing it (13:17). (Joseph Blenkinsopp, *The Pentateuch: An Introduction to the First Five Books of the Bible*, The Anchor Bible Reference Library (New York: Doubleday, 1992), xxx.

possess it. This first statement provides a point of reference throughout the narrative (18:18; 22:18; 26:2-4; 28: 13; 35:12; 46:2-3).[65]

The Promises to the Ancestors

For Noth, the theme *'Promise to the Patriarchs'* includes both the promise of posterity and the promise of the land from the very outset.[66] The promise theme is the most extensive within the Abraham story. It first occurs in the call of Abraham (12:1-3). The primary emphasis is on the divine promise of blessing that will make Abraham and his offspring into a great nation and will make them prosperous and at peace with other nations, to whom they will be a blessing.[67] The most recurrent promises are of children and land.[68] The land promise (12:7; 13:14-17) is given to Abraham when he arrives in the land of Canaan, and the extent is spelled out after he separates from Lot, who chooses the Jordon plain. The promise of land is already implicit in the call to 'go to a land that I will show you' (12:1), and the extent of the land is national and corresponds to the size of the descendant population that will inherit it. In fact, the two promise themes cannot be separated.[69]

Yahweh's first and last words to Abram (12:1; 22:1) begin with an imperative ('Go ... Take...'). Both times the imperative is followed by a triple object: "Go forth from (1) your country, (2) your Homeland, (3) your father's house"; "Take (1) your son, (2) your only son whom you love, (3) Isaac."[70] Motifs of divine promise and present blessing are very subtly employed a key points in the traditions to impart a sense of continuity that links saga to saga and generation to generation.[71] In both Chs. 12 and 22, God's directive to Abraham falls short of supplying explicit directions; Abram is simply pointed in the light direction. About the terminus point of that pilgrimage he is unclear. Here he is told to go to a land "while I will show you." In Ch. 22 he is told to take Isaac to a mountain 'of which I shall tell you.'[72]

---

65 Blenkinsopp, *The Pentateuch...*, 110-111.

66 M. Noth, *A History of Pentateuchal Traditions,* trans. with an Introduction By Bernhard W. Anderson (Englewood Cliffs, N.J.: Prentice-Hall Inc., 1972), 55.

67 J. V. Setters, *The Pentateuch, A Social-Science Commentary* (England: Sheffield Academic Press, 1995), 125.

68 Gottwald, *The Hebrew Bible...*, 156-157. Sometimes, the promise has to do with a single son, such as Isaac promised to Abraham, while in other contexts the promise is of many descendants. At points the promise of land has to do with immediately needed land for cultivation and pasturage, while elsewhere the vast territory of the later Israelite Kingdom is foreshadowed.

69 J.V. Setters, *The Pentateuch, a Social-science Commentary,* 125.

70 V.P. Hamilton, *The Book of Genesis, Chs. 1-17* (Michigan: Wm. B. Eerdmans Publishing Company, 1990), 370.

71 Gottwald, *The Hebrew Bible...*, 156-157.

72 Hamilton, *The Book of Genesis...*, 370-371.

God's first words to Abraham, in which he commands him to leave Haran and proceed to an unknown destination, initiate a theme which recurs several times and dominates these 'patriarchal' stories; the promise, in this case (12:1-3) that Abraham's descendants will become a great nation and that he will be especially blessed. In subsequent passages[73] the promise is repeated, first to Abraham himself and then to Isaac and Jacob, in somewhat different words, and with one notable addition: a promise of possession of the land of Canaan.[74] The patriarchs are never pictured as owners of the land.[75] The Canaanites (12:6; 13:7) and other peoples (Ch. 23) were in possession; Abraham and his family are described as resident aliens (23:4; 35:27), passing through reader than settling. The promises of possession of the land, then, were not for immediate fulfilment but for the future.[76] Here the promise of posterity is clearly labled earlier, associated with the nomadic period, while the promise of the land is associated with the claims of settlers.[77]

There are two fundamentally different approaches to the theme of the patriarchal promises. The one stresses the basis unity of the theme within the source J and the impact that the theme has on the shaping of the Pentateuch as a whole. The other looks for the origin and growth of the promises theme by dividing it into small units and then relating their evolution into more complex forms to successive stages in the growth of the patriarchal tradition as a whole.[78] The traditions have been intensively studied by form critics with a view to unravelling the many types of divine blessings anticipated by promise or conferred in activity.[79]

This is clear from 35:12, where in renewing the promise God says, 'the land that I *gave* to Abraham and Isaac, I will give to you, and I will give the land to your offspring after you' - when in fact he had *not yet* given possession of the land at all, either to Abraham or to Isaac. The Hebrew verb נָתַר (*nathan*) '*give*', here used in the past tense, clearly means something more like promise to give in this passage at least.[80]

73 Especially 17:4-8; 22:17-18; 26:3-5, 24; 28:13-15; 35:10-12.

74 Whybray, *Introduction to the Pentateuch...*, 4.

75 The promise of possession of the land of Canaan, to which Abraham (or his father) had moved from Ur of the Chaldeans (15:7), was in fact never fulfilled in the course of the book of Genesis. (Whybray, *Introduction to the Pentateuch...*, 53).

76 Whybray, *Introduction to the Pentateuch...*, 53.

77 C. Westermann, *The Promise to the Fathers, Studies on Patriarchal Narratives,* trans. David E. Green (Philadelphia: Fortress Press, 1980), 6.

78 Setters, *The Pentateuch, a Social-Science Commentary,* 64.

79 Gottwald, *The Hebrew Bible...*, 156-157.

80 Whybray, *Introduction to the Pentateuch...*, 53.

Relevance of Migration Motif in Present Day Context

The Ancestors of Israel were not looked from the perspective of Migrants due to the reverence the biblical narrations give to them. The sources of the Ancestors portray that they have esteemed value to the History of Israel from the faith perspective than the migrant's perspective. Søren Kierkegaard discusses Abraham from ethics and faith perspective than migrant's perspective. The Ancestors migrating from one place to another cannot be considered as a faith aspect. Migrating from one place to another brings social, cultural and economical dislocations including the life threatening experiences. Migrants who leave their place were exposed to be attached, chances of losing their belongings, sexual harassments etc. In this context, the Ancestors were vulnerable to their own existence.

The Ancestral narratives presents a numerous social issue while they attempt to settle down in Canaan. There was an identity crisis, conflict with neighbours, disputes over well, land, and belongs were the issues that were associated with Ancestors. The Ancestral narrative also conceals the silent suffering of the women who were with the Ancestors, carrying heavy loads, caring the children, feeding all those who were with them. The women were kept asunder from political and economic roles and confined to be the caretakers. The similar issues of the migrants could be seen in various parts of our globe, people migrate on want of job, due to terrorism, exclusivist parochialism etc. The biblical texts gives impetus to the migrants issues in the present day context not only from the faith perspective but also from social and ethical perspective as well.

Conclusion

The Ancestral narratives begin with the background of Abram who was called by the Lord to go to the place where the Lord shows him to go. This probably would have happened at the end of the Second Millennium BCE. During this period there were many people who moved from place to place for various reasons. For some it is due to famine, finding pastures for the cattle, seasonal business, caravans who move from one place to another and sell their products of the desert on their way, etc. Some Biblical scholars call this as movements in the Ancient West Asian regions during the end of the Second Millennium BCE.

The Biblical scholarship struggle with many issues in the patriarchal narratives such as the age of the patriarchs, their sojourn in the Ancient West Asian world, the process of their life-style, their wealth, economical status, and above all their seclusion from the society for the cause of the divine. One of the major issues of the Ancestors is that of the nomadism. It is a clear fact that the Ancestors moved from place to place, tented at the places where the Lord asked them to do so, and also removed their tents according to the directions of the Lord moved to other places. They moved from place to place, mainly the outskirts of the City-States of the Canaan and Egypt. They did not live totally in the desert as it was argued by some of the biblical scholars. Certainly, they moved from one place to another place not for the commercial purposes like that of the *great* nomads or the Caravans. But they solely travelled from place to place under the divine guidance. In other words, it is the divine who asked the Ancestors to move from placed to place. During this movement, the promise of the child(ren) and the land was assured to them. Though the process to acquire the promise of the child(ren) and the land to some extent took shorter or the longer period, in all this endower, the divine guidance was the cause behind the Ancestors.

4

Justice for the Ger (*rg*) in the OT Traditions against the Exilic Context

S. Jaganathan

It is no more a matter of discussion that most of books of the Old Testament took a sort of written form when the people of Judah were Exiled in Babylon. So the books of the Bible, reflecting various traditions or sources had a common platform of experience, i.e. their bitter experience of being Exiled in Babylon, an expedition carried out under the Babylonian King Nebuchadnazzor. The 'alienation' motif is at the root of all Biblical books to whatever source or tradition we may ascribe to the book. The focus of this article is to show that the aliens '*ger*' in the Old Testament is the fundamental experience of the people of Israel and on the basis and scale of this experience how they should extend their social relations to the aliens who were in their land for one reason or other.

1. Vocabulary

The marginalized or the impoverished group is referred to various groups of people at various historical periods. The landless poor who depended on the rich were the marginalized and during the monarchical times but such a group can't be identified during the period of Israel's settlement in the land of Canaan when everybody had their share of land. But there are three groups of people who were identified as marginalized and who deserved justice and compassion – the widows, the orphans and the strangers. Our present debate concerns the third group, the strangers or the aliens. The Hebrew Bible uses three terminologies to denote the 'stranger'. The word ***nokri*** (yrkn) denotes a foreigner, who follows his/her own religion without much involvement in the tribal system of the Israelite covenant community, as it is found in Psalm 144:7 ".... set me free and rescue me from the mighty waters, from the hand of the aliens (nkr – rkn). They neither are included in the Passover sharing nor enjoy the remission of the 7th year debts. This word is used in Is. 2: 6 "For you have forsaken the ways of your people, O House of Jacob. Indeed they are full of diviners from the east and of soothsayers like the Philistines and they clasp hands with foreigners (yrkn)" clearly points out a negative picture of this group of people. Slightly different, the word ***tosav (bvwt)*** is used in pair with ***ger.*** These ***tosavs*** seem to represent a group of temporary residents without much involvement in the socio-economic and religious life of the Israelites. But the *ger* are those who are considered to be resident aliens who remain with the Israelites permanently or for a longer duration who seem to deserve justice and compassion from the Israelite community.

2. Being in an Exile: Threat of Losing one's own Identity

The '*ger*' experience of the People of Israel: The prophet of social justice had a prophetic look beyond the prosperity of the northern Kingdom ruled by Jeroboam II and saw a doom of captivity and deportation, which we might call a forced migration that took place under Sargon II, the Assyrian King in 722. Amos could clearly see that '*Gilgal shall surely go into Exile and Bethel shall come to nothing*' (Amos 5:5b). Interestingly both the places mentioned by Amos were places of God experience when the protagonists Jacob and the people of Israel were in migration. Jacob experienced God in his migration from Beersheba in the place called Bethel (Gen 28:10-13) was the place of Yahweh-experience when Jacob was fleeing from Beersheba and Gilgal was the place of God-experience when the people of Israel were migrating to the land of Canaan in the place called Gilgal (Joshua 4:19-24). These places of God-experience have deprived people of true God-experience and so they no more deserve to have these spaces, they need to be deprived of these places and go in migration, as a punishment. In other instances like Gilgal and Beersheba are cities which were destined for Exile and destruction (Gen 21:14, 32-33; 26:23-25).

In Ninth Century BCE, prophets were voice of critique against individuals and their individual abuses which was paving way for social chaos and disasters. But in the Eight Century BCE, the prophets began to challenge the cultic, political and social institutions as well. They dared to challenge these institutions in the name of Yahweh and foresee and forecast the destruction of these institutions which were insensitive to the unjust practices prevalent in their institutions. Amos, Hosea and Micah in the North and Isaiah in the South were compelled to question the conventionality. The most daring prophet was Amos who was a migrant from the Southern side and prophesied in the North. Throughout Israel, whether it be North or South, a prosperous aggressive rich landowners placed themselves over the small land-owners and developed the philosophy of self-sufficiency and prosperity which forced the small landowners stand at the brink, unable to cope up with the recurrent tragedies of agriculture with a heavy debt on their head. This made them permanently impoverished and prophets called them *dal* (weak) and *anaw* (the wretched). This social injustice was prevalent in the Northern side since it was more fertile but was no less found also in Judah. Amos who was a farmer, a shepherd and dresser of sycamore trees was such a *dal* who lost his land in such a tragedy and goes to the North to condemn this social atrocity of the large landowners and the social institutions which support them.

In all his condemnation of injustice and sin, the Lord reminded Israel of their state of being migrants from the land of Egypt '*Yet I destroyed his fruit above and his roots beneath. Also I brought you up out of the land of Egypt and led you forty years in wilderness.....' (Amos 2:9-10).* The series of social sins narrated in Amos 2:6 *viz,* selling the righteous for silver, the needy for a pair of sandals, trampling the head of the poor into the dust of the earth, pushing the afflicted out of the way, etc., invoke a heavy gravity and seriousness because these social evils against the marginalized were committed by the Israelites, a group of people who were in the form of oppression, namely a band of landless, impoverished slaves who were on migration to a land promised by Yahweh. So prosperity and wealth of the reign of the kings of Israel came to an end with the Assyrian Captivity and with the deportation of the people of Israel into Assyria and with part of the population fleeing to the Southern Kingdom, Judah and settling in the suburbs of the Judaean cities. Miller and Hayes summarises the consequences of this destruction of the North (Samaria) as follow:

> A significant portion of the population was deported, along with the cultic symbols of the Israelite deity. One of the goals of deportation, in addition to punishment for rebellion was to remove those in leadership and thus to lessen the likelihood of nationalistic uprisings in the future. A second goal was to supply populations for use in other areas of the empire. Deportees were utilized in various ways by the Assyrians, as settlers in sparsely populated areas, especially in depopulated areas, especially in areas needing agricultural improvements as skilled workers in various crafts, and as general labourers throughout the empire. According to II Kings 17:6, the Israelites were resettled in Halah, and on the Habor, the river of Gozan and in the cities of the Medes. Foreign populations were resettled in Samaria, especially from Babylonia, Syria. Samaria continued to be the recipient of new settlers for several years.

So, Israel was forced out to be a migrant outside its own territory because it forgot its migration from the land of Egypt and failed to support the similarly marginalized, especially failed to protect the rights of those who had suffered the fate of migration. It must be also noted that some of the northern population might have fled south to avoid deportation. It is in this way that many of the northern traditions were also brought to the South.

The '*ger*' experience of the People of Judah

The fall of Samaria threatened Judah to the extent that Hezekiah who began to intensify Yahwistic reform in the South. A General summary of Hezekiah's life and ministry is provided in II Kings 18-20, II Chronicles 29-32 and Isaiah 36-39. Hezekiah is presented as a good king, sandwiched between his predecessor Ahaz and successor Manasseh, who were not upheld as good kings. He intensified Yahwism in the land and this would be later taken by Josiah who would launch the Deuteronomistic reform based on the scrolls (Part of the book of Deuteronomy) called as the Book of the Law. The unexpected death of Josiah in 609 BCE resulted in the Deuteronomistic reform entering into a 'coma' stage, unfunctional although very important personalities of the royal court and of the general population and priestly and prophetic groups, like Jeremiah the priest and prophet, were part of it. Jeremiah's temple sermon (Jer. 7) was a severe criticism of Jehoiakim and in 605, in the fourth year of his reign, Jehoiakim was warned by Jeremiah that Yahweh would send for all the tribes of the North and for Nebuchadnezzar and would bring them against the land of Judah and utterly destroy it. He also predicted that Yahweh will utterly destroy the land the whole land shall become a ruin and a waste and these nations will serve the King of Babylon seventy years (Jer. 25:11). The severe criticism of Jeremiah against Jehoiakim who undertook building projects and harassed the poor predicted the destruction of Judah and the Exile. It was during Zedekiah's time that the final Exile had taken place. The royal palace, temple, city homes of citizens were burnt. The walls of Jerusalem were felled. City was ravaged. Treasuries were carried away (II Kgs 25:13). The leading priests, royal officials and commanders and province-leaders were taken to Riblah and executed before Nebuchadnezzar (Jer. 52). The leading citizens were taken to Babylon (II Kgs 25:11-12). Yahweh himself forced out his people in migration to a far-off land. A part of the people also migrated to Egypt. A vulnerable group of common people remained amidst destroyed ruins of Judah. The deportation affected the upper class. The people who were left in the land suffered on account of constant confrontation from the surrounding countries since they had neither military power to confront them nor leaders who could guide them to face these pressures. So even in their own land, they lived like migrants, without their territorial and social integrity and identity.

A voluntary group migrated to Egypt and settled along the upper and Lower Egypt, in the military cities like Migdol, Memphis and Daphne and many of them served as soldiers in the Egyptian Military. They began to integrate themselves into the society well and they formed their place of worship. The theology of renewal, revival and restoration which sprang up in Babylonian circles was not seen in a favourable light in the Egyptian Gola.

Those who were migrated to Babylon, had lost their land, culture and religion. It was a social uprooting. The sense of being removed from their land against their will was a traumatic experience. So the identity of the people of Judah was totally lost due to this Exile, the force migration. There were some who could integrate themselves with the new society without giving up their national ethnicity. Here levites, priests and prophets, though not functioning as such, had their own loyalties. They were placed in groups in abandoned places for agriculture and hence were in simple employment. Although, there was no inhuman treatments, absence of the temple, sacrifice, being away from their homeland, etc... made them constantly grieve over their situation.

To summarise, few facts appears clear about Exile of Israel. **First**, Exile was a forced migration whether it be the Exile of the people of Samaria in 722 or the Exile of the people of Judah in 587. The Migration of one group of people, made the left-over in the land suffer more on account of insecurity, constant confrontation with the surrounding countries, lack of leadership, etc. S**econdly**, Exile has resulted in the loss of identity of the people of Israel. They became people without a land, people without a king, people without temple and cult, people without destiny and goal. They become a vulnerable group without identity. **Thirdly**, this forced migration was done by Yahweh himself. A faith-struggle was among those who were Exiled who could not reconcile their invincible Yahweh with their present state of defeat and despair. **Fourthly and finally**, this forced migration has divided the Israelites all the more, who were already divided as people of Judah and People of Israel. The on, a further division enters: people who were Exiled and who were in the land. This led to series of struggles and confrontations among these groups in the latter history of Israel.

Towards Reconstructing Identity: Various Revival Groups (Traditions) and their Theology

The ideological struggle of the migrant groups in Babylonian Exile

The agony of the Exiled ones can't be easily understood by a generation like us who are separated from the event by several centuries. It is not an exaggeration that the people of Judah who had witnessed how Yahweh delivered his city and his temple, from the Assyrians hoped till the end that Yahweh would somehow miraculously deliver His city and His House, the Temple. For them, the Zion-theology itself became a question. How could the temple, in which Yahweh took his abode be desecrated and destroyed by his enemies? The veracity of the truths and beliefs transmitted through the priests and prophets was therefore questioned.

The Deuteronomistic Ideology

If we look at the developments at the early post-exilic period, we can identify three main rival schemes which were trying to reshape the Jewish community in an effort to regain the identity of the Exiled Israelites. They were the Deuteronomistic group in its basic and developed form (DtrG and JerD), the priestly reformed theology and the salvation-tradition of Deutero Isaiah. Of these, we can easily understand that the basic form of Deuteronomistic theology was from a lay group who were more interested in the land. For example, the whole book of Judges is from this tradition, and the book of Judges is nothing but a struggle of the local heroes of some tribes to possess the land, retain and land and preserve and protect the land from the enemy tribes or nations. It not only paves the way for a freedom for land, it emphasizes also the lay-administration of the land. For them, the only way to the restoration of the Jewish identity was to regain the land as the land was obtained by Joshua, as it was protected and quite often redeemed by Judges. The basis of this Deuteronomistic tradition goes back to Hezekiah's reform who had some sort of accessibility to an oldest strata of Deuteronomy which is called the Book of the Covenant. This book of the covenant (Ex. 20:23-23.19) is seen as the legal basis for Hezekiah's reform. There can be no hesitation regarding the precedence of this book of the covenant before the Deuteronomistic reform since, the book of the covenant gives a special concentration on the protection of the sojourner (migrant) or alien (22: 20, 23:9) which is a reaction to the increasingly serious problem of the migrants which Judah was to confront especially after the fall of Samaria in the North. The post exilic Deuteronomists brought a remarkable insight to be instilled in the minds of the people that they should learn from the mistakes of the past. This prophetic Deuteronomistic movement first began to integrate and systematize the prophetic opposition theology into the Jewish religion. It this post exilic, or a migrant community which brought in the concept of a sacred historiography that God acts in History. The Deuteronomists are convinced that the Law of Moses was a gift. But the Land was the saving gift. So, it can be said that even the establishment of Kingship in Israel, the David-cycle of D stories were intended to reinstate the fact that the supreme gift of Land should not be lost and even if Kingship is to be removed from Yahweh and given to an earthly human, Yahweh desires that this land be preserved and protected for the sake of the people. So, Deuteronomists began to think on the problem of land at the time of their Exile, when they lost their land and were in Exile, i.e. when they faced the dangers of migration in Babylon.

The Priestly Ideology

Any surface reader of the Old Testament would understand what is meant by Priestly source. It is one of the ancient sources of the Pentateuch and it gains its name from the fact that the priests and cultic personnel were behind these writings. Today, many scholars hold on to the idea that even though some oral priestly sayings had a pre-exilic origin, the written and the theological priestly document comes from the post exilic times. This is from the priests who wanted to preserve their role and identity. After the destruction of the temple, the priests faced the threat of the destruction of priesthood and the sacrificial system. So, the priestly documents are an attempt on the part of the priestly group to reinstate their honour and dignity in the Israelite community. It is also said that the priestly writings do not refer back to the system of sacrifices and priestly functions during the monarchical period but are admonitions how the priestly system is to be restored in the post-exilic situation. The priestly laws are to be considered as post-exilic innovations in the rituals to be introduced in the second temple period. Passages that deal with purity and defilement, theophany, sacrificial systems, priests, etc. naturally have P writer beneath them. Very important is the P source in Exodus 25-31, 35-40, Lev. 1-16. For this tradition, the Jewish identity can be restored and revived only by Priests, only by the sacrificial system and only by maintaining the laws of Purity. The priestly tradition material has several layers of formation by editing and redacting which took place simultaneously or successively. Among such developments we have a unique block of material in Leviticus 17-27 which is called Holiness Code. While P restricts to priests and Nazirites (Numbers6:5-8), H refers to all of Israel. For P spatial holiness is confined to the sanctuary while for H the spatial holiness is extended to the whole land. This development should have taken place only when the Israelites were in Exile, when there was a question on their sanctity and holiness beyond the holy temple, city and land. It is also to be noted that that the priestly holiness is static and confined to rituals while the Holiness of the H school is dyanamic, pervading into the structures of the society. As for P traditions, defilement is confined to rituals and sanctuary but for H, defilement is in the social evils such as idolatry, depriving the land of its rest, incest, social injustice, etc. The forced migration of the Judahites into Babylon, made them re-reflect on the concept of defilement. While the P tradition tries to regain the their identity by reviving their cult in Jerusalem, the Holiness School tries to formulate alternate modes of re-establishing their identity, i.e. by a new holiness which is inclusive, society and justice oriented. The context of being in the foreign land, made the priestly group and Holiness school re-formulate the concept of Holiness in their ideologies although basically they believed that the Jewish identity lies in the fact of their being Holy to the Lord.

The Salvation Tradition of Deutero Isaiah

The disciples of the prophets who had some fragmentary forms of the prophetic sayings of the prophets were constantly making a critique of the monarchy, the temple and priesthood and the political affairs of the state. But in the exilic (migration) context, this prophetic tradition was trying to give more reasons as to how this Exile happened. The prophetic traditions ideology has to be retrospectively reconstructed basic justice in the society and purity in cult. But the Salvation tradition of Deutero Isaiah is a new light that appeared in the midst of the post-exilic Jews. Though the Babylonian community had no overt animosity over the Judahites, the Exiles had a deep psychological distress mixed with the feeling of impotence and religious regression. As years passed by, the return to their homeland seemed almost impossible. The generation who became active in Babylonia were more attracted to the Babylonian gods and images which grieved the older generation. A small group of people, behind the name, 'Deutero Isaiah' began to perceive a new beginning behind these political chaos. The ideology of this group of salvation-propagandists is preserved in Is. 40-55. So by Deutero-Isaiah, we can understand a group of theologians from the background of temple singers, cult prophets and pro-salvation groups from the laity. According to them, Yahweh was at work in the miraculously victorious in the course of history. He will end the days of gloom and sadness. He will bring salvation in unpredictable way and in an unpredictable time using unexpected humans like Cyrus the Persian and the Suffering servant. The concrete sign of this salvation is their return back to their land, rebuild the temple and live in harmony and peace.

Apart from these dominant theological ideological controversies, there were many small groups which were labelled together as non-priestly sources but which did not go much in hand with the Salvation tradition or Deuteronomistic tradition. While the later Deuteronomists questioned the validity of the temple worship and the Israelite rituals, there were sections of people who began to question the relevance of the Deuteronomistic tradition itself. They trusted that all was well as long as Yahweh was worshipped with Asherah and that disaster fell on them when these god-figures were removed by the Deuteronomists starting with Josiah (Jer. 44:17-19)! This paved the new way for the family piety which is devoid of temple and cult. This comes closer to J source which is more human-centred, family centred, society oriented, etc.

The state of Exile made them think of a religion which is family centred. This type of religion does not require a temple or a specified place for God experience. It is from this type of source many family-stories in Pentateuch took its shape. The God-experience of Abraham is narrated in Gen. 18 where Abraham entertains three men who were 'standing' at the entrance of his tent. The word, 'standing' literally refers to the state of being on motion, journeying. Similarly the J story of creation and Adam and Eve being cast out of the Paradise, is a post exilic reflection of the holiness of the creation of Humankind, obedience to God as the state of being in the land, disobedience as the state of being in Exile. The J story of Cain ending in his fate of being a wanderer is a post exilic reflection of violence (*hamas*) making Israel wanderer!

If we take the Exile as a migration, the post exilic migration experience has led various groups come up with their reflections to restore the identity of the people of Israel once again. This type of divergence and mutual challenges set in motion two opposite movements, i.e. integration and disintegration. The most important example of integration is the formation of the Biblical books in the written form. So the migration experience of the people of Israel lies at the bottom of this integration, although the presentations of these often contradicting ideologies are expressed in tense and rigid dialogues. It is this migration experience, which gradually excluded the kingship theology and prophecy (although against kings and priests) was gradually included into the formation of the Biblical corpus. So consciously or unconsciously, the migration experience of the Exilic community lies at the bottom of all traditions be it priestly, Deuteronomistic or salvific. This is collective integration of the experiences, feelings, reflections prayers and hopes of a community which was thrown out of its land. The disintegrating element is the later development at the end of the fourth and beginning of the third centuries which once again gave an important place to the Davidic Kingship and covers the monarchy (Joshua - II Kings) in general canonization in the Third Century

Select Texts Reflecting on Justice to the Migrants

Exodus 22:21:- *"You shall not wrong or oppress a resident alien, for you were aliens in the land of Egypt"*

Exodus 23:9 :- *"You shall not oppress a resident alien; you know the heart of an alien, for your aliens in the land of Egypt"*

These verses are from D Source with its origin in the Book of the covenant (20:23-23:9). This seems to be the oldest legislation of the Bible. As we have seen earlier, Hezekiah based his reform on this basic precept. It is interesting to note that the earliest written laws of in the Bible, i.e. the Book of the Covenant consisted only of social laws except for the introductory section 20:22-26. The components of this section are: (i) Laws concerning the slaves (ii) Laws concerning Violence (iii) Laws concerning property (iv) Laws on restitution (v) Social and Religious Laws (vi) justice for all. The laws on the aliens (*rg*) comes under the section of Justice and forms an inclusion 22:21 & 23:9. The section begins with the alien and proceeds justice to the widow, orphan, poor, and concludes with aliens (*rg*) once again.

Though the book seems to be part of the instruction in the Sinai narrative, this section is to be taken as a separate unit, interrupting the Sinai narrative and it betrays a settled culture. So, the social and community laws which existed at the time of the initial settlement were retrospectively taken back to the time of Moses to gain moral authority and power. Most of the verbs are in the second person plural imperative form which shows that these were dictated to a group either in common gatherings or even in public cultic places. So, even in the heart of the cultic and communal functions, the most important laws were laws of social justice and a special emphatic place is given to the alien (rg) both in the beginning and at the end.

The word ger *(rg)* alien is placed as the first word of the sentence and is in the emphatic position, and the literal translation would be 'and the stranger, do not oppress him'. The alien is not to be oppressed for he is vulnerable for he lacks the support or protection of his clan. The word 'ger' can be taken to mean traveller, stranger, sojourner, temporary dweller, new-comer etc. And the word oppress is in the *hifil* form which is causative, meaning to say that you don't become ever the cause for the suffering of the alien. The word 'oppress' (hgn) is not a very strong word, it can even mean maltreat. Even such unpleasant treatment of the alien or migrant is not tolerated in the ancient law of the Israelites. With the migrant are added the other vulnerable such as the widow and the orphan. The style shifts to the first person where God says, "I myself will head their cry, my wrath will burn and I will kill you. The ancient law says that maltreatment of the vulnerable, of whom the sojourner or migrant is the first, deserves death penalty directly from God. The ground for this law is three fold: (1) Israel knows from her past experience what is to be a migrant or a sojourner. (2) God is compassionate to these vulnerable as they don't have any one to support them and they become the property of God (3) the fact of covenant relationship with Yahweh excludes any type maltreatment of the sojourner.

So the earliest 'law narrative', which served as a basis for the Hezekian reform and for the reform of Josiah, articulates social comfortability and relations as the foundation of Jewish religion and among the socially marginalized the aliens or migrants stand out miserably.

Lev. 19:33-34 :- "*When an alien resides with you in your land, you shall not oppress the alien. The alien who resides with you shall be to you as the citizen among you; you shall love the alien as yourself, for you were aliens in the land*".

This text is from Holiness Code – a further development of Priestly Tradition. The Holiness in the Old Testament is not to be taken merely as 'unapproachability' as the God of Old Testament who was unapproachable. Holiness is neither absence of sin. It is a positive concept and a goal associated with God's nature, a internal power gained by uniting oneself to Yahweh and to his fellow humans. The Holiness Code talks of holiness for all without restricting it to a select few. It is a participation of the life-giving power of God. "Be holy, as I am holy" (Lev. 19:2).

Leviticus 19, part of this holiness code deals with respect for God's creation. 19:2-10 sets the foundation principles for Holiness. The primordial principle that Yahweh states is: "I am the Lord, your God (v. 3, 4, 10). The second section (19:11-18) deals with relationships and the founding virtues which underlie good relationships *viz*, integrity (vv.11-12), no exploitation (vv. 13-14), justice (vv.15-16) and Love (vv. 17-18). The second part (vv.19-37) dealing with respect, talks about respect for boundaries (v.19), respect for people (20-22, 29, 32-36), respect for nature (23-25) and respect for God (26-28, 30-31,37).

The commandment to withhold oneself from oppressing the alien and to love the alien comes in the section which deals with respect for the people. The Old Testament speaks as much as 36 times with regard to protecting the alien and admonishes the Israelites to love them. The Holiness code amplifies the basic form which is the Book of the Covenant. The distinction between the Book of the covenant and the Holiness code is that the Book of covenant deals with a prohibitive law that one should follow in order to avoid punishment. In the Holiness code, the people are not only commanded to withhold from oppressing the aliens but also positively love them in order to share in the Holiness of Yahweh. Developing on the theme of holiness which the priests insisted as purity from defilement that comes through impure elements and sins, the Holiness school improves on the theme of holiness that is beyond the space of the sanctuary, well into the world where an alien, however impure he/she might be, lives with them.

Psalm 137

This is a Lamentation Liturgy. Alienated from the temple and thrown away from the cultic superiority, the Exiled Judahites had all the dangers of losing their relationship with God but for the lamentations that are preserved as some lamentation psalms in the Psalter as well as in the some lamentations in the prophetic books. We are unaware how the Judahites managed to maintain their faith in Yahweh without the official cult or sacrificial system. However, as far as we see, the main cult of the exilic period was the lamentation. Even after the Exile was over, the practice of fast and lament continued, especially on 9th of *Ab*, the day when Babylon desecrated and destroyed the temple. The occasional laments which were not part of Israelite cult in the pre-exilic times came to be incorporated into the official cultic program of the Israelites. Crossing the barriers of wretchedness of human condition, the migration experience opened up the cultic doors for the expressions of human mourning. The temple in Jerusalem needed purity cult namely the *hattat*. The post exilic community, crossing these barriers, had the boldness to bring as songs for the cult. Psalm 137 is a typical psalm of this time. We can find these types of lamentations in various books of the Bible. Jer. 41:5, I Kgs. 8; 46, Psalms 44, 60, 79, 89, Lamentations 5 are some examples of this phenomenon. These lamentations betray a struggle for a theological re orientation.

> Psalm 137 has an exilic Babylonian setting, it brings out the emotional outbreak and a depressive nostalgia towards their homeland. This is a community lament for God to destroy the oppressors and enemies.

The utter desolation and mourning is brought out by the expressions 'sat and wept'. Sitting is the posture for lamenting in the funeral house. The root word underlying 'wept' means to break out emotionally, cry aloud with accusations. River is a place of joy and exhilaration. But the rivers of Babylon have been the setting for the Israelites to cry aloud. The harps were hung in the willows, meaning to say that they were not used as an accompaniment. Harps were used as an accompaniment in joyful praises of God. Exiled from their homeland, the Judahites complain that their captors and tormentors asked them for a song. The Zion songs were sung as they were on pilgrimages to the Holy city and they sang such songs on the days when they celebrated the Kingship of Yahweh. Now that they are far removed from the temple, the temple being destroyed and ravaged, they were not able to sing such songs of Zion.

Plea against the enemies and prayer for their annihilation is part of the lamentation Psalms. Here the migrants pray for the total destruction of Edomites, who were their enemies. They joined the Babylonians in the sacking and pillaging of Jerusalem and handed over fleeing survivors to the Babylonians (Ez. 25, 35, Ob. 8-14).

Conclusion

Many books of the Old Testament gained their written form during the post exilic times. Though it was a period of agony and despair, their situation as Migrants made them to reflect on their identity and how they could re-form, and stabilize that identity. This migration experience was the compelling experience which pushed them for reflection and reintegration. Though there were opposing ideologies, they had grown to the level of incorporating all these ideologies for the restoration and revivification of their Jewish heritage. They looked back their first migration from Egypt with the eyes of this Exile. This exilic experience is reflected in every part of the Bible. So, the Migration perspective is not one of the many perspectives with which we must read the Bible, it should be taken as the indispensable author context of nearly the entire Bible.

5

Strangers and Aliens in 1 Peter Towards Constructing a Symbiotic Community

K. Balakrishnan

"Wherever there is social life, there is conflict"[1] Conflicts are ubiquitous phenomena which cause devastation, displacement and disruption to people. As a result, human lives are jeopardized to a great extent. People who live in the conflict-torn zone make their vigorous attempts to leave their native place or country in order to find safety and shelter elsewhere. The predicament of the refugees is precariously increasing more and more due to multiple reasons. It is in fact true that migration has been a constant feature of not only humanity and human history, but also the God of the Bible is the God of migration. The Biblical God is always on the move along with the people of God. Both the Old Testament and the New Testament are filled with stories of migration and the migrants as well as challenges of offering hospitality to the migrants. In this section, an attempt is made to identify and locate the fact and issue of migration through the metaphors of strangers, alien and diaspora as found in 1 Peter as author addresses the Petrine Christians with these metaphors who encountered displacement, homelessness and alienation probably because of their faith and the resultant persecution and dispersion. Further, this section also explores possibility of constructing and consolidating an *oikos* or a symbiotic community through the interweaving threads of these metaphors.

Historical Locations of the Migrants in 1 Peter

Prior to identifying and locating the Strangers and Aliens in 1 Peter, it is important to have a glimpse of the historical settings of the Epistle of 1 Peter. From the first chapter verse one we come to know that the Letter of 1 Peter is addressed to Asia Minor comprising Pontus, Galatia, Cappadocia, Asia and Bithynia which were under the Roman provinces. The amount of territory covered by these provinces is approximately, 129,000 square miles. Thus, 1 Peter is addressed to a

1 B.J. Malina, "The Social Sciences and Biblical Interpretation," *Interpretation* (1982): 235.

larger area than any other letter of the NT.[2] It appears that the People addressed in these localities belonged to the Jewish dispersion. For it is probable that the commercial, economic and educational opportunities in those places attracted immigrants, both Jews and Greeks. We can see the diverse population of Asia Minor in the following description:

> The attraction of educational opportunities (such as the university at Tarsus) and health spas (at the renowned Asclepian spring shrines) and athletic and dramatic festivals, religious pilgrimages, mass movements of deported groups, the banishment of individuals, and the peregrinations of assorted itinerant philosophers and religious missionaries.[3]

This illuminates that the immigrants were attracted to these places due to multiple advantages that offered to the immigrants. Further, the Epistle also provides glimpses of the suffering the Petrine community experienced (1:6; 4:12; 19; 5:9, 12) and the Christians were challenged (3:15), abused (3:16; 4:4) and put into suffering. This gives us an impression that the Petrine community experienced suffering. However, the epistle does not shed any further light on who were responsible in causing a fiery trial (4:12) to these community. It is also not clear whether they suffered under the Roman Emperors. In this regard, it is important to note that the persecution of the Christians took place under four Roman emperors: 1) Nero, 54-68 CE; 2) Vespasian, 69-79; 3) Domitian, 81-96; and 4) Trajan, 97-117.[4]

While the NT Scholars were sees to locate more precisely the historical situation that surrounded the context of the writing, they generally points to the period of persecution of Christians under Nero in the 60s. This would make sense of references made to malice and the "fiery ordeals" and the general feeling of apprehension that characterises the document as a whole. (4:4, 12, 16).[5] However, the Nero's persecution, as it is assumed, was confined to the vicinity of Rome. In this respect, Achtemeier observes: "While Nero's persecution of the Christians was certainly "official" to the extent that the emperor ordered it, it was local, affecting only the Christians in Rome."[6] This view vitiates the contention that the Roman persecution did not affect the location of the Petrine community. If so, the Neronian persecution did not affect the areas as mentioned in chapter

2 J.H. Elliot, *1 Peter- A New Translation with Introduction and Commentary* (New Haven/ London: Yale University Press, 2000), 84.

3 J.H. Elliot, *Home for the Homeless: A Sociological Exegesis of 1 Peter- Its Strategy and Situation* (Philadelphia: Fortress, 1981), 67.

4 P.J. Achtemeier, *1 Peter* (Minneapolis: Fortress, 1996), 29-33.

5 As cited in J. B. Green, *1 Peter: Two Horizons New Testament Commentary* (Grand Rapids/ Michigan: Eerdmans, 2007), 8.

6 Achtemeier, *1 Peter…*, 33. See Green, *1 Peter…*, 8.

one verse one, the persecution of the community could be located under the reign of Domitian (81-96 CE).

Domitian indeed was known as a second Nero who caused a widespread persecution and put a number of Christians into death. While some scholars like Baur and Wand argue that Domitian did not persecute the Christians, there is ample evidence that the Christians did in fact fall victim to Domitian's lethal wrath.[7] This suggests that the Christians seem to have suffered under the reign of Domitian. At the same time, there are certain difficulties in locating the suffering of the Petrine Christians under the reign of Domitian: 1) it will question the authorship of the Epistle by Peter, the apostle; and 2) it will rule out Peter's direct involvement in its content. Green on this remarks that "if it is impossible to associate the historical situation of I Peter with official persecution under Nero, the same may be said of other actions against Christian believers under the emperor Domitian (CE 81-96)."[8] This suggests that it is too difficult to precisely locate the persecution of the Petrine community under any particular Roman Emperor. Green again observes:

> In fact, the situation presumed by 1 Peter is easy to place throughout the Roman Empire, and therefore difficult to pinpoint more precisely on a timeline. Periods of hostility toward the Christians, such as that experienced under Domitian, were only intensifications of a more pervasive menace toward foreigners, especially from the East, with their non-traditional religions.[9]

This suggests that the Christians faced persecution throughout the Roman period. Green also indicates that there were immigrants from the Eastern part to Rome. The immigrants were dumped like sewage in Grand River according to satirical Juvenal (saturate 3.60-65, written in a second century). Lucian of Samosata (born at CE 120) narrates a disdainful account, narrating a person who was converted to Christian faith and then he rejected the Christian faith. Further, he speaks of the man who was crucified in Palestine and later he introduced a new cult to the world. The significant aspect of that writing is seen against the Christians as worshipping *the crucified sophist.*[10] This indicates the fact that the Christians were treated with utter contempt. Moreover, 1 Peter is silent about the Roman sponsored programme of persecution.[11] Although, it is very difficult to establish the official persecution of the community by the Roman Emperor, the suffering of the Christians in the Roman Empire cannot be denied.

---

7 Achtemeier, *1 Peter...*, 31; Green..., *1 Peter*, 9-10.

8 Green, *I Peter...*, 8.

9 Green, *1 Peter...*, 9.

10 As cited in Green, *1 Peter...*, 9.

11 Green, *1 Peter...*, 9.

The letter does attest to suffering: (1:6; 3:14; 4:1, 12, 16, 19; 5:9, 10), revile (3:9, 16; 4:14). If the persecution of the community lacked the official policy of the Roman government, the local authorities or people may have been responsible in instigating and causing the persecution. Perhaps, the withdrawal of the Christians from the social and cultural activities of the local populace might have incurred the animosity of the local people (4: 16; 4:14). It is likely to believe that the Christians failed to take part in religious activities and, particularly the emperor's worship which assumed more importance by the local elites than the Emperors themselves. It was in the context of such religious fervour accorded to the emperor cult and to the local gods that the Christians might have been accused of disloyalty and malefactors.[12] In particular, the suffering of Christ on the tree would have incurred aversion from the Roman government. As a result of this aversion, the local citizens would have brought social pressure on the Christians.[13] Not only did the Christians suffer physical violence but they also encountered social discrimination. Whatever might be the situation behind the persecution, the reality of suffering accompanied by social abuse and discrimination becomes indubitable. This gives a clear indication that the Petrine Christians suffered both the physical and social discrimination.

Strangers, Aliens and Diaspora in 1 Peter: Migration and Social Alienation

Having located the historical ambience of the Petrine community, it is important to locate and identify a number of images such as strangers and aliens and diaspora which may serve as social indicators of the Petrine Community' migrant status. The employment of these images is interesting and illuminative to understand the status of the Christians as displaced, disinherited, despicable and alienated. Hence, it is imperative for us to explore into these images: 1) Strangers and Aliens; and 2) Diaspora.

Strangers and Aliens

Another issue that one needs to look at the Petrine community is the social status accorded to them. Although, their social status were not explicitly described in the letter, terms such as strangers and exiles can offer useful insights about the social status of the community. In this connection, one needs to consider two terms used to refer to Christians in 1 Peter: 1) strangers παροικος and 2) aliens (παραπι/δημοϖ) in 1:1; 2:11. In order to ascertain its probable meaning, it is important to understand the Greek word, πα/ροικοϖ. While the verbal form πα/ροικε/ω suggests the meaning of a stranger, dwell or sojourn as a stranger, to dwell at a place only for a short time; the noun form πα/ροικε/ω means a sojourner, one who dwells in a foreign country, a temporary dweller not having a settled

12 Achtemeier, *1 Peter...*, 35. Green, *1 Peter...*, 9.

13 Green, *1 Peter...*, 9-10.

habitation in the place where he/she currently resides.[14] These words suggest that the community as πα/ροικουϖ did not have settled place or country. Does the usage suggest strangeness or alienation? According to J.W. Proyor, both the Greek words "πα/ροικοϖ" and "παραπι/δημοϖ" are used in a spiritual sense and should not be understood literally. From the heavenly perspective, the earthly existence of the community is perceived as strangers and aliens. In addition, he avers the contention that the believers in 1 Peter are the new People of God not the strangers and the aliens.[15]

Although this view helps us see the spiritual identity of the community, it purely relies on the heavenly existence of the community; such view fails to take into view the social and cultural implications of the terms. But, the use of these words seems to point to the audience' despicable and homeless identity. In this connexion, it would be better to consider Elliot's analysis of the Greek words. For Elliot, these terms epitomise "the literal social status of the resident aliens whether of Jewish or pagan lineage."[16] In addition, the "*Paroikoi*," according to him, were "strangers, aliens, uprooted transients, and dangerous nonconformists;"[17] they had become Christians in order to get rid of their despicable status. Unfortunately, their action went against their expectation in understanding about the status of the Christians as a disparaged and discriminated group[18] who lacked decorum and respect in the eyes of the society in which they lived. With reference to their social status, Elliot provides useful data as follow:

> As noncitizens, they were unable to vote, to hold public office, and to own land. Excluded from voting and landholding, privileges as well as from the chief civic offices and honours, they enjoyed only limited legal protection, were restricted in regard to intermarriage, commerce, transmission of property, land tenure, could be pressed into military service, and were susceptible to severer forms of civil and criminal punishment. While allowed limited participation in local cities, they were excluded from priestly offices, but still shared full responsibility with the citizenry for all financial burdens, such as tribute, taxes, and production quotas.[19]

14 πα/ροικε/ω (Lk. 24:18; Heb. 11:9; Sep.: Gen. 20:1; 24:37) and πα/ροικοϖ Acts 7:6, 29, Sep.: Gen. 15:13; Ex. 2.22); Spiros Zhodiates, ed. "πα/ροικε/ω " and "πα/ροικοϖ" in *CWSDT* (Chattanooga; AMG, 1992), 1121.

15 Cited in T.R, Schreiner, *1, 2, Peter & Jude: The New American Commentary*, volume 31 (Nashville, Tennessee: Broadman & Holman Publishers, 2003), 41.

16 Elliot, *Home…*, 49.

17 Elliot, remarks that the *paroikoi* were despicable fanatics, lowly slaves, Christ- lackeys, obsequious advocates of humiliation. *Home…*, 226.

18 Elliot points out that the area in which these *paroikoi* live is predominantly rural and agriculture in their main occupation. They were largely tenants, farmers, slaves, and artisans. *Home…*, 49.

19 Elliot, *1 Peter*, 94.

This brings to the fore the social situation in which the Petrine community placed was despicable. They lived in a status of not possessing citizenship. Moreover, their different languages, clothing, customs, religious traditions and forgotten roots set these aliens apart and exposed them to suspicion and hostility. The native population charged to charges such as wrongdoings and conduct hazardous to the life of the society. (2:11, 3:16; 4:12-14, 15).[20] As viewed in light of 1 Pet. 2:12, 23; 3:9, 16; 4:14, it is clear to note that the members were undergoing verbal abuse and social discrimination. It is important to note as to why the community earned the status of being called as strangers and exiles? Were the community called as the strangers and exiles because of their homeless condition or spiritual status as the people of God? Donald P. Senior holds the view that their identity as Christians would have compounded the social alienation

> The Christians are aliens or strangers because their Christian values and community identity put them at a distance from the pagan society around them. They are "exiles' not simply in the sense that they are living an earthly existence while awaiting the full revelation of God at the end of the world (1:6-7), but because their non-Christian neighbours are perplexed by their manner of life and "speak evil" of them, thereby giving the Christians a sense of alienation and displacement from the surrounding society.[21]

This illuminates the point that it was their manner of life and Christian values which earned the status of strangers. Whatever might be the situation that characterised the community as strangers and aliens, the status of the community as displaced and dismantled people cannot be ruled out. This helps us to understand the community's despicable situation marked by alienation and strangeness.

Diaspora

In addition to the stigmatised status as cited above, the metaphor, Diaspora is another indicator of the migrant status of the Petrine community. In order to consider the implication of this word in 1 Peter, it is important to look at the literal meaning of the term Diaspora. The term is derived from the Greek word, διασπειρειν (to scatter about or disperse) which is from two root words – *dia* (about, across) and *speirein* (to scatter). The Greek Septuagint used the term in Deuteronomy 28:25 to refer Israelites will be in the hands of enemies because of disobedience.

20 Elliot, *1 Peter*, 94.

21 Donald P. Senior, *1 Peter, Jude and 2 Peter* (Collegeville/Minnesota: The Liturgical Press, 2008), 66.

In the NT, it refers to the dispersion of the Jews.[22] In its literal sense, it is strictly used to refer to the Jews living outside Palestine. But then Peter's use of the term in 1 Peter 1:1, "To the pilgrims of the Dispersion in Pontus, Galatia, Cappadocia, Asia and Bithynia" suggests the point that the term involves both Jewish and Gentile Christians who were scattered throughout the provinces in Asia Minor. We know from the context of 1 Peter that he is writing to both Jewish and Gentile Christians. If it is so, the word Diaspora refers to Christians in general, both Jewish and Gentile. In this regard, number of scholars such as James Moffatt, Martin Dibelius, James Hardy Robes, Recike and Leslie Mitton[23] cogently argue that the Diaspora was a metaphor used to refer to the Jesus movement among the Jews and Gentiles.[24]

Now, if the term refers to Christians in general, the question is whether Peter used the term Diaspora in 1 Peter to delineate social discrimination faced by the community. In Green's view, "Diaspora" has become a metaphor for social ostracism and other forms of harassment and is associated with notions of exile."[25] This indicates the point that the diasporic experience witnessed by the community inflicted upon them a sense of ostracism associated with exile. In fact, there is no basis within the letter itself for suggesting that Peter's audience occupied any social mobility or rung on the ladder of economic measurement. These are the people whose commitments to the Lordship of Jesus Christ led to transformed dispositions and behaviours that placed them on the margins of respectable society. Their allegiance to Christ earned animosity, scorn, and vilification. Their lack of acculturation to prevailing social values marked them as *misfits worthy of contempt.*[26] This explains the point that the community were socially marginalized and discriminated in the larger society. Their social marginalization probably was due to their failure to follow the mores of the society. Their refusal to take part in the native religious festivals might have earned the distinction of being strangers and pilgrims.

22 Jas 1:1; 1 Pet 1:1. In particular, it is used in Jn. 7:35 to refer to the Jews living among the gentiles. See Rhodes, "διασπορα/" *Word Study*, 440. In modern parlance, "Diasporas" is used to refer to the Jews who live throughout Europe.

23 Cited in John S. Kloppenborg, "Diaspora Discourse: The Construction of Ethos in James," *NTS* 53. 2 (2007): 243.

24 Kloppenborg remarks that the term, diaspora could refer to persons who belonged to the various ethnic Diasporas that could be found in most cities of the Empire – Judaeans, Syrians, Phoenicians, Phrygians, Egyptians, and so forth. But these Jesus groups did not comprise a single ethnic Diaspora. See "Diaspora Discourse," 243-44."

25 Green, *1 Peter…*, 15.

26 Green, *1 Peter…*, 15-16.

A Constellation of Images as Interweaving Threads towards Community Solidarity

Having perceived the social situation and the status of migrants in 1 Peter, it behoves us to ascertain the remedial strategy undertaken by the writer of the letter to deal with the uprooted status of his readers. In this process of ascertaining the community vision, a plethora of metaphors such as conversion, brotherhood, *oikos*, hospitality, etc. are explored bellow in order to recognize the author's community interweaving threads and how the employment of these metaphors serve to construct and consolidate the coherence of the community.

Conversion

Having explored the suffering and social discrimination and alienation of the Petrine community, it is now important to ascertain the Petrine author's conception of the community. One of the key factors employed by the writer to build up the community is the language of conversion or new birth (1:1, 2:1). In Peter 1:3, the writer indicates that the Petrine members have been born into a living hope. The language of new birth is an interesting metaphor used to convey the idea of newness here. There is newness entailed in the concept of new birth, although some scholars detect herein an implicit baptismal theology or a baptismal liturgy.[27]

But, the author's use of the metaphor is a step removed from such a specific liturgical or baptismal reference, even though its theology certainly lends itself to a theology of baptism.[28] The concept of new birth is used to describe both God's sovereign power (God alone can give life) and the radical change salvation brings (from non-existence to existence). The metaphor seems to suggest a notion of radical change. In this sense, the thought of new birth imparts them a new understanding of life. Green observes:

> New birth, then, is a dramatic metaphor for the decisive transformation of life that has come in accordance with God's mercy and by means of the resurrection of Jesus. What Peter announces, then is a conversion of the imagination: personal reconstruction within new web of relationships, resocialization within a new community, and the embodiment of a new life-world evidenced in altered dispositions and attitudes.[29]

In the light of this view one can understand that the thought of new birth provides access into the new world of relationship that necessitates the reversal

27 As cited in Donald P. Senior, *1 Peter, Jude and 2 Peter* (Collegeville/Minnesota: The Liturgical Press, 2008), 35.

28 Elliot, *1 Peter…*, 333.; Goppelt, *1 Peter…*, 91.

29 Green, *1 Peter…*, 26.

of attitudes. Since the members have been born into a new life, they have been urged to dissociate themselves from destroying vices. In 2:1-3, the writer seeks disengagement from these vices. This could be seen in v. 1 wherein the writer uses the verbal root of participle (αποτι/θημι) which means putting off clothing (baptismal frame of reference for the passage). The verb is regularly used to refer to the elimination of sins, often in connection with lists of vices. These vices are understood as community destroying forces.[30] In particular, Davids calls these vices as community destroying vices of paganism.[31] These three groups of vices are mentioned in correspondence to 1: 22. The kind of vices mentioned is inimical to the love command in that verse. Thus, kakia is surely a power that destroys the community.

The next set of three vices: deception, hypocrisy, and envy point to acts intended to serve the individual at the expense of the neighbour.[32] The final vice, καταλαλια refers to habitual disparagement of others. These vices produce attitudes or actions which resist the new community which is based on love.[33] What the writer intended is the formation of the community's new identity marked by conversion. Conversion in antiquity might have connoted either transition from one religion or moving deeper into one's own religion. For Peter, conversion is not merely looking back into the former lives but it is a moving forward. At the same time, it is a social act which effects social consequences such as withdrawal from the pagan practices. In particular, conversion engages the members into a new community of brotherhood/sisterhood, which in Green's opinion is called as a new community. Conversion, according to him,

> ...involves incorporation into a new community with its distinguishing practices, signified in the present text with the imagery of no longer clothing oneself (α)ποτιθημι, "take off, Rom 13:12; Col 3:8; Jas 1:21) in evil, deceit, and the like (2:1), but giving oneself rather to deep and unceasing love for those within the community. To love entails a group ethos of solidarity and loyalty, an essential disposition favouring others in the community and so refusal to harm, a commitment to harmony within the group.[34]

30 D.L. Bartlett, "The First Letter of Peter," in *NIB*, Vol. XII (Nashville: Abingdon Press, 1998), 238-39; P.H. Davids, *The First Epistle of Peter: New International Commentary on the New Testament* (Grand Rapids, Michigan: Eerdmans, 1990), 83-84.; Achtemeier, *1 Peter...*, 144.

31 *Davids, The First Epistle of Peter...*, 84.

32 Achtemeier, *1 Peter...*, 144.

33 Achtemeier, *1 Peter...*, 145.

34 There entails a strong sense of family identity. In fact, Peter uses a constellation of familial terms in order to depict the community of believers: new birth, new born babies, and children, father (1:2, 3, 17). Of special interest is Peter's use of the term φιλαδελφι/α. This concept of familial love is a significant because it serves to counter *the most pervasive experience of*

This suggests that taking off of old sins ought to be accompanied by taking plunge into the community. Through the gift of salvation the Christian takes on a new existence. Like in the books of James, Paul and 1 John, concern here is community solidarity. For "Christian life is not solitary, but gives the believer a new identity as part of the people of God bound together in mutual love."[35] The call to "earnestly love each other from the heart" is based, therefore, on the very nature of Christian existence. It is one's total response to God's love that effects the purification of one's life from the self-indulgent and dead-end desires that make human life shallow (1:14). "Being open to God's love," according to Senior, "means leading a life that is now capable "genuine mutual love" for the members of God's people."[36] Peter's discourse on conversion counters the mind set of exclusivism and exclusion of other and thus provides legitimation to the alienated so as to affirm a symbiotic existence.

Brotherhood/Sisterhood

Peter's vision for a collective community is further seen in Peter's concept of brotherhood/sisterhood. This kinship language is expressed through a plethora of familial metaphors.[37] In order to understand the concept clearly, perhaps we need to look at the importance given to brotherhood (*sic*) in the Greco Roman society.

In the Greco Roman society, the love of blood brothers (*sic*) and siblings was a highly celebrated virtue as a sign of harmonious and mutually supportive household/family and its signal of honourable character and public reputation. One can note a strong group-bond existing among the people. Whenever a group was converted to another group, the group was expected to make new bonds. Such brotherly (*sic*) love is also present in the works of Philo. In particular, brotherly (*sic*) love finds significance in Philo's injunction both to the Proselytes and the Jews. Philo avers: "Thus, while giving equal rank to all in-comers with all the privileges which he gives to the native born, he exhorts the old nobility to honour them not only with marks of respect but with special friendship and

---

strangehood. This makes us perceive that Peter is engaged in the formation of identity. See Green, *1 Peter*, 51

35 Senior, *1 Peter, Jude* and *2 Peter…*, 50.

36 Senior, *1 Peter, Jude and 2 Peter…*, 50.

37 1 Peter uses a plethora of familial metaphors and household terms: *oikos* and its cognates: household of God (4:17), household slaves (2:18), sharing the home with others (3:7), stewards (4:10), deployment of the household code (2:13-17), images of new birth (1:3,23) and new growth (2:2), together with the identification of God as Father (1:2,3, 17) and familial language and terms of endearment: children (1:14), brotherly love (1:22, 3:18), born anew (1:23), parentage (1:23) new born babies (2:2), mature as Children (2:2), brotherhood (2:17; 5:9) hospitality (4:9), brother (5:12), son (5:13) and the kiss of love (5:14). I Pet 2:17-18). In particular, the writer seeks to draw attention to mutual love in 1:22.

with more than ordinary good will."[38] This makes it clear that brotherly love to proselytes is seen as an attempt in Philo's notion of brotherly (*sic*) love. Philo also indicates that at conversion the proselytes at once became friendly and loving. Brotherly (*sic*) love is thus a mark of true proselyte as well as native born Jews.[39] While Philo's brotherly (*sic*) love relates to both Jews and proselytes, Peter's notion of brotherhood (*sic*) includes all.

This helps us understand Peter's description of brotherly (*sic*) love which is marked by ethos of solidarity, and commitment to social harmony.[40] In Israel too, such fraternal affection and familial solidarity was prized.[41] While the word 'Philadelphia' properly implies the affection and support shared by both brothers of the same kin or surrogate group kin group, the word, *periadelphon* includes both male and female. While it is strictly used to refer to those who are related by blood siblings,[42] terms such as *adelphikos, adelphoi, adelphotes,* and *philadelphoi* were metaphorically used to identify the compatriots or members of religious groups. According to contemporary interpretation, these terms in Israel were applied not only to natural siblings but to co-religionists who had converted and observed the Mosaic Law.[43]

People in the first century lived in close-knit societies in which collectivism was highly honoured. Whenever a group was converted to another group, the group was expected to make new bonds. In light of such group-bond mind-set and practice prevalent in the Mediterranean world, Peter's message assumes greater importance in his depiction about his community in 1:22; 2:17; 4:8. It is interesting to note that the concept of Philadelphia becomes a salient feature of the Petrine community. Even it more interesting to note that fraternal love denoted by Philadelphia included both brothers and sisters. By accentuating mutual love, the Petrine writer, thus brings to the fore the sense of brotherhood/sisterhood. The use of the word, *Philadelphia* in 1 Peter unfolds the author's perspective of the community. The community, which is a believing community is called a "brotherhood/sisterhood" (2:17; 5:9). Herein, the concept of brotherhood/sisterhood seeks to cement the relationship of the members whose identity was centred on the experience of alienation and strangeness. In constructing the solidarity of the community, the Petrine author injects the necessity of enhancing sincere love of the brothers/sisters in 1: 22-23. By doing so, the members are asked to preserve a familial identity. The intention behind the use of the brotherhood/

---

38 Cited in Torrey Seland, *Strangers in the Light: Philonic Perspectives on Christian Identity in I Peter*, Biblical Interpretation Series 76 (Leiden: Brill, 2005), 75.

39 Seland, *Strangers…*, 75-76.

40 Green, *1 Peter…*, 51.

41 *4 Macc. 13: 19-4:1; also T. Gad 6:1-2;* Philo, *Virt.192; Mos. 1.150; Legat 12.*

42 *4 Macc.* 13;9-14;1

43 *Lev.* 25;35-36; *Deut.* 15:3,12; 23;19;2 *2 Macc.* 15:14; *IQM*M XIII 1; XV, 47; *CD* VIII 17,19; IX 16; Philo. *Spec.* 2.79-80.

sisterhood language is to form the Petrine community and to serve to form and to consolidate the solidarity of the community elsewhere in Asia Minor. Through the language of brotherhood/sisterhood, the author constructs a social and religious bond between the Christians of Rome and those of Asia Minor. This bonding, for M.C. Elliot, is shared through brotherhood/sisterhood. Elliot observes:

> Reference to commonly known persons, commonly shared kergmatic, liturgical, catechetical and parenatic traditions, common experience of suffering and estrangement, common enjoyment of dignity and hope, and common membership in the household of God. Thus, through 1 Peter the Petrine community is promoting and acting as stimulus for the distinctive identity and unity of the Christian brotherhood / sisterhood throughout the world.[44]

This serves to establish the identity and unity of the Christian brotherhood/ sisterhood throughout the world. Moreover in the ancient Mediterranean World, the family or household relations indicated relations of status and power. But the kinship language in 1 Peter is used to include all children and slaves in the household of God.[45] Thus, for the author, the language of brotherhood/sisterhood serves the purpose of promoting, building and maintaining the community who were called as born anew (1:3). Such strong sense of familial love signifying family identity can serve as counter culture against the pervasive experience of strangehood[46] and one imagine an embracive community that affirms the ethos of solidarity, love and equality for all members.

Oikos

Alongside the concept of brotherhood/sisterhood, it is important to note yet another metaphor called *oikos* or the house of God used in 1 Peter where spiritual house is used as another identity maker to depict the community. In 2. 5 the community who are called as God's elect, precious are said to be built into a spiritual house. It is not clear whether the spiritual house is used as a reference to temple. In this regard, some scholars such as E. Best, Green and Michaels support the contention that the use of *oikos* in v. 5 has the implication of the temple.[47] However, this does not mean that the writer refers to the material building of the temple. The notion of non-material is not something which is foreign to the Jewish and the Qumran community.[48] NT texts such as Mk 14:58; 15:29;

44 M.C. Elliot, *Freedom, Justice and Christian Counter Culture* (London: SCM Press, 1990), 31-32.

45 Green, *1 Peter…*, 78.

46 Green, *1 Peter…*, 51.

47 E. Best, "1 Peter 2: 4-10: Reconsideration," *NTDT* (1969): 280-81; Green, *1 Peter…*, 61; Michaels, *I Peter...*, 10.

48 The picture of the church was not only common in the NT, but was also known in Judaism, especially in the Dead Sea community. (IQS 5:6 - Israel pleads to the house of Truth; 8:5, a

Jn. 2:19; 4:21, 23-24; Acts 7:48; 17:24 attest to the concept of the non-physical church replacing the material temple in Jerusalem Thus, the house of God is no longer to be thought of as a physical building, but, as a living house in which God lives. Envisaging the believers as a house, the writer seeks to offer comfort to an oppressed Christian group. There is a certain meaning of comfort given to the oppressed people evident in the notion of house rather than the material temple and meeting place.[49] This shows that the concept of house is used as a means of concretising fellowship among the members of the church. In this respect, F.V. Filson points out the fact that the house church functioned as a vital factor in the early church's development: It provided the setting in which the primitive Christians achieved a mental separation from Judaism before the actual open breakdown occurred. It gave an added importance to Christianize the family relationships. It served as the house of family which provided the means to what has been regarded as church of the dispossessed.[50] This view illuminates the point that it was through the conceptualisation of the house image that the writer may have infused a sense of belongingness and comfort into the Christians who were dislocated. Since the community were depicted as homeless, one can understand that the notion of the church as house reinforced solidarity of love, care and nurture in the lives of the dispossessed and oppressed.

While trying to understand the social situation of the Petrine community, Elliot has studied two correlated terms "παροικοι" and "παροικοι του Θεου." For him, these terms epitomise the literal social status of the resident aliens whether of Jewish or pagan lineage.[51] The Christians are described as παροικοι seeking a οικοϖ. In Elliot's analysis, the aim of 1 Peter was therefore to reconcile the community which suffered at the hands of the outsiders. The members were thus, encouraged not to give in to hostility and persecutions. To this end, 1 Peter 2:5 uses the image of the house as οικοϖ πνευματικοϖ. The use of the term "*oikos*" is thus, designed to satisfy the deepest longing of the homeless and the discouraged addressees of the letter (2:4-10).[52]

Here a theological idea is used to legitimise a social reality. The image of a house is particularly good for this purpose because the community was in fact organized in house churches.[53] Having embraced Christianity, the community

---

house of Holiness for Israel, 1QS 6:25-28, where the teacher of righteousness is the house into which the community is built). It is the spiritual house in that the Spirit forms; it is not physical. See Davids, *First Epistle of Peter…*, 87.

49 Davids, *First Epislte of Peter…*, 87.

50 F.V. Filson, "The Significance of the Early House Churches," *JBL 58* (1939): 112.

51 Elliot, *Home*, 49.

52 As cited in Edwards, "Sociology as a Tool," 443-44.

53 T. Schmiller, "Sociology and New Testament Studies," in *DBI*, vol. 2, ed. J. Hayes (Nashville: Abingdon Press, 1999), 400.

found themselves as resident aliens exposed to despise and aversion.[54] In this context, the image of the church as the house has far greater significance than the church being viewed as the cathedral (building). It engenders fellowship, belongingness and wholeness. The church as the house creates a vibrant sense of community in which all members are bound together. In this respect, P.S. Minear has drawn attention to the task of rethinking the essential structures of the community in terms of its simple constituents such as faith and obedience, grace and forgiveness, hospitality and love. Human relationships, for Minear, ought to be conceived in terms of their sociological, ecclesiological and ontological experiences.[55] This view underpins the core value that the Christian relationship finds its authentic place when it accords importance to one's very being, church, society and God.

However, Elliot sees the household as a separate entity for the communal identity of the Christians. The concept of the household in 1 Peter should not lead one to endorse the separate identity detached from the society. In this respect, D. Balch remarks that Elliot has polarized the state and culture in an inaccurate way and it does not do justice to the more complex picture of the relation Peter implies. There is seemingly a correspondence between the household code and the Hellenistic code. By means of this correlation, the Christians in Asia Minor were induced to make a greater accommodation and integration with the Roman society. By accommodating to generally accept social norms in relation to πολιτεια and οικονομια, the Christians could counter the slander of outsiders.[56] Although there is a correspondence between the household and the Hellenistic code, the household in 1 Peter unfolds the writer's intention in the formation of the community which is corporate and inclusive. Both Balch and Elliot seems faulted in their views in failing to perceive theological crux of the *oikos*. In particular, Elliot's trenchant view[57] repudiates the relation of *oikos* with the temple. Hence, it is important to understand the theological notion of *oikos*.

The concept of *oikos* is not merely a sociological paradigm drawn from a contemporary culture; rather, it is the divine household of the church as a holy society. The controlling factor for the role of the church in 1 Peter is the new vision that construes the Christian community as the people of God.[58] Although the implication of house is present in the concept of *oikos*, it is also called as a spiritual house. It is this concept that construes house as a temple. The house is

54 Elliot, *Home...*, 201-16.

55 P.S. Minear, *Survey of Images of the Churches in the New Testament* (Philadelphia: West Minister Press, 1966), 172.

56 As cited in S.C. Barton, "Social Setting of Early non-Pauline Christianity," in *DLNT*, eds. R. I. Martin & P. H. Davids (Leicester: InterVarsity Press, 1997), 1105-07; D.L. Balch, *Let Wives be Submissive: The Domestic Code in Peter* (SBLMS 26; Chicago: Scholars Press, 1981), 109.

57 See Elliot, "The Elect and the Holy," 157-75.

58 Martin, *Theology of Jude, 1 Peter, and 2 Peter*, 127.

portrayed as the temple because God is resident in the community. It is God's presence that signifies the community. In Senior's words, "the temple is no longer a building or an institution, but living community or "household."[59] Similarly, community, according to Green, is called as the new temple; the new temple is the mark of the community that symbolizes God's power and presence.[60]

Hence, as the term house alludes to the temple, the Christians could be described as the temple in view with other NT passages.[61] The designation of the Christians as the priesthood in 2: 5 could concur the point that the new identity of the Christians as the temple. The picture here is of a house in which believers constitute the building stones. For which is called a house in the OT (2 Sam. 7:13; 1 Kgs. 3:2; 6:8) is called as a house in the NT (Mt. 21:13; 23:38; Jn. 2:16-17; Acts. 7:47, 49). In particular, when a verb is combined with house (*oikos*) in the Septuagint, the temple is in view. The house is spiritual because it is animated and indwelt by the Holy Spirit. Despite the hesitation of some scholars, Peter seems clearly identifying the church as God's new temple[62] and people as living stones. The purpose of such imagery is that Christians function as a holy priesthood[63] which is indicative of collectiveness and community of solidarity.

Hospitality: A Network of Enhancing Social Space

Another image used in 1 Peter with regard to the construction of a collective community is hospitality. The network of hospitality is closely tied to the house churches. In fact, the house churches were identified as centres of hospitality. For examples, 1 Peter 2:11, 12 4:8, 9; 1 Timothy 3:2, and Titus 1:8, and Hebrew 13:2; 12:12; 13:1-3; 16; 2 John 10, 3 John 3-4 speak about the extension of love based hospitality in the community. I Timothy 5:10 informs us that the widows had opened their house for missionaries, teachers and other Christian travellers.[64]

The Greek world for hospitality is φιλο/χενια which means love for the strangers. The exhortation of hospitality assumes greater significance in the conflict-torn community. Both the Epistles of Hebrews and 1 Peter reflect the pressure of a persecuted church. In such a context, hospitality to refugees and exiles and visitation of prisoners was essential. For early Christians, love for brothers and sisters, hospitality to strangers, and visitation of those in prison were all part of

59 Senior, *1 Peter, Jude, and 2 Peter*, 59. See Eph. 2.20-22; 1 Cor 3.16-17; 2 Cor. 6.16; 1 Tim 3.15; Heb. 3.6.

60 Green, *I Peter*, 61.

61 Mk. 14:58;15:29; Jn. 2:19; 1 Cor 16-17;6:19; 2 Cor 6:16; 1 Tim. 3:15; Heb. 3;6;10;21;12:18-24; Rev 3:12; 11:1;cf. Acts 7:48;15:29.

62 T. Seland, "The Common Priesthood of Philo and 1 Peter: a Philonic Reading of 2:5, 9," *JSNT 57* (1995): 111. See Elliot, *Home...*, 165-266; Gopelt,, *1 Peter...*, 141; Michaels, *1 Peter...*, 158-59.

63 Seland, "Common Priesthood of Philo and 1 Peter," 105.

64 Osieck, *Families...*, 208.

one piece of ministry (Heb. 13:1-3). The focus was primarily set on the needs of other believers. In 1 Pet. 4:8-9 the connection between deep love for one another and hospitality to one another is clearly brought out. It is interesting to note that the act of hospitality appears to be one of the divine gifts (1 Pet 4: 12-19). In 1Timothy 3:2; Titus 1:8, although the hospitality was the responsibility, it was particularly the duty of the bishops or overseers of the household of God. Even widows were known for hospitality and good deeds (I Tim 5:9-10). Hospitality was an established practice to provide food, lodging, money, encouragement to the needy. The early Christians undertook to care for all their needy.

However, the early Christian hospitality was not limited to taking care of poor, widows and the persecuted. It was practiced as dissemination of the Gospel tradition.[65] The practice of hospitality entailed the mobility of the travellers and the travellers availed themselves of the hospitality wherever they could find even in the inns. Christian hospitality was further manifested in the phenomenon of the house church. In fact, the early Christians grew as it found strong solidarity in the hospitable homes.[66] It is interesting to note the expansion of the Christianity and social process went side by side. In this process, the early household as a pilgrim body served as a charming and effective aspect of Christian life. The extension of hospitality not only did cause the dissemination of the gospel, it also served to transform the strangers into friends.

Such kind of hospitality is defined by Malina as "…the process by means of which an outsider's status is changed from a stranger to guest…. The outsiders need hospitality, for otherwise they would be treated as non-human because they are potentially a threat to the community."[67] In the light of this view, we can see that the extension of hospitality was not reciprocated between the individuals, but it was reciprocated between the communities. This also indicates that the extension of hospitality has the transformative function in changing the strangers into friendship. It entails the extension of love to the strangers and offers resistance to the forces of alienation and strangeness. Here any claim on the privileged status by individuals becomes incompatible with the gospel of Jesus Christ shared at the meal. For one cannot remain in a state of strangeness when he/she enters into the Lord's Table of fellowship which shares the very life of Christ. In the words of Witherington, "The Christians are called to be strangers in the world aware of our own essential otherness so that fear of strangers gives way to divinely enabled *philoxenia* (the love of stranger). Therefore, distinction of "weak" and "strong" disappear in the face of love and hospitality.[68]

65 Riddle, "Christian Hospitality," 144-45.

66 A.J. Malherbe, *Social Aspects of Early Christianity*. Second Edition. Philadelphia: Fortress Press, 1983), 96.

67 Malina, "III John and Hospitality," 173- 94.

68 B. Witherington III, *Paul's Letter to the Romans: A Socio Rhetorical Commentary* (Grand Rapids: Eerdmans, 2004), 349.

It is explicit here that the fear of xenophobia and difference can be dissipated in the context of love-filled hospitality. The Christian hospitality has potential to create a space for coming together. Through the extension of hospitality both the host and the strangers can be brought into a network of relationship. A host of NT scholars such as Malina[69] and Palmer and envisage the possibility of enhancing one's social space in the context of hospitality. According to Palmer,

> Inviting the stranger into our private space whether that be the space of our home or the space of our home or the space of our personal awareness and concern. And when we do so, some important transformations occur. Our private space is suddenly enlarged; no longer tight and cramped and restricted, but open and expansive and free. And our space may also be illumined. ... Hospitality to the stranger gives us chance to see our own lives afresh, through different eyes.[70]

Similarly, Witherington also observes that

> When hostility is converted into hospitality then fearful strangers... become guests revealing to their hosts the promise they are carrying with them. Then, in fact, the distinction between host and guest proves to be artificial and evaporates in the recognition of the need found unity. Thus, the biblical stories help us to realize not just that hospitality is an important virtue, but even more that in the context of hospitality guest and host can reveal their most precious gifts and bring new life to each other.[71]

When our social space is enlarged by hospitality, we can shed off our differences and dissipate aloofness. This allows us to see the differences of other people rather as complementary. Hence, this is a Christian imperative that we create a network of hospitality across the boundaries that will be help to address the issues around migration, particularly the struggles of migrants.

Convergence of Identity and Integration

One of the issues in migration is that the very name or identification of people as 'refugees' and 'migrants' expose them to a situation of vulnerability, strangeness, alienation and social discrimination and thereby stripes them of from their self-worth and dignity. For the core issue that refugees or migrants encounter is the

69 B.J. Malina, "The Received and what it cannot do: III John and Hospitality," *Semeia* 35 (1986): 73- 94.

70 P. Palmer, *The Company of Strangers: Christians and the Renewal of Americas Public Life* (New York: Crossroad, 1981), 65.

71 Witherington III, *Paul's Letter to the Romans*, 349. See also H. Nouwen, *Reaching Out: The Three Movements of the Spiritual Life* (New York: Doubleday & Co., 1975), 47.

identity-crisis. Identifying them as refugees or migrants fragments their meaning of life and disintegrate from family life. Further, the social discrimination they undergo at the hands of host society is very precarious.

Such situation of refugees and migrants of our times today perhaps can be connected with the strangers and aliens of 1 Peter. The social discrimination and alienation they underwent and undergo are almost the same. For more than anything else, the Petrine community suffered social discrimination and isolation[72] as refugees and migrants of our times face because of their very identity. Apart from social discrimination and alienation they also undergo social stigmatization and verbal shaming which perhaps is the main weapons in the arsenal of social ostracism. As alluded by author, the Petrine community underwent this experience as refugees and migrants undergo. In fact, suffering from such social evils is more dehumanizing than persecution and the physical sufferings. Accordingly Johnson,

Persecution and martyrdom, after all, have a certain clarity and comfort. Lines of allegiance are obvious. However painful the choice, it need be made only once. But scorn and contempt are slow- working acids that corrode individual and communal identity. Social alienation is not trivial form of suffering. Persecution may bring death, but with meaning. Social scorn can threaten meaning itself, which is more subtle form of death.[73]

This view makes it clear that verbal shaming is more difficult to deal with than physical violence; it obliterates individual and community identity. It exposes the community to precarious and vulnerable situation. Therefore, the author of the 1 Peter attempted to redefine their identity. In redefining the identity of the community, the writer is keenly engaged in reconstructing their identity. Further, the writer adds a constellation of corporate community images such as elect race, God's possessions and the people of God, nation, royal priesthood etc. and metaphors so as to reconstruct and reinvigorate the community bonds, and thereby promote a sense of belongingness, solidarity and kinship. For the Petrine community were at the periphery of acceptable society. They did not belong and their deepest loyalties and inclinations were not very well lined up with what matters most in the world in which they live.[74] The experience of the community as pilgrims and sojourners is closely thus connected to the writer's interweaving community threads by which they are integrated into a collective community. Considering all these, the message of 1 Peter becomes highly relevant not only to issue of migration, but also to the Church.

---

72 Because the letter excludes the possibility that its author or community find themselves in an officially initiated persecution. Instead, it is a question of social discrimination and isolation." Stegemann. E.W., and Stegemann, W. *The Jesus Movement: A Social History of Its First Century.* Translated by O. C. Dean (Minneapolis: Fortress Press, 1999), 337.

73 Johnson, *Writings...*, 435.

74 Green, *1 Peter...*, 18.

Today, the collectiveness of the church is disrupted due to divisive forces such as caste, gender, power and wealth. The politics of holiness and power continue to wreak a wounded psyche into the displaced, despicable and vulnerable people. The serious threats that confront the church include materialism, consumerism and individualism. The challenge to the Church is resistance against such life-negating forces and strive towards unity, fellowship and brotherhood/sisterhood of all. The Church must be *oikos*, a symbiotic community where there is inclusivity, love and commonality. The Church must have social space for all strangers and aliens, refugees and migrants, people pushed out into the periphery because of their social identity.

Conclusion

It is conclusive that the Petrine community is a migrant community which was scattered throughout the Asia Minor. The strangers and aliens of 1 Peter were migrants who suffered multiple problems: social alienation, displacement, despicability, homelessness and sufferings both physical and psychological. In many ways, the predicament of the Petrine Christian is analogous to the experience of the migrants today. Although the idea of migration is averse, but it remains inevitable in the precarious contexts of war, conflict-zone, homelessness and unemployment. In this situation, the *oikos* model of community as delineated in 1 Peter can transform the marginality of the migrants. As the Christians were empowered by the concept of *oikos* in 1 Peter, we as the collective members of the love-infused *oikos*, are called to promote fellowship, brotherhood/sisterhood and reconciliation thereby welcoming the strangers and aliens. This necessitates the church to be a place of hospitality, healing and wholeness that dispels aloofness and acrimony in the lives of the people. In this task, the church has dual role to play: 1) witnessing to the life-renewing values; and 2) offering resistance the pseudo values of the world. In sum, the Church being an *oikos* of God is the agent of transformation and restoration of broken people and the broken world!

6

Challenges from the Migrants to the Church-in-Mission

K. David Udayakumar

In the present day context, migration has become part of life. People in the past have migrated from one place to another for good and bad reasons and this phenomena continues in the present also. Migration refers to the movement – either forced or by choice – of people across boundaries. Movement and migration is a sign of our times – some people moving across the countries (*international migration*), and some others moving within the country (*interstate migration*). Christian faith and tradition are deeply rooted in the narratives and stories of migrant peoples – Abraham's long journey out of Ur; Moses leading the people of Israel out of Egypt; Joseph and Mary with baby Jesus fleeing to Egypt, and many more examples. The early church was born in a context of migration and movement – the disciples and early followers of Christ scattered around the Roman Empire due to persecution. In this phenomenon one could observe movement of people across the religious boundaries and also movement of Christians across the denominational borders. When it comes to movement of people to Christian faith, we could see migrants being assimilated into the ecclesiastical traditions and structures, but at the same time one could also notice people remaining true to their own faith traditions and thereby maintaining dual status. Here I am referring to unbaptised believers and churchless Christianity or what we call '*Hybridity*'.

An Overview

In such a context engaging in mission today is not the same as it was in the past. The image of a missionary from the West coming to the East with a passion to transmit his/her faith and also culture is gone, though not totally disappeared. Understanding of the West as the primary mission player is slowly diminishing. Mission today includes the recognition of the vital role of the global and also glocal church coming of age and learning to assume its role in mission. From a missiological perspective there is a growing consensus that the 'dynamism of mission', is shifting from those who have historically been '*above*' to those who are now coming '*from below*'. In the WCC document "*Together Towards Life*" the emphasis is on '*mission from the margins*'. In the words of Samuel Escobar[1]

> *there is an element of mystery when the dynamism of mission does not come from people in positions of power or privilege, or from the expansive dynamism of a superior civilization, but from below, from the little ones, from those who have few material, financial, or technical resources but who are open to the prompting of the Spirit.*

To put it in the words of David J. Bosch[2]

> *it is apparent that God in his sovereignty works in ways beyond human comprehension and the dynamic social and cultural revolution in the world is a reminder again that the 'mission of the church needs constantly to be renewed..."*

This article is an attempt to understand the Church-in-Mission positively responding to the challenges from the migrants and especially concentrating on mission together with migrants and migrant communities. It is dealt in three sections – an overview of contemporary migration situation, church's response to the issues related to migration and finally concluding with the challenges from the migrant communities to the present day church and how church-in-mission could be involved in mission together with the migrants and migrant communities.

Some Preliminaries

Renowned Roman Catholic missiologists, Stephen Bevans has mapped shifts in missiology and Robert Schreiter, has noted contemporary sites for missiological attention. Bevans[3] identifies four significant missiological shifts that have taken place over the last century. He says the present study of missiology has i) *a new context*, ii) *a new attitude*, iii) *a new means* and iv) *a new content*. That is to say, mission no longer works on a euro-centric, West-to-the-rest trajectory but is informed that mission is from everywhere-to-everywhere (to use WCC term "Mission in Six Continents), which is *a new context*; secondly, development of post-modern attitudes that critique the enlightenment values, which claimed universality and gave certainty to the modern western world is *a new attitude*; thirdly, understanding of mission as *mission Dei* rather than an activity of mission specialists and churches which ultimately led to perceiving Christ-like mission

1 Samuel Escobar, *A Time for Mission* (Leicester: InterVarsity Press, 1995), 17.

2 David Bosch, *Transforming Mission, Paradigms Shifts in Theology of Missions* (Maryknoll, Orbis Books, 1998), 519.

3 Stephen Bevans, "From Edinburgh to Edinburgh: Towards a Missiology for a World Church," in *Mission After Christendom: Emergent Themes in Contemporary Mission*, edited by Peter Vethanayagomony, *et al.* (Louisville, Kentucky: Westminster John Knox Press, 2010), 1.

in vulnerability, that is doing mission in Christ's way is *a new means*; and finally missiology has developed a multi-faceted understanding of mission, as evangelism, as contextualization, as liberation, as inculturation, as interfaith witness and so on which is *a new context*.

Such shifts in missiology inform and are informed by new sites of mission, providing multiform responses to most complex and at the same time very slippery situations. Robert Schreiter[4] identifies four such missiological sites namely, i) *secularity*, ii) *poverty*, iii) *interfaith* and iv) *globalization*. Schreiter is of the opinion that these sites provide new opportunities for missional engagement. Therefore he calls for a) reimagining secularity in the light of changing world scenario; b) identification and accompaniment with the majority who are poor; c) radical new understanding and involvement in our inter-religious interface; d) and study, understand and respond to the impacts, effects and consequences of globalization, etc.. Along with these we also need to give a serious thought to the environmental degradation in the light of globalisation and wars.

Interestingly each one of these sites relates to the migration of people. In the context of international migration, people are migrating from relatively poor countries, some of which are experiencing drastic climate change, civil war, ethnic violence, etc. to countries where secularism is a prominent part of their culture. Some migrations are taking place from countries of longstanding religious pluralism to countries with a relatively recent history of religious pluralism. In most of the cases globalisation that include modern communication systems which contributes to exchange of goods, services and people across the globe and also modern transportation system has become an important site related to migration.

The biblical focus on responsibility of Israelites towards *aliens* in their midst suggests that a concern for the physical, social, and spiritual well-being of migrants and refugees should not be peripheral to Christian life, mission, and witness; instead, it should be central. Therefore some are challenging traditional Christian models or responses for addressing migration such as showing sympathy, involving in social work, assimilation into an existing ecclesiastical systems and structures, etc.

An Overview of Contemporary Migration

During the last two decades, movement of people and at the same time displacement of people due to various reasons have risen to unprecedented levels. According to UN International migration report 2017 the number of international migrants worldwide has continued to grow rapidly reaching 258 millions in 2017 an increase of 40% since 2000. In 2014 the total number of refugees in the world

4 Schreiter, Robert, "Mission from the Ground up: Themes in Contemporary Mission," in *Mission After Christendom…*, 16.

was estimated at 19.5 million.[5] International Migration Report 2017 (Highlights) states that 3.4% of the world's inhabitants today are international migrants. This reflects a modest increase from a value of 2.8% in 2000. By contrast, the number of migrants as a fraction of the population residing in high-income countries rose from 9.6% in 2000 to 14% in 2017.[6]

Discussing on international migration theories, Douglas Massey[7] identifies some theories about the nature, origins, and processes of international migration:

- The *neoclassical economic* perspective, explains international migration in terms of the supply of and demand for labour.
- The *historical-structural* approach focuses on the unequal distribution of economic and political power as reasons for migration.
- Theories that emphasize *social capital* draw attention to the network connections on which potential migrants draw and the self-perpetuating nature of migration networks. Such a theory proposes that migratory movements generally arise from the existence of prior links between sending and receiving countries based on colonization, political influence, trade investment, and cultural ties.

These diverse theories attest to the complexity of contemporary international and internal migration. One of the best summary evaluations holds that[8]

> *the increase in migration is due to rapid processes of economic, demographic, social, political, cultural and environmental change, which rise from decolonization, modernization and uneven development. Furthermore, these processes seem set to accelerate in the future, leading to even greater dislocations and changes in societies, and hence to even larger migrations.*

We are aware that people have been on the move from the earliest times, and when people move they also carry their ideologies, cultural beliefs, and religious practices along with them. Thomas Sowell, in his study on migrations, observes that each group has its own cultural pattern. These patterns do not disappear upon crossing a border or an ocean. Historian Peter Stearns describes *people movements as culture in motion.*[9] It is true that religious beliefs and spirituality are vital to the survival of migrants in a new land.

---

5 https://www.un.org/development/desa/publications/international-migration-report-2017.html

6 https://www.un.org/development/desa/publications/international-migration-report-2017.html

7 For a useful treatment of international migration theories, see Douglas Massey, "Why Does Immigration Occur? A Theoretical Synthesis," in *The Handbook of International Migration: The American Experience,* edited by Charles Hirschman, *et al.* (New York: Russell Sage Foundation, 1999), 34-52.

8 Ibid., 139.

9 Peter Stearns, *Cultures in Motion: Mapping Key Contacts their Imprints in World History* (New Haven: Yale Univ. Press, 2001).

Challenges of Peoples' Migration to the Church-in-Mission

The challenging question in such a complex and at the same time fluid context is – how can the church be engaged in mission in a world which is dominated by the forces of globalisation, cultural alterations, secularisation, religious and ideological pluralism, technological advancements in communication, social and economic inequality, which are some of the reasons and consequences of migration?

This leads us recognise that there is a need for the church to rethink its traditional understanding of engaging mission and to lay more emphasis on 'holistic mission' whereby the Good News of Jesus impacts on every facet of human life. Holistic mission implies demonstration of the love of God to all humanity impacting the 'spiritual, social and environmental.'[10]

Meeting Spiritual and Physical Needs

When we study and understand biblical passages, in its own context, carefully it is an obvious reality that God has always been mindful of both the physical and spiritual needs of his people, who were a migrant community most of their life. By and large, most of the migrants especially the refugees are poor, persecuted, displaced, marginalised, discriminated and deprived of social justice and have little opportunity to improve their situations. Many a time the church and Christians remain silent towards such realities migrant people encounter. We read in Isaiah 58:1-10 that one of the accusations the prophet against God's chosen people, Israel was for her sin of ignoring the poor in their midst. This was because Israel failed to act as a picture of the coming king when she neglected the poor. When the church neglects holistic ministry and chooses to address only the spiritual needs of the people, the church may be repeating the same error that Israel committed. The church is the body, the bride, and the fullness of Christ, unlike Israel, who was just a shadow of the coming king. This means that there is a greater responsibility for the church than whatever Israel was called to do.

The church needs to be sensitive in working with and among the migrants and migrant communities because many Christians and church leaders see these people, especially coming from other faith traditions as potential converts because of their vulnerability. It should also be noted that church has more responsibility to meet the needs of migrant communities than their own because we are prone to look after our own sheep and whatever we do to the others that do not belong to us, as charity.

Injustices and Violence

Life as a migrant worker or a refugee is hard. Migrant workers and refugees suffer injustice and are oppressed in numerous ways. In the Bible, there is a constant call to seek justice for the oppressed. In Isaiah 1:17, the Lord says: "*Learn to do*

---

10 Martin Goldsmith, *Get a Grip on Mission: The Challenge of a Changing World* (Grand Rapids, InterVarsity Press, 2006), 183.

good; seek justice, rescue the oppressed, defend the orphan, plead for the widow." The principle here is to provide justice for everyone who is suffering injustice. Many times, unfortunately, we shy away from this responsibility. The church thinks and acts that it is the work and responsibility of the government and non-government organisations. Christians and their leaders are more concerned about their own problems and the problems of the people in the church. Christine Pohl says that[11]

> *... the biblical focus on responsibility to aliens suggests that a concern for the physical social and spiritual well-being of migrants and refugees should not be peripheral to Christian life, mission and witness instead it should be central.*

In the words of Samuel Escobar[12]

> *[P]erhaps the biggest challenge is a prophetic task of being a mouthpiece for the poor and downtrodden and pronouncing an unpopular prophetic word for a society that seems to be taken over by panic from seeing these waves of foreigners who have come to stay.*

Again Escobar[13] expresses

> *...there is an element of mystery when the dynamism of mission does not come from the people in positions of power or privilege, or from the expensive dynamism of a superior civilisation but from below, the little ones, those who have few material, financial and technical resources but for open to the prompting of the spirit.*

Rising to the Challenge

As a church we have to seriously think about these complex issues and develop appropriate responses. Samuel Escobar[14] observes that migration produces four primary challenges for the Church:

i. How to be compassionate Christians and have loving attitudes that are frequently contrary to popular culture?
ii. How to educate inside the churches that ensures that people are informed of the issues and have their negative (sinful) attitudes challenged and corrected?

---

11 Christine D. Pohl, "Biblical Issues in Mission and Migration," *Missiology: An International Review*, vol. XXXI, no. I (January 2003): 9.

12 Samuel Escobar, "B*iblical Issues in Mission and Migration*," *Missiology: An International Review*, vol. XXXI, no. I (January 2003): 19.

13 Samuel Escobar, *A Time for Missions...*, 17.

14 Samuel *Escobar,* "Migration: Avenue and Challenge in Mission," *Missiology: An International Review*, vol. XXXI, no. I (January 2003).

iii. How to have a prophetic ministry to the society at large? Christians should be speaking up for those who are suffering and seeking to create solutions and to combat political ideologies that sometimes seek to make the strong stronger at the expense of the weak.
iv. How to make migration an avenue for the evangelistic mission? (*Here one needs to be careful!) David Bosch states that 'evangelism should not be equated with mission'* and Samuel Escobar states that *'migration is an avenue for the evangelistic mission'*. Paul Freston[15] says that 'effective evangelisation of Europeans by diaspora churches would presuppose both, a) a fundamental reorientation of priorities and rethinking of strategies on the part of the diaspora churches and b) a fundamental attitudinal change on the part of native Europeans.

Missions today include the growing impact of the global South's role in missions. A significant part of this role is what is happening through migration and diaspora contexts as many of these people are devout Christians and many are going to the West, where the church is in decline. The impact of being a migrant allows us to question our own identity and challenges us to "define, demark, or defend our own sense of personal and cultural territory. We must develop a sense of where we belong, the values we want to live by, the kind of person we want to be, how we want to communicate, and so on."[16]

Challenges from the Migrants

Amid these contentious debates, much has been written about the social, political, economic, and cultural dimensions of migration. But surprisingly very little has been written from the vantage point of the migrants themselves.

The notion of God's mission as originating from the margins is powerfully depicted by the Cuban-American scholar Miguel De La Torre[17]

> *God's self-revelation to humanity does not occur from the centres of world power but in the margins of society. It is not from the court of Pharaoh that God's laws are revealed to humanity but from their slaves. Nor does the incarnation occur in the imperial palace of Caesar, or to the household of the high priest in Jerusalem. Rather, God is made flesh among the impure Galileans ... [in] a region where the unclean Gentiles outnumbered the Jews.*

15 Paul Freston, *Reverse Mission: A Discourse in Search of Reality, Pentecostal Studies*, vol. 9, no. 2 (2010): 162.

16 J., *A.* Shaules, *Beginner's Guide to the Deep Cultural Experience Beneath the Surface* (Boston, MA: Intercultural Press, 2010), 81.

17 Miguel A. De La Torre, *Reading the Bible from the Margins* (Maryknoll, N.Y.: Orbis Books, 2002), 31.

However ambiguous is the experience of migration, from a missiological perspective, as stated at the beginning of this article there is a growing consensus that the 'dynamism of mission', is shifting from those who have historically been '*above*' to those who are now coming '*from below*'.

JAB Jongenel[18] identifies three important ways various missionary and evangelistic activities of the Christian migrants and their congregations and churches in Europe engaged in:

1. *Internal Mission (Mission in Non-Western Circles):* The non-Western Christian migrants are part of their own ethnic, national, and linguistic communities. Consequently, they witness primarily in their own circles. For instance, some Chinese, Korean, Spanish congregations in Europe and North America consist of new converts; the other members of these congregations migrated as Christians from Hong Kong, Singapore, Indonesia, Latin America and other Asian countries. Many newly converted people are young. The Christian migrants tell their conversion stories to other people and it is called 'internal mission'.
2. *Reverse Mission:* Some of the migrants to Europe and North America do not confine their witness to their own circles. They are convinced of their call to preach the Good News of Jesus Christ to nominal or festival Christians of Europe and North America. Ter Haar[19] has referred to "*the common sight today of African missionaries preaching in public places in the big cities of Europe, Bible in hand, which seems to suggest that a reverse mission might be in progress. This is indeed so. Just as European missionaries once believed in their divine task of bringing the gospel to Africa, African church leaders in Europe are today convinced of their mission to bring the gospel back to those who originally provided them with it.*"
3. *Common Mission:* Mission can also be done by members of established congregations and churches in cooperation with members of migrant congregations and churches – the so called '*common mission*'.[20] Werner Kahl[21] has referred to "*the vision of a common missionary vocation*," which he regarded as justified by the biblical perspective as well as by the contemporary predicament of the national churches in Europe and North America. The

18 Jan A.B. Jongenel, "The Mission of Migrant Churches in Europe," *Missiology: An International Review*, vol. XXXI, no. I (January 2003): 32.

19 Gerrie Ter Haar, *African Christians in Europe* (Nairobi, Kenya: Action Publishers, 2001), 166-170.

20 Claudia Wiihrisch-Oblau, "From Reverse Mission to Common Mission ... We Hope: Immigrant Protestant Churches and 'the Programme for Cooperation between German and Immigrant Congregations' of the United Evangelical Mission," *International Review of Mission*, 89: 467-483.

21 Werner Kahl, *A Theological Perspective: The Common Missionary Vocation of Mainline and Migrant Churches* (Unpublished Conference Paper, 2001): 6-10.

realization of this new vision is not an easy task; from the European point of view, it requires a broad knowledge of European culture and a deep intuition of European life-experience; from the non-Western point of view, it requires a committed understanding of the missionary zeal to reach out to non-Christians.

Having said that, let us try to identify some of the challenges the migrant Christian communities pose through their involvement in missionary engagement. Under this section I want us to look at three areas:

Diaspora Mission

Diaspora community has been defined as those who

a) have migrated from a homeland and settled in a new place,
b) have taken the time and trouble to form a separate community there, and
c) still maintain connections with the homeland[22]

JAB Jongeneel[23] observes that protestant migrants have indeed not only affiliated themselves with existing congregations and churches in Europe (both as individuals and as groups), but have also - and even mostly – established new and independent communities such as Bible and prayer groups, congregations and churches, and ecclesiastical societies and foundations recognized by the government.

It is also observed that most migrant congregations and churches do not belong to the Ecumenical Movement, but to the Lausanne Movement, the Pentecostal Movement, and the Charismatic Renewal in the various mainline churches. In many ways, they prove to be more dynamic and expansive than the established congregations and churches in Europe and North America.

- Diaspora community as cross-cultural missionary

It is not a question of whether or not the Christian diaspora community should be involved in mission, but a question of "how?" Among many, misiologists have identified four different ways how the diaspora community are involved in mission:[24]

22 M. Rynkiewich, *Soul, Self, and Society: A Postmodern Anthropology for Mission in a Postcolonial World* (Eugene, OR: Cascade Books, 2011). 207.

23 Jan A. B. Jongeneel, "The Mission of Migrant Churches in Europe," *Missiology: An International Review*, Vol. XXXI, No. I (January 2003), 30.

24 S. George, "Diaspora: A Hidden Link "From Everywhere to Everywhere," *Missiology*, vol. XXXVI, no. I (2011): 52-53.

i. Diaspora community's mission is to *focus on reaching out within their own social networks*. Since they share common experiences they easily understand the difficulties of '*leaving and adjusting*' that other migrants are dealing with. As Christian migrants are forming a new cultural identity, they are in a better situation to position themselves to assist other migrants in finding their new identity in Christ.
ii. Diaspora community is also engaged in mission beyond their immediate community, by reaching out to other diaspora or migrant groups. These may be peoples that the dominant culture may not be sensitive to reach but with which the diaspora church could identify. Each of these avenues for ministry requires the diaspora community to embrace their identity as exiles and aliens rather than leaving behind who they are. It is not to say that they should not assimilate or integrate, but rather recognize their affinity with God's call to be pilgrims and participants in his kingdom.
iii. Diaspora community are also involved in missions to the host culture. This may be the hardest, but is very important. First and foremost, the new immigrant congregations are performing a vital missionary function by their very presence.
iv. Diaspora community focuses on cross-cultural witness. By embracing the attitude of pilgrim, diaspora Christians recognizes that what they have learned through adapting to a host culture is preparation for cross-cultural missions. One context in which migrants have an advantage in missions is in what we consider to be creative access countries. When Christian migrants establish their community in these settings they also establish the church. This community, particularly through the assimilation of their children has the opportunity to reach out to the hosts.

This is also true in Indian context. We do have different 'diaspora congregations'[25] quite actively engaged in diaspora mission. How are we responding to that? Do we see them as a threat? or as accompaniment in our own mission engagement?

Enoch Wan[26] has described missions from the diaspora as being either "*Missions through the diaspora*" which is reaching out through social networks or "*Missions by and beyond the Diaspora*" which is "*cross-cultural missions to other ethnic groups in their host countries, homelands, and abroad*". Another dimension of the missionary role of the diaspora community is described as reverse missions

25 For example, Naga Christian Fellowship, Mizo Fellowship, Korean Congregations, many Hindi Fellowships in South India, etc.

26 Enoch Wan, "Introduction," in *Diaspora Missiology: Theory, Methodology and Practice,* edited by E. Wan (Portland, OR: Institute of Diaspora Studies, 2011), 5.

"*when non-Western churches return with the Gospel to societies that initially brought the Gospel to them.*"[27]

- *Diaspora Missiology*

During the November 2009 Lausanne Diaspora Educators Consultation held in Seoul,[28] South Korea (*the 'Seoul Consultation'*), participants produced an enhanced definition of diaspora missiology which states "[*D]iaspora Missiology is a missiological framework for understanding and participating in God's redemptive mission among people living outside their place of origin.*"[29]

Diaspora missiology as an interdisciplinary field refers to

a) the study of their geographic or demographic mobility of people in various parts of the globe,
b) viewed through the lens of God's redemptive plan for all nations (*panta ta ethne*) and
c) it also refers to the exploration of how the body of Christ can participate in this redemptive purposes and work.[30]

The church, especially the local churches, are challenged by migrant Christians missionaries to actively participate in diaspora missions by,

- Recognizing and responding to the missional opportunities presented by global migration and diaspora communities, in strategic planning, and in focused training and resourcing of those called to work among them.
- Bearing counter-cultural witness to the love of Christ in deed and word, by obeying the extensive biblical commands to love the stranger, defend the cause of the foreigner, visit the prisoner, practice hospitality, build friendships, invite into our homes, and provide help and services.
- Discerning the hand of God, even in circumstances they may not have chosen and listen and learn from immigrant congregations, and initiate cooperative efforts to reach all sections of people with the gospel.

---

27 Hun Kim, "Receiving Mission: Reflection on Reversed Phenomena in Mission by Migrant Workers from Global Churches to the Western Society," in *Transformation*, vol. 28 no. 1 (2011): 63.

28 Read about this consultation at http://www.lausanne.org/diaspora-2009/consultation-on-diasporamissions.html

29 See 'The Seoul Declaration on Diaspora Missiology', available at www.lausanne.org/documents/seoul-declaration-on-diaspora-missiology.html (accessed, 10.4.2018).

30 Chandler H. Im and Tereso C. Casino, "Introduction," in *Global Diasporas and Mission*, edited by Chandler H. Im and Amos Yong (Oxford: Regnum 2014), 3.

Reverse Mission

The subject of reverse mission, that is, missionaries and pastors from former mission field now ministering in Europe and North America is becoming a phenomenon that is attracting the attention of both academics and the media. In mission circles this has become termed as the '*reverse-mission agenda*'. Although it is relatively new phenomenon, the validity of the observation has become ever more apparent with missionaries from Africa, India, Philippines, Korea, China and Latin America arriving in Europe and the North America, as well as taking a more active part in some of the more traditional areas such as the Middle East and South Asia.

What is the theology behind reverse mission? For me personally, among many there are *two theological reasons for reverse mission.*

- The understanding that God is a missionary God. In the Old Testament we see God making known himself through Israel to the Nations. It was this understanding that also sees God sending Jesus, to redeem humanity from their fallen nature. As we see it in the Acts of the Apostles, the redemptive work of God continued through the work of the Holy Spirit in the Church. In essence the Triune God is a missionary God. As we read in John's gospel, Jesus sends his disciples and later the church to continue the redemptive work of the Triune God. Jesus sends his disciples and later his followers into the world.[31] It is within this understanding that the church must see her mission - participating in God's mission (*mission Dei*) and not ours (*mission ecclesia*). One implication of this is that just as some people from European North American context obeyed God's call and went to the South as missionaries, these former recipients of the Good News of Jesus are now hearing the same God calling them to go to Europe and North America.
- The global mission has no headquarters, and permanent address. Earlier global mission used to have a permanent address in Europe and North America, but this is not the case anymore because mission is now understood as from "*everywhere to everywhere*". It is in this framework that we talk about reverse mission. Asia, Africa, South America and the Caribbean are no longer just receivers but givers and contributors to global mission. This does not mean that Europe and North America have stopped sending missionaries or should stop sending missionaries into the global south or the rest of the world, but it only means that the previous monopoly on world mission is no longer acceptable.

31 John 17:18 *As you have sent me into the world, so I have sent them into the world*; John 20:21 Jesus said to them again, *Peace be with you. As the Father has sent me, so I send you.*

Intercultural Mission

Fornet-Betancourt[32] suggests that migrants provide the church with a '*school of inter-culturality*', meaning the opportunity to learn how to relate inter-culturally in a "community of worlds that are different and yet in solidarity with each other... that are reshaped by means of the interaction of their members... (where) the organizing principle... is the leading and normative idea of mutuality." Intercultural mission sees mission as a two-way process from the very beginning, establishing a mutuality of relationships that, as Fornet-Betancourt suggests, will reshape both sides.

The WCC document '*Together Towards Life*'[33] states, "*Migration has become a worldwide, multi-directional phenomenon which is reshaping the Christian landscape*" (TTL5).[34] All the WCC documents refer to issues of justice that are raised by migration as well as implications for the life of churches. TTL goes further in critical missiological thinking by suggesting that "*God's hospitality calls us to move beyond binary notions of culturally dominant groups as hosts and migrant and minority peoples as guests. Instead, in God's hospitality, God is host and we are all invited by the Spirit to participate with humility and mutuality in God's mission*" (TTL71). Are migrants the missionaries of today?

Let me conclude with some of the observations (*not all are listed)* by Richard Evans on Migration and Mission: Through a Boschian Lens[35] presented at the Global Connections Mission Educators Forum on 15 June 2016.

1. ***Mission as Church with Others*** (*God's Pilgrim People*): Two important motifs in Scripture have been identified: i) continuing experience of the people of God as aliens or exiles on earth therefore being a stranger is normatively central to Christian identity, ii) as strangers themselves, the people of God welcome strangers and embody hospitality as a way of life. This motif of

32 Raul Fornet-Betancourt, "Hermeneutics and the Politics of Strangers," in *A Promised Land, a Perilous Journey: Theological Perspectives on Migration*, edited by Daniel Groody and Gioachhino Campese (Indiana: University of Notre Dame Press, (2008), 219.

33 For full text see, https://www.oikoumene.org/en/resources/publications/TogethertowardsLife_MissionandEvangelism.pdf

34 *The history of Christian mission has been characterized by conceptions of geographical expansion from a Christian centre to the "unreached territories," to the ends of the earth. But today we are facing a radically changing ecclesial landscape described as "world Christianity" where the majority of Christians either are living or have their origins in the global South and East. Migration has become a worldwide, multi-directional phenomenon which is reshaping the Christian landscape. The emergence of strong Pentecostal and charismatic movements from different localities is one of the most noteworthy characteristics of world Christianity today. What are the insights for mission and evangelism—theologies, agendas and practices—of this "shift of the centre of gravity of Christianity"?*

35 https://www.globalconnections.org.uk/.../gc_mef_migration_mission_through_a_bosc...

'*strangers welcoming strangers*' suggests significant implications for mission and migration and addresses some of our contemporary challenges.[36]

2. **Mission as m*issio Dei*** – (*Mission beyond the church*): The history of the expansion of the Christian church, past present and future, has to be understood and explained from the historical reality of God's sovereignty moving over the nations and at the same time God's people moving everywhere.[37] While referring to 'migrants', we are not merely talking about people, who are 'other' than ourselves, rather we are talking about ourselves.
3. **Mission as Mediating Salvation**: As David Bosch rightly observes, from the tension between the '*already*' and '*not yet*' of the reign of God, from the tension between the '*salvation indicative*' (salvation is already a reality) and '*salvation subjunctive*' (comprehensive salvation yet to come) there emerges the '*salvation imperative*' - get involved in the ministry of salvation here and now.[38] Enoch Wan[39] calls it "missions to...", "missions through...", "missions by and beyond...". JAB Jongeneel[40] identifies it with "internal mission...", "reverse mission...", "common mission...". This is a challenging task the migrant communities pose to the church everywhere.
4. **Mission as the Quest for Justice**: As stated earlier the observation of Christine Pohl, the Biblical focus on responsibility towards strangers and foreigners among us suggests that a concern for the physical, social and spiritual well-being of migrants and refugees should be central to Christian life, mission and witness not at the peripheral level. In such a context the biggest challenge is the prophetic task of being a voice for the poor and downtrodden. This is very important task of pronouncing a prophetic word to a society that is panicking from seeing flood of foreigners who have come to stay with them.[41]
5. **Mission as Evangelism**: There is a strong notion prevailing in mission studies called '*witness of presence*', which many do not notice or recognise. Though migrant community congregations all over the globe do not make attempts to attract the people among whom they are living as aliens, yet their presence itself makes a difference and many call this as 'silent evangelism'.

36 Pohl, "Biblical Issues in Mission and Migration...," 5.

37 Lausanne Diaspora Educator's Consultation, "Seoul declaration on Diaspora missiology," in *Scattered to Gather – Embracing the Global Trends of Diaspora* (2009), 28.

38 David J. Bosch, *Transforming Mission* (Maryknoll, NY, Orbis, 1991), 400.

39 Enoch Wan, *Diaspora Missiology: Theory, Methodology and Practice* (Portland, OR: Western Seminary, 2011), 138.

40 Jan A. B. Jongeneel, "The Mission of Migrant Churches in Europe," *Missiology: An International Review,* vol. XXXI no. I (January 2003), 32.

41 Escobar, "Biblical Issues in Mission and Migration...," 19.

> The very presence of such congregations is a testimony to the dynamic quality and significance of migrant community evangelical witness.[42]

The primary focus in this article has been to see what challenges the migrants bring to the church-in-mission. To arrive at this, I have tried to understand the phenomena of migration in the present day context and how missiologists have attempted to address the complex and yet fluid situation called 'migration'. While understanding the challenges of peoples' migration, it has been noted that the church-in-mission should be prepared to meet both the physical as well as spiritual need of the people, and at the same time be bold enough to address injustices and violence done to the migrant people. It has been noted that '*diaspora mission*', '*reverse mission*' and '*intercultural mission*' are some of the challenges from migrants to the church-in-mission.

42 Paul Freston, "Reverse Mission: A Discourse in Search of Reality," *Pentecostal Studies* vol. 9, no. 2 (2010): 162.

7

Is God Still the Refuge for Refugees
An Interfaith Perspective

J.M.P. Thomas Birla

About three thousand years ago, a Tamil poet and philosopher – Kaniyan Poongundranar in the Tamil classic *Purananuru* wrote: "All places in universe is our place and all citizens in universe are our relations…"[1] Many other philosophies and ideas of universal-friendship and relation such as this could be cited from the ages past. A similar concept is applied in the world economy like 'globalization[2]' where all places are considered as our market and all people are considered as our customers.[3] However, a question arises as to whether such life-giving religio-cultural and embracive secular concepts are relevant to humanity troubled by the complexity of migration. Considering this fact, an attempt is made in this article to look at global migration as a religious challenge and quest for humanhood of all. For all categories of people[4] affected by migration undergo certain common

1 http://tamilnation.co/diaspora/index.htm (accessed on 18 February, 2018).

2 Noam Chomsky defines as "the extension of trans-national corporate tyranny. These are tyrannical, totalitarian institutions, mega corporations. They are huge command economies, run from the top, relatively unaccountable and interlinked in various ways. This first interest is profit. But it is does not end there. Its deeper objective is to construct an audience of a particular type, one that is addicted to a certain life style with artificial wants." Pascal Alan Nazareth, "Inaugural Address," in *Gospel and Globalisation in Gospel and Globalisation: 2nd South Asia Christian Youth Conference, e*dited by Adrian Watkins and Leslie Nathaniel (New Delhi: CMS/ISPCK, 2006), 6.

3 http://thamizhamizhthuinimai.blogspot.in/2011/02/yaathum-oore-yaavarum-kelir-kaniyan.html (accessed on 17 February, 2018).

4 Different categories such as "migrants", "refuges" Asylum seekers" are generally used. "Migrant" is a person who is engaged in a remunerated activity in a State of which he/she is not a national.. http://unesdoc.unesco.org/images/0014/001435/143557e.pdf (accessed on 28 March, 2018). "A refugee is someone who is unable or unwilling to return to their country of origin owing to a well-founded fear of being persecuted for reasons of race, religion, nationality, membership of a particular social group, or political opinion." Convention and Protocol relating to the status of Refugee, UNHCR – The UN Refugee Agency. http://www.unhcr.org/3b66c2aa10.

challenges such as identity crisis, suffering, pain and trauma which certainly requires response from interfaith relation perspective. It is assumed that the role of interfaith relation can play as a catalyst for instilling a spirit of embrace and see the whole world as a single family. To arrive at this conclusion, the article highlights the inseparable connection between religion and migration, the various challenges facing humanity today.

Religion and Migration

Migration is not a new phenomenon in the human history. From the time immemorial humans have been on the move for one reason or the other. The phenomenon of migration was very much there in the ancient religious writings. In fact, the perspective in which religion describes migration and migrants is vital.[5] For religion decides the attitude of people belonging to different religious traditions over against the migrants. Perhaps some of the serious theological questions in this regard are: Does religion looks at migration as a punishment for the past sins or law of karma at work? Does religion offers hope to the homeless? Is God still the refuge for refugees?[6] What should be the attitude of a religious person towards migrants? Such theological questions and challenges on migration can be found in various religious traditions.

In Christianity, the Holy Bible begins with the story of creation, and the climax of the story is that Adam and Eve had to migrate from the Eden Garden because of sin.[7] Similar story continues throughout the Bible. The history of Israel is perhaps the history of captivity and exiles.[8] For instance, the king of Assyria captured all the land of Naphtali and carried people into captivity (2 kings 15:29). Similarly, the king Nebuchadnezzar captured Jerusalem, Judah captivated and huge number of Jews taken into exile in Babylon (Jeremiah 52:28-30). These narratives in the context of our times today is nothing, but the narratives of formed migration.

The Ramayana,[9] one of the ancient Indian epics, also is a story of migration. The story of Rama's exile beautifully depicts the struggles and hardships

---

pdf Accessed on 27 March, 2018. The terms "asylum seeker" is the one who asks for protection after arriving in the host country."http://www.unesco.org/new/en/social-and-human-sciences/themes/international-migration/glossary/asylum-seeker/ (accessed on 29 March, 2018).

5 Mohan Doss, "Migrants in Theological Perspective: Strangers No More, in Migration and Mission in India," in *Migration and Mission in India,* edited by L. Stanislaus and Jose Joseph (Delhi: ISPCK, 2007), 197.

6 Doss, "Migrants…," 190-197.

7 Doss, "Migrants…," 198.

8 Exile means forced removal of a large population from their homeland to a foreign land. Duane A. Garrett, *The Exiles of Israel: A Closer Look. http*://www.christianitytoday.com/edstetzer/2012/april/exiles-of-israel-closer-look.html (accessed on 3 March, 2018).

9 The traditional and orthodox understanding is that Valmiki wrote the Ramayana during the life time of Ramachandra. Valmiki gave structure to a story that has been transmitted by oral

encountered by the migrants as well as good relation between migrant community and the host society. Here too, it is a story of forced migration. For the King Dasharatha decided to make his eldest son Rama as a new king. But because of his second and favourite wife Kaikeyi who wanted her son Bharatha to be on the throne Rama the rightful heir of king Dasharatha was sent into exile in forest for fourteen years.[10]

The Islamic history has testified that the early Muslim converts and Prophet Muhammed too were not exceptions to this forced migration experience. The early Muslim converts were subjected to ruthless torture by their own people for embracing Islam. They were forced to leave their home land for survival.[11] At this juncture, they had migrated to a Christian kingdom called Abyssinia. After some years, the situation became so worse that it compelled Prophet Muhammed and the rest of the Muslims to migrate from Mecca to Medina.[12]

Migration: Its Issues and Challenges

Migration takes place for various reasons. Some are forced to migrate from one place to another due to lack of livelihood, protection, and basic human rights. They are also forced to migrate due to persecution, poverty, and natural calamities. People migrate from their country of birth to an unknown land for mere survival. Others migrate willingly to another place looking for better fortune, to gain wisdom and to spread their ideology and culture. Besides, one of the strongest waves of migration the human history ever witnessed is the migration for promotion of religion. There are number of issues and challenges these migrations pose which calls for looking at whole issue or migration from interfaith relations perspective in our times.

Migration for Promotion of Religion

The faith communities belonging to different religious traditions have migrated from one place to the other to promote of their religion. Christianity for instance have basically been promoted by the migrant missionaries like St. Thomas, one

---

traditions. C. Rajagopalachari, *Ramayana* (Bombay: Bharatiya Vidya Bhavan, 1979), 15.

10 Raj Balkaran and A. Walter Dorn, *Violence in the Valmtki Rämäyatta: Just War Criteria in an Ancient Indian Epic,* http://web.b.ebscohost.com/ehost/pdfviewer/pdfviewer?vid=1&sid=9b10f0a8-b2d7-4a71-aaf0-1492f65252ff%40sessionmgr104 Accessed on 4 March, 2018.; http://blessingsonthenet.com/indianculture/hindugod-hindugodess/articles/65/exile-of-lord-rama (accessed on 2 March, 2018).

11 Maulana Muhammad Ali, *Muhammad: The Prophet* (Lahore: Ahmadiyyah Anjuman Ishaat Islam, 1951), 93.

12 Hakim Mohammed Said, *The History of the Islamic Calendar in the Light of Hijra,* http://web.b.ebscohost.com/ehost/pdfviewer/pdfviewer?vid=1&sid=59055b52-a646-4f2e-bebb-1c302814b98d%40sessionmgr104 (accessed on 4 March, 2018).

of the disciples of Jesus Christ, who migrated to India.[13] Many other Christian missionaries like Francis Xavier, Robert De Nobili, Zeigenbalg, the Serampore trio – William Carrey, Joshua Marshman and William Ward were migrated from their native place to a foreign land to spread Christianity.[14]

In Hinduism too, A. C. Bhaktivedanta Swami Prabhupada, the founder of ISKCON[15] travelled to New York in the year 1965 to fulfill the vision and mission of his spiritual master Srila Bhaktisiddhanta Sarasvati Thakura.[16] Similarly, the migration of Sufis to India especially in the 13th century[17] played a significant role in the spread of Islamic faith in India.[18] Migration of Sufi saint Khwaja Qutb-ud-din Bakhtiyar to Delhi can be cited as evidence for such religious motif of migration.[19] Likewise, under the patronage of great king Ashoka, Buddhist monks migrated to different places both within and outside India and spread the teachings of Buddha. The spread of Buddhism from India to Sri Lanka, Burma, Nepal, Tibet, China, and Japan are all because of migration.[20] Such migration for the promotion of a particular religion is not just a past history but also a present reality till today.

This sort of migrations in the past and present times have not left nations and societies without trouble. Such migration not only brings new religion and culture, but also makes the host society fragile. The vulnerable native religious traditions, cultures and belief systems are certainly disturbed and threatened by the migrant ones. Since the host society is treated by the migrants as a mission field, there is no subject to subject relation. Instead, subject to object relation at

---

13 Nectaria McLees, "Witness for An Apostle: The Evidence for St. Thomas in India," *Road to Emmaus* 6/2 (2005): 47-61. http://web.b.ebscohost.com/ehost/pdfviewer/pdfviewer?vid=1&sid=1d6b4ea2-aed7-424c-b96a-f9a6aa81e37d%40sessionmgr103 (accessed on 7 March, 2018).

14 Ulrike Gleixner, "Remapping the World: The vision of a Protestant Empire in the Eighteenth Century," *Migration and Religion*, vol. 46 (2012): 77-90. http://booksandjournals.brillonline.com/content/books/b9789401208116s005 (accessed on 7 March, 2018).

15 ISKCON – The International Society for Krishna Consciousness. It is also known as the Hare Krishna Movement.

16 John M. Bozeman, *Field Notes: ISKCON's Extensive Reform Efforts.* http://web.a.ebscohost.com/ehost/pdfviewer/pdfviewer?vid=3&sid=bdecf554-7bc8-48d1-9c52-4dc382460f7b%40sessionmgr4008 (accessed on 21 February, 2018).

17 Nazeer Ahmed, *The Sufis of India and Pakistan.* https://historyofislam.com/contents/the-post-mongol-period/the-sufis-of-india-and-pakistan/ (accessed on 20 February, 2018).

18 Rubina Ramji, "The global migration of Sufi Islam to South Asia and beyond," *Religion, Globalization, and Culture,* vol. 6 (2007): 473-484. http://booksandjournals.brillonline.com/content/books/10.1163/ej.9789004154070.i-608.165 (accessed on 12 February, 2018).

19 http://www.columbia.edu/itc/mealac/pritchett/00islamlinks/ikram/part1_09.html (accessed on 9 March, 2018).

20 http://www.ushistory.org/civ/8d.asp (accessed on 21 February, 2018).

play. As a consequence, there emergences religious fundamentalism[21] leading to religious intolerance and violence between the natives and migrants.

In fact, such kind of migration develops transnational linkages.[22] People from the host society gradually starts to visit the migrants' country and vice versa. However, there is not much mutual learning that takes place. It is always the members of the host society who are at the receiving end. An important point to be noted here is that in the process of such migration, the members of the host society are made migrants in their own land.

Spatial Conflicts

One of the major issues people face as a result of migration, particularly in the situation of forced migration[23] is displacement or dislocation from their land. The land is not just a property, but it is people's identity. It also has deep religious meanings and people's sentiments are attached to it. Therefore, when people are displaced and dislocated they not only become landless and homeless, but undergo identity crisis and lose of dignity. As a result, the migrants try to use multiple identities depending on the circumstances. For example, while one's family name is used as an identity within a locality, one's ethnic group's name is used as an identity within the country.[24] And when it comes to international forum, it is the national identity which is used. In most cases, people uses these multiple identities interchangeably in order to gain support by identifying themselves with a larger group. While in the host society or country, the migrants/refugees often seek for same identity and dignity. Whereas, the host society often resists to it and any attempt of including the outsiders within the host society's identity in most cases results into spatial conflicts.

One of the important facts to be noted in such spatial conflicts is that it is not always the migrant population who loses their land or become homeless; but it all depends on who are the migrants and with what purpose they migrate? For

---

21 According to Anson Sharpe and Jeffrey Hadden, "Fundamentalism is a truly modern phenomenon: modern in the sense that the movement is always seeking original solutions to new, pressing problems. Leaders are not merely constructing more rigid orthodoxies in the name of defending old mythical orthodoxies. In the process of undertaking restoration within contemporary demographic/technological centres, new social orders are actually being promulgated. Malsie Ruthven, *Fundamentalism: A Very Short Introduction* (New York: Oxford University Press, 2007), 125.

22 Jacqueline Hagan and Helen Rose Ebaugh, *Calling Upon the Sacred: Migrants' Use of Religion in the Migration Process.* http://onlinelibrary.wiley.com/wol1/doi/10.1111/j.1747-7379.2003.tb00173.x/abstract (accessed on 24 February, 2018).

23 Forced Migration includes refugees, asylum seekers and internal displacement. Stephen Castles, *Towards a Sociology of Forced Migration and Social Transformation.* http://journals.sagepub.com/doi/abs/10.1177/0038038503037001384 (accessed on 10 March, 2018).

24 Patta Devaraja and Esther Kathiroli, "International Displacement in Asian Countries," in *Rights of Internally Displaced People: Asian Churches' Response,* edited by Mathews George Chunakara (Hong Kong: International Affairs CCA, 2000), 66.

instance, one might refer to the ancient Indian history Aryan migration. It was perhaps not migration, but invasion.[25] They got hold of the land, towns and cities and made the native people migrants in their own land. The natives were pushed to the periphery[26] and made refugee in their own land.[27]

Social Conflicts

After migration, both the migrant population and the indigenous population have to share all their social aspects such as natural resources, job opportunities, economy and political interest. The social conflict possibly arises during this process of sharing their livelihood resources. This happens when one start to blame the other group for their misfortunes and untoward incidents.[28] Generally, the host society takes advantage of the vulnerable condition of the refugees by employing them for less salary.[29] They work more but earn less. This particular struggle could indicates various other problems such as poverty, malnutrition, denial of basic human rights and illiteracy. The differences between these two groups could be misused for political interests and they could be polarized to serve as a vote bank for some political parties.[30] Inter-marriages among these two communities hardly happen and if at all it happens very often it creates social conflicts. It is due to the low status or the second class citizen treatment given to the migrant people. However, it is not always the common people who decide upon the refugees, but the government and its policies. When the government

25 Arvind Sharma, *Dr. B. R. Ambedkar on the Aryan Invasion and the Emergence of the Caste System in India.* http://web.b.ebscohost.com/ehost/pdfviewer/pdfviewer?vid=0&sid=e539ea35-c4f0-478a-b687-9bbc1e12c4e8%40sessionmgr102 (accessed on 7 May, 2018).

26 Karl Ivan Solibakke, "Muslim Migration to Germany: A Response to Thilo Sarrazin's Deutschland Schafft Sich AB," in *Migration and Religion*, vol. 46 (2012): 219-235. http://booksandjournals.brillonline.com/content/books/b9789401208116s013 (accessed on 22 February, 2018).

27 Stephen Castles, *Towards a Sociology of Forced Migration and Social Transformation.* http://journals.sagepub.com/doi/abs/10.1177/0038038503037001384 (accessed on 12 March, 2018).

28 Ngambouk Vitalis Pemunta and Atock Brice Aristide, "Socio-spatial occupation, conflict and humanitarian assistance for Bororo cross-border migrants in east Cameroon," *International Journal of Development Issues* 12/3, 2013. http://www.emeraldinsight.com/doi/abs/10.1108/IJDI-03-2013-0032 (accessed on 23 March, 2018).

29 A.K. Gupta, *Sociological Implications of Rural to Rural Migration* (Allahabad: Vohra Publishers, 1988), 63.

30 Keith Harper, review of *A Nation under Our Feet: Black Political Struggles in the Rural South from Slavery to the Great Migration,* by Steven Hahn (Cambridge and London: Belknap Press of Harvard University Press, 2003). http://web.a.ebscohost.com/ehost/pdfviewer/pdfviewer?vid=0&sid=7aba6ff9-5b0a-416c-9a3e-a01ce9088164%40sessionmgr4007 (accessed on 22 March, 2018).

turns its back on them there arises lot of untoward incidents such as sexual assault, violence and suicide etc.[31]

Religious and Cultural Conflicts

Relation between the religion of the land and the religion of the migrant population is very crucial. Religion plays a significant role in shaping the community's culture and vice versa. The life style, religious practices, customs, food habits, dress code and many other aspects of a particular community has its roots in their religion and culture. Therefore, the relationship between the religions is determined by people's culture. As refugees bring along their religion and culture alien to the host society, number of tensions that emerges between the two. Firstly, it distinguishes the refugees from the indigenous population. Secondly, the arrival of a new religion could be seen as a rival to the native religion. Thirdly, if any element in their religious practices is contrary or offensive towards the religious sentiments of another group then it might instigate conflicts. Fourthly, if one has superior claims over another religion and culture then it provokes religious tension.[32] Finally, having lived in the host society for generations, the impending danger is that the future generations of the migrant population may not know either their language or their culture in fullness as their land, language and culture are heavily influenced by the host society. Perhaps, it produces a typical generation without any distinct identity of their own. Often they are they are in between and as a result they are even considered as 'No People'.

Religious Insights on Migration

As it is hinted above, religions, particularly the Christianity, portrays migration as a punishment and a result of the migrants' sins. For example, the Exile or migration is the outcome of God's anger for people's unbelief and disobedience. In other words, it is popularly understood that God sends people in exile. However, it is also evident that God never sends people alone, but goes along with them and stands with them as refuge and bring them back to restoration.[33] For it is written,

> For I know the plans I have for you, says the Lord, plans for welfare and not for evil, to give you a future and a hope. Then you will call upon me and come and pray to me, and I will hear you. You will seek me and find me; when you seek me with all your heart, I will be found by you, says the Lord, and I will restore your fortunes and gather you

31 Sarah Malik, *Syrian Refugee Crisis: This is about Humanity, Not Religion.* http://www.abc.net.au/news/2015-09-07/malik-syrian-refugees/6755696 (accessed on 21 March, 2018).

32 Ilangovan Rajasekaran, "The ways of the Parivar," *Frontline,* 21 (July 2017): 12-15.

33 Hans Walter Wolff, "Prophecy from the Eighth through the Fifth Century," *Interpretation* 32/1 (January, 1978): 17-30.http://web.a.ebscohost.com/ehost/pdfviewer/pdfviewer?vid=1&sid=848036c1-fba6-4a8b-bb6d-edf8f978be08%40sessionmgr4007 (accessed on 5 May, 2018).

> from all the nations and all the places where I have driven you, says the Lord, and I will bring you back to the place from which I sent you into exile. (Jeremiah 29:11-14)

The Biblical narratives, in both Old Testament and New Testament, are filled with the stories that God constantly moves along and identifies with the migrants. The story of Abraham, Jacob, Moses to cite few, and more distinctly, the very narrative of Jesus' incarnation is the crystal clear evident of this fact. According to Johannine narrative, "The Word became flesh and made his dwelling among us. We have seen his glory, the glory of the one and only Son, who came from the Father, full of grace and truth. (John 1:14)." This is how God revealed his love to the world that "He sent his one and only Son into the world that we might live through him (1 John 4:9)."

To connect into our language of discourse, the 'Word' which was in the beginning migrated to the womb of Virgin Mary migrated and became flesh. More practically, the Gospel records: *Rise, take the child and his mother, and flee to Egypt… (Matthew 2:13-23).* Here God becomes a refugee and experiences the experience of refugees and migrants.[34] Further, to its climax, the suffering of Jesus on the cross elucidates the fact that in the context of migration, suffering is inevitable. In this, Jesus' cry "*My God, my God, why have you forsaken me?" (Matthew 27:46)*, perhaps is the cry of migrants today.

In Ramayana too, Rama is the avatar of Lord Vishnu, and his wife Sita is an avatar of Sri Lakshmi a Hindu goddess. Rama and Sita are the manifestations of God who went on exile and thereby experienced and identified themselves with the struggles of migrants. Lord Rama was unlawfully forced to leave his homeland. Along with Lord Rama, his wife and brother Lakshmana too migrated and faced so many untold persecutions and struggles which are figuratively depicted in the form of Rakshasas and Rakshinis.[35]

Though there were many kind-hearted people such as saints, seers, the common folks, Hanuman[36] who stood in solidarity with the migrant family of Rama, an important aspect in this narrative is that the sufferings and challenges

34 Daniel G. Groody, "Homeward Bound A Theology of Migration for Fullness of Life, Justice and Peace," *The Ecumenical Review* 64/3 (October, 2012): 299-313. http://web.b.ebscohost.com/ehost/pdfviewer/pdfviewer?vid=2&sid=f3f419b8-8bd3-4b2b-9c7c-a3531759634c%40sessionmgr120 (accessed on 15 March, 2018).

35 Rakshasas would denote male demons. Rakshinis would denote female demons. The terms 'Rakshasas' and 'Rakshinis' in our times can be compared to the oppressors who had reduced the common people to the status of forced migrant and refugee, but figuratively it is taken to refer struggles, pain and suffering of the migrants.

36 Hanuman is the so called Monkey-god. A zealous devotee and the servant of Lord Rama. Philip Lutgendorf, *Hanuman's Tale: The Message of a Divine Monkey* (New York: Oxford University Press, 2007), 47.

faced by both men and women in the migrant population are not the same.[37] It is strange that Rama wanted to test the purity and honour of Sita[38] by making her to walk through the flames of fire.[39] In fact, while all other women failed, Sita proved her purity. However, the fact is that Sita underwent double struggle and suffering. This is how the pathetic condition of migrant women are. They are not only oppressed, forced and sexually abused by the 'Rakshasas' of the host society but also humiliated, mistrusted by their own family members. The migrant woman had to undergo such Agni Pareeksha daily.[40]

Despite negative aspects, one needs to learn that the relation between the migrant family and the common people of the host society were very good. Mutually they were always ready to support each other in all the possible ways. At times of trouble, the migrant family stood with the host society and that builds mutual trust. For example, the kindness showed by the host society has been reciprocated by Rama by protecting the people in Dandhaka forest as a guardian for ten years.

In the Islamic history too we see such healthy relationship that though the inhabitants of Abyssinia and their king Negus were Christian by faith, they did refuse to accept the early converts migrant Muslims.[41] When Prophet Muhammed and the rest of the Muslims had migrated to Medina, the Prophet faced great challenge of looking after the helpless migrants who were once very wealthy. In order to address such situation of migration, Prophet Muhammed established a brotherhood/sisterhood between the inhabitants or 'Helpers'[42] and the refugees. Each Helper is bound to one of the migrant family in a bond of brotherhood/ sisterhood. At the request of Prophet Muhammed, every inhabitant of Medina has accepted one migrant as his/her sibling by bond. Each helper took a migrant family to his/her home and shared their possessions as they would do with their lawful siblings.[43] The land, wealth and other resources became secondary concerns whereas life has become the prime concern.

37 G. Julie and M.A. Rani. "Migration and Women: Ways of Empowerment," in *Migration and Mission in India,* edited by L. Stanislaus and Jose Joseph (Delhi: ISPCK, 2007), 180.

38 Since Sita was abducted by Ravana and he kept her enslaved for a short period, until Rama won the battle and freed her.

39 Raj Balkaran and A. Walter Dorn, "Violence in the Valmiki Ramayana: Just War Criteria in an Ancient Indian Epic," *Journal of the American Academy of Religion* 80/3 (September, 2012): 659-690. http://web.b.ebscohost.com/ehost/pdfviewer/pdfviewer?vid=1&sid=2bc8136a-9a55-49f4-b590-7a1bfa536e9f%40sessionmgr101 (accessed on 21 February, 2018).

40 Agni Pareeksha is the fire test that Sita underwent to prove her chastity. See, https://www.youthkiawaaz.com/2013/12/never-want-husband-like-ram-far-maryada-purushottam/ (accessed on 22 March, 2018).

41 Maulana Muhammad Ali, *Muhammad: The Prophet...*, 69.

42 Helper - The inhabitants of Medina is popularly known as Helpers.

43 Maulana Muhammad Ali, *Muhammad: The Prophet...*, 104-105.

Though this brotherhood/sisterhood was only within the Muslim community, it can very well be the model of universal brotherhood/sisterhood transcending the borders of religion, ethnicity, caste, race and so on. The embracive and tolerant attitude and action of the inhabitants of Abyssinia and Medina can be the model for initiating interfaith relations in our times today.

All these religious insights suggest that migration is not God's punishment for the sins, but it is God's identification with humanity.[44]

Who is my family?

The core issues in all the migration related problem is the separation between 'We' and 'They' or 'Us' and 'Them'. The Abrahamic religions such as Judaism, Christianity and Islam claim that God created only one man Adam and one woman Eve, which emphasizes that all human beings irrespective of race, colour, creed etc. come from a single family.[45] It is to this parent, the whole humanity could trace their roots and find a common identity. This is nothing, but the identity of one humanity that all human beings are created in the image of God.

According to Advaita, reality is one, there is no two but one. It is from this single ultimate reality that all human beings came into existence and it is to this single supreme reality all human souls will be merged. So, the entire humanity is nothing but the manifestation of the Supreme Reality. There is a potential divinity in every human being. This philosophy certainly negates all the differences that exist among human beings.

The inter-connectedness of the creation is well-explained in all other religious traditions as well. Such common religious beliefs of the oneness of humanity challenge us to come out of our narrow understanding about family, and humanity. If all peoples and communities understand and follow such kind of religious belief, the selfish love where one loves his/her family, tribe, culture, nation; but hates or not extending the same love to others' family, tribe, language and culture can be overcome.[46] This also can reduce the gulf between the "self" and "other" that exists among the migrants and host society can be reduced.

---

44 Patrick Mwania Musau, "I Was a Stranger and You Welcomed Me: A Christian Pastoral Response to Migration and Displacement," *AFER* 59/1 - 2 (March – June, 2017): 4-25. http://web.b.ebscohost.com/ehost/pdfviewer/pdfviewer?vid=1&sid=c68d50bb-cbb9-45f4-89a7-50879270503a%40sessionmgr103 (accessed on 21 February, 2018).

45 Patricia Wilson-Kastner, "Contemporary Feminism and Christian Doctrine of the Human," *Word & World* 2/3 (Sum, 1982): P. 234-242. http://web.b.ebscohost.com/ehost/pdfviewer/pdfviewer?vid=1&sid=d49e4ccb-8e99-45dd-aca3-aec2da2bc262%40sessionmgr104 (accessed on 22 February, 2018).

46 Sri Amritanandamayi, *The Awakening of Universal Motherhood* (Amritapuri: Mata Amritanandamayi Mission Trust, 2003), 12.

God Alone Owns

Since the migration and the issue of migrants are closely related to the issue of land or space, it is important to know who ultimately holds the land. According to various religious traditions, especially Christianity, the land belongs to God alone. All religious traditions speaks of land as gift of God to humanity. It is God who created the land, and it is humans who created borders. For example, in Genesis 1:28, God said to human, "Be fruitful and multiply, and fill the earth and subdue it..." According to the description of Swami Vivekananda, the exponent of practical Vedanta, Lord Shiva is the master of the world. If anyone wants to please Shiva then he/she should serve the poor and homeless. Similar admonition can be found in Islam that Allah takes the side of the meek and helpless.

It is not just the land that belong to God but also all that we have and all that we are belongs to God alone. The entire creation and all the natural resources are freely given to humanity for care and use for their needs. However, greediness and unwilling to share with others are the main reasons for spatial conflicts people around the world are facing today. The individuals' intention to occupy and accumulate more wealth hinders the opportunity to share with others.

All these suggest that each and every people irrespective of their identity, status as migrant or host population or indigenous people have the right to land and the natural resources there in. Hence, no one should be deprived of land, water and other natural resources that are essential for life. As all human beings are constantly on the move from one place to another, the claim over a particular piece of land based on the virtue of being native is debatable. For today's natives were yesterday's migrants.

Interfaith Relations a Potential Remedy

In the previous sections, an attempt has been made to find out some of the major issues and problems that refugees or the migrant population and the indigenous population encounter with. Each and every dimension of their private and public lives are faced with multiple difficulties due to different factors such as land, language, culture, economy, religion and politics etc. While discussing on the issue of migration, religion is identified as one of the major factors that causes unrest and oppression among people. However, it is also noted that the role of religion per se is not the problem, but the misuse of it by certain people or people groups. In its true sense of the meaning, the ultimate aim of any religion is to bring peace and harmony among people. Each religion has life-giving values to offer.

Therefore, looking at the issue migration from interfaith perspective[47] is inescapable necessity. Certainly, the power of religion and inter-faith relations can

47 Interfaith Perspective is to ponder upon a particular topic/issue from different religious traditions drawing out insights from their religious resources and to address the issue which

play a potential role in bringing remedy to the conflicting situations and issue on and around migration.

Religion could be one of the best supportive systems for the refugees and the migrants. If rightly used, religion can unite people from different walks of life and help live together in harmony, rather than creating havoc among the faith communities. It also can provide spiritual and psychological support to the refugees who undergo agonizing struggles. It can be the source of courage, healing and hope. In fact, such kind of religious values and solidarity are witnessed in our society in times of emergency situation caused by natural calamities.

Perhaps, the religion can shape strong socio-political ideologies and action especially towards reforming and reinstating the lost identity of the refugees or migrants.[48] There can be a mutual enrichment between religion and the migrant population. Religion, on the one hand, can empower the suffering masses, and on the other it can play as a medium to communicate their views and mobilize peace-loving people from different backgrounds in rebuilding their community.

Interfaith Relations for Co-existence

Migrants bring along their own religion, culture and values to the host society. Both the people of host society and the migrants mutually see each other's religio-cultural practices as alien and as a threat to their own. Such tension perhaps can be overcome through interfaith relations. For all religious traditions have certain common belief about humanity, land and life-giving values such as love, forgiveness, and tolerance. The untoward incidents unfortunately happen just because the 'other' is always unknown. So, the interfaith relations can certainly set a platform for representatives from both the group to interact, to know and to develop a true relation which otherwise hardly happens. It can serve as a catalyst to initiate peace and harmony among the host community and the migrants. If such interfaith relations are established and religious insights are embodied in the hearts and minds of people, even the forced migration itself can be prevented at the first place.

Interfaith relations can bring positive effects on whole issue of migration. It can make people and their society open-minded and overcome the exclusive claims about their own faith and respect other religions and people, and thereby ensure treating migrants and refugees having equal human right and dignity and co-exist as one family of God.

---

affects human beings. Timothy H. Robinson and Nancy Ramsay, "Interfaith Perspectives on Religious Practices," *Theological Education* 47/2 (2013): 35-38.

48 Elzbieta M. Gozdziak and Dianna J.shandy, "Editorial Introduction: Religion and Migration in forced Migration," *Journal of Refugee Studies* 15/2 (2002). http://heinonline.org/HOL/LandingPage?handle=hein.journals/jrefst15&div=16&id=&page (accessed on 18 March, 2018).

Conclusion

All religions demands seeing image of God in the 'other' irrespective of their status as stranger, migrant or inhabitant. Unfortunately, very often such religious teachings are practiced only within a narrow scope of one's own religion. Therefore, one of the ways out for rescuing religions from such narrow and close-mindedness is inter-faith relations. The efforts of inter-faith relations can make people of all religious walks realize that God alone owns the entire creation and the whole human race the members of one family. The mutual embrace and co-existence among the refugees/migrants and the people of host society depends on such realization. Finally, the answer to the question "is God still refuge for refugees?" lies with openness of our hearts and minds to see God in and among migrants and refugees. Further it calls for our discernment, whether God is refuge or God Himself/Herself is refugee in the religious camps.

8

Immigrants or Inhabitants
A Search for Identity from the Margins

Anthony Jeevaraj

FIFA 2018 World Cup been won by France with great expectation. One of the interesting facts which astonished me was that most of the famous football players like Zinedine Zidane, Zlatan Ibrahimovic, Robert Pires and others are all migrants. This has kindled the thoughts that when the globally the human race are not able to make flexible to other or struggling to fit themselves in some other place, how come these players could do and achieve. Migrants gets their identity through the jobs and talents. Then the limpidity was that they were famous because of their identity, which is football. There are lot of legends can be found in the world's history who are migrants at once.

On the other hand, the history also tells the narratives about the people who lost their identity because of their migration. In particular the history of Dalits and Adivasis of India can tell many of those and it was not some incidents of the past but also present and future phenomena. The collective agony and expected desire of Dalit and Adivasis is to get their identity back and live a life of equality. In order to respond effectively to the issues of Dalits and Adivasis, one needs to identify the root-causes and visible manifestations both at the micro-macro levels. Because only the historical roots of the margins can provide the evidences to the lost identity of the margins.

History of the Margins

History can be used for many purposes. As humans, we tend to take possession of histories within history and identify ourselves in them. Everyone believes that it says something about the background and helps us to know our identity. For Dalits and Adivasis the history has been used to denote on the negative sense. It has been used to give them an identity as those who are impure, outcastes, untouchable, illiterate and marginal and excluded communities. Romila Thapar points out that, the writing of early Indian history has until recent times reflected social, political and economic interests other than those of the Dalits,[1] it is same to the Adivasis. The absence of the right materials and it is very difficult to write and find the history of the Dalits and Adivasis. However there are some archaeological evidences and literary sources which can lead to possible historical roots of the margins, i.e., Dalits and Adivasis.[2] Therefore, the history of Dalits and Adivasis should be studied and understood from below. The facts used the find the roots of the Dalits and Adivasis had been discussed on the same floor by the James Massey and Nirmal Minz, so it would be fair enough to discuss on the same tune.

Indus Valley Civilization

The margins of India today had surely been similar beginning like any other human beings on the Universe. The Indus valley civilization of which impressive remains have been discovered at Mohenjo-Daro in Sindhu and Harappa, in the Western Punjab, is the earliest picture that we have of India's past. It is much older than 5000 years before the Vedic period. Until when Sir John Marshall excavated these places, he was the Director General of Archaeology. These excavations have revolutionized the conception of ancient history.

Mohenjo-Daro and Harappa are far apart. There can be little doubt that there lie many such buried cities and other remains of the handiwork of ancient man in between these two areas; that, in fact, this civilization was widespread over large parts of India, certainly of the North India. The inscriptions found at Mohenjo-Daro have so far not been fully deciphered. But what we know, even thus far, is of the utmost significance. The Indus Valley Civilization, as we find it highly developed and must have taken thousands of years to reach that stage. The archaeological evidences which been founded since AD 1920 at various sites at Harappa and Mohenjo-Daro find there was a civilization even before the arrival of Aryans in India.

Initially, the Aryan invaders were pictured as the one who brought the civilisation to India. But after the discovery of the ruins of the Indus Valley civilisation (Harappa and Mohenjo-Daro) in the 1920's, the scenario was altered sharply: the Aryans became the nomads who destroyed the earlier civilisation in India. Their Sanskrit language, their Brahmanical priesthood, their Vedic religion, came to be described as primitive and as foreign impositions on India. All kinds of divisive forces jumped on the Aryan Invasion Theory as the perfect tool to cut slices out of Hindu society and out of Indian state. This theory became the basis of attempts to pit Dalits against Aryans, high caste against low castes, Adivasis against mainstream Hindus.[3]

---

1 Romila Thapar, *Cultural Pasts – Essays in Early Indian History* (New Delhi: Oxford University Press, 2000), 3.

2 James Massey, *Roots of Dalit History, Christianity, Theology and Spirituality* (Delhi: ISPCK, 1996), 1.

3 Koenraad Elst, *Indigenous Indians: Agastya to Ambedkar* (New Delhi: Voice of India, 1993), 3.

The central thesis of the Aryan and the Inhabitants opposition between the Indus Valley civilisation, matriarchal, source of all valuable things in Indian culture; and the Aryans patriarchal and destructive, who came to oppress the original Indus population through the caste system. In the Indus Culture, racism is unknown: in the graves, skeletons of different race have been found side by side, proving that there were mixed marriages.[4] The Dalits and Adivasis were grouped together and pushed and scattered due to the invasion of the Aryans. The invaders (Aryans) said in their scripture that they defeated the people of Indus Valley Civilisation and occupied this country. The Dalits and Adivasis were driven away from their hearths and homes and they fled deep into the jungles and other places of India. The dominant group of the Indian society had destroyed socio-economic, cultural and political history. All classical Hindu languages, literatures, traditions and customs have been consequently been despised and denigrated.[5] After independence Dalits faced two dimensional framework of adjustment with Indian social system and newly born Indian republic. Due to conception of a-varna (untouchable) they felt a disassociation from a brahmanic dominant and brahmanic favourable Indian system and due to reservation policies of Indian government they felt association with system.[6] Due to the lack of evidences the Dalits and Adivasis the inhabitants became immigrants in search of their identity which they have lost.

Reasons for Migration of the Margins

Migration have resources allocation framework, because migration of the people is require resources to migrate. Study considered that migration is investment of human which have some costs and returns. It also elaborate complex of in-migration and out migration. Net migration is better tool to analysis of the costs and returns of the migration rather than gross migration. It categorised costs into two parts one is money cost and non-money cost. Money cost is related to food, lodging and transportation cost, which we can measure in money. ***First***, the non-money cost is constituted by opportunity cost, loss of earnings during finding job and learning new job. ***Second*** it related to psychic cost, which difficult for measurement. Study is argued that migration would be high if the psychic cost is zero. Migrants compensate psychic costs with the resource allocations, and it used for migration. Money returns of migration are gets in positive or negative increment in real income. It will enhance from in nominal earnings, cost of employment and price. Non money returns influence behaviour and they cannot

4 James Massey, *Dalits in India* (New Delhi: Manohar Publlishers, 1995), 35.

5 Joseph Marianus Kujur and Sonajahria Minz, eds., *Pearls of Indigenous Wisdom* (New Delhi: Indian Social Institute & CISRS, 2007), 57.

6 Bhoopal Singh, "Dalit migration, Urbanization and language change," https://www.academia.edu/755526/Dalit_migration_Urbanization_and_language_change (accessed on 30 August, 2018).

separated from money returns. Migrants will not bear all cost of and not receive total reward of migration.[7] Migration of Dalits and Adivasis in India involves both the causes and it would be discussed on detailed manner.

Untouchability

The Article 17 of the Constitution of India reads: *"Untouchability" is abolished and its practice in any form is forbidden. The enforcement of any disability arising out of "Untouchability" shall be an offence punishable in accordance with law.*

The situation is the same despite the new Constitution, which the people of India gave unto themselves in 1950, loudly proclaiming the explicit abolition of "Untouchability" and its practice in any form (Article 17). Notwithstanding Parliament's enactment of the Protection of Civil Rights Act (PCR),1955, "Untouchability" based discrimination against Dalits has been rampant through all these years regardless of the gradual advancement of Dalits and Adivasis in education and economic status. Studies have revealed the prevalence of more than 150 forms of the most heinous and inhuman "Untouchability" practices. Although significant contributions toward understanding untouchability have been made in each of these areas, it is difficult to comprehend the scope and pervasiveness of the problem without combining the tools of all three. The term should not be taken in a literal sense. It is a cultural manifestation, which been coined at the beginning of this century to collectively describe a complex of cruel and humiliating discriminatory practices and disabilities which may or may not include prohibition of physical contact to which members of Dalits and Adivasis were and still are subjected by the rest of society. It is regarded both as an important feature of Dalit and Adivasi existence and also as mechanism whereby, as an integral part of the India caste system.

There are few laws which been formulated like *Protection of Civil Rights Acts 1955,* which was enacted in 1976 to rename and amend the *Untouchability* (Offenses) Act, 1955. But even the enumerations in this Act are not exhaustive. It is not possible to exhaustively catalogue all instances of behaviour which come within the ambit of untouchability. The larger sect of the Indian population who are considered to Dalits and Adivasis been kept down as agricultural labour, leather workers, deprived of the right to own or hold or cultivate land, scavenging, drum beaters, etc. through the centuries that from their point of view, make the history of India. For many centuries untouchability was able to operate as a perfect instrument to keep the untouchable Dalits and Adivasis under total subjugation as providers of labour. Many of the cases in regard of with Dalit and Adivasi atrocities arise from all the issues with the Dalit and Adivasis.

7 P. Deshingkar and J. Farrington, *Circular Migration and Multilocational Livelihood Strategies in Rural India* (New Delhi: Oxford University Press, 2009), 64.

Atrocities

We have been noticing over the years Dalit and Adivasi communities increasingly and powerfully asserting their rights and entitlements. This has resulted in further increase of the atrocities against them. Whenever they wanted to access legal services and natural resources (land, water, livelihood, etc.), made claim to occupation of their choice, just and fair wages, participation in cultural life of the community, demanded their right to vote and to govern, voiced their right to dignity and self-respect, they have been subjugated to atrocities. These have ranged from verbal abuse, physical assault, mass attacks, social and economic boycotts, torture, custodial violence, rape and gang rapes and even mass murders.

As many as 47,338 cases of crime against Dalits and Adivasis were registered across the country in 2016; Minister of State for Home Hansraj Gangaram Ahir said that according to information provided by National Crime Records Bureau, a total of 40,774 cases were registered under the Scheduled Castes and Scheduled Tribes (Prevention of Atrocities) Act and other sections of law over alleged crimes against Dalits and Adivasis in 2016. Of these, charge sheets were filed in 78.3 per cent of the cases, and the conviction rate was 25.8 percent.[8]

On October 9, 2015 A Dalit family was stripped naked on road including a woman by none other than police in Greater Noida near the Capital. Gautam and his brothers were robbed on gun point on Tuesday evening while they were watering their farmland. Their motorbike besides some cash was also taken by the robber about which Gautam went to police to get a FIR registered on Wednesday morning. Gautam demand speedy action against the robbers and his demands irked police official at Dankaur police station who allegedly stripped member of family and threw them out on road.

"In the violence that erupted on 2 April, members of the upper-caste were involved," said social activist and Dalit leader Sushil Gautam. "The police had arrested them on the spot but later released them due to pressure from the BJP. Releasing the upper-caste members and leaving the Dalit boys behind bars for two months only shows the two-faced nature of the administration. All this is being done to break the social and political movement of Dalits." There are several incidents are related to the untouchability been projected in everyday life of the Indian society. Data of the Indian government clearly states that every minute atrocities against Dalits and Adivasis been recorded and raised due to untouchability.

Despite the deterrence assured by the earlier PCR Act and the later SCs & STs [PoA] Act, the numerical increase in atrocities has not stopped. Nor has the response from the different governance agencies in the country (police, district and state level monitoring committees, district and state level vigilance committees,

8 Atrocities against Dalits: "47,000 cases of crime against SC/ST lodged in 2016, Lok Sabha told," The Indian Express, New Delhi: April 4.

public prosecutors, special courts, etc.) been satisfactory. The following recent official data attest to this:[9]

Atrocity affected Dalits and Adivasis: A rough estimate for 1995-2010 puts the numerical population of Dalits and Adivasis facing atrocities at around 1.5 cores and the number is increasing day by day at the annual rate of 2.8 per cent.

Top 10 Dalit atrocity prone States in 2010: 10 States, namely, Uttar Pradesh, Rajasthan, Andhra Pradesh, Bihar, Madhya Pradesh, Karnataka, Orissa, Tamil Nadu, Maharashtra, and Gujarat cumulatively account for 93.3% of atrocities against SCs.

Registration of cases: The police do not register many instances of atrocity. During the last 15 years (1995-2010), a total of only 5, 58, 103 cases (4, 71,717 against Dalits and 86,386 against Adivasis) were registered in police stations.

***Non-Registration under PoA Act*:** In 2010, only 11,682 (34.2%) out of 34,127 atrocity cases were registered under the PoA Act at all-India level. In Madhya Pradesh & Rajasthan over 95% of the cases were not registered under the PoA Act, and instead were registered under IPC and other legal provisions.

High pendency rate of Cases: With 1, 01,251 crimes against Dalits and Adivasis (80%) pending for trial by 2010-end. This showed no significant improvement since 2001, when the trial pendency rate was 82.5 per cent. By 2010 end, many states had more than 80% of pending cases of atrocities against Dalits: Gujarat (90.9%), West Bengal (89.2%), Rajasthan (86.6%), Maharashtra (86.2%), Kerala (85.5%), Bihar (84.3%), Himachal Pradesh (82.9%), Delhi (81.7%), and Orissa (80.7%).

Closure of Cases under PoA Act: In 2010, police closed 2,150 (13%) out of 16,601 cases of atrocities against Dalits registered under PoA Act. As regards cases of atrocities against Adivasis, 223 (13%) out of 1,714 registered cases were closed.

Economic

According to Hindu theology, all are born in a particular *jati* or caste. Currently, around 3000 castes are in existence in India. Caste is hierarchical, hereditary and endogamous in nature, and has historically been linked to specific occupations. A study of occupational concentration by caste groups indicates that marginalized groups such as the Dalits and the Adivasis are disproportionately concentrated in skilled and semi-skilled occupations in the informal sector of the economy. The economic dimension of the identity is very much present in the religious and social order of India. Ambedkar has also examined and exposed the fact that, the caste system is a division of society into four classes within certain social and religious rights conferred on each of them. It is also a division of people

9 Sirivella Prasad, "Atrocities against Dalits and Adivasis," National Coalition for Stringhening SCs & Sts (PoA) Act.

into specific economic activities.[10] The important economic features of these economic divisions are:-

- Fixation of occupation for each caste group and continuance thereof by heredity.
- Unequal distribution of economic rights and privileges among the caste groups.
- Occupation is fixed in an unequal manner, i.e., a particular caste must do assigned job without any question. It thus maintains a hierarchy of occupation based in the stigma of high and low.
- The Brahminic Hindu religious order recognised slavery and extended the principle of graded slavery across caste groups.

The first and foremost principle of caste based fixation of occupation and continuance thereof by heredity implies that every member just follows the occupation assigned to the caste into which he or she is born. It leaves no scope for individual choice, individual inclination and inter-caste occupational mobility.

Dalits and Adivasis have been the main providers of labour which created the ancient Indian agricultural civilisation. In order to force them to remain permanently tied down as villains providing agricultural and other labour, Dalits and Adivasis were denied the right of owning or cultivating land on their own account.[11] Along with their economic control, the caste system had been devised. The Dalit and Adivasis farmers are forced to use contaminated water. This led to soil degradation. Soil pollution couple with air pollution led to decrease of yielding and change in the cropping pattern due to continues use of contaminated water, cultivable land of some farmers became barren. Acquisition of land by the company which leads to soil pollution reduced some responds to coolies from Dalit and Adivasis. Cattle rearing, goat and pig keeping, fishing etc. activities were gradually given up. Rate of unemployment is higher in Dalits than any non-Dalit communities. Social, economic and political inequalities are based for untouchability. Usually Dalits are offered dirty and unclean occupations. They are refusing to do these occupations now days, but they do not have power or other alternative means. Youngster Dalits are finding new way escape from these traditional jobs, they migrate to town, cities and try to do different (modern) jobs. Dalits are excluded from the social, political, economic and cultural activities. Prohibition on consumption of goods like milk, Ghee, not allow space for

---

10 Sukhadeo Thorat, "Ambedkar and Economics of the Hindu Social Order: Understanding its Orthodoxy and Legacy," in *The Emerging Dalit Identity: The Re-assertion of the Subalterns*, edited by Walter Fernandez (New Delhi: Indian Social Institute, 1996), 10.

11 P S Krishna, "Untouchability and Atrocities," in *The Emerging Dalit Identity: The Re-assertion of the Subalterns*, edited by Walter Fernandez (New Delhi: Indian Social Institute, 1996), 127.

vending with non-Dalits. Increasing atrocities, women rapes, humiliations are major concerns.[12]

Dalit and Adivasis women were feeding their cattle, working in the fields, shoulder to shoulder with their husbands and assisting them in all their requirements. Hindu castes are having control over means of production. But after the industrialisation and development projects they become idle.[13] Some who were willing to work in the areas other than agriculture filed becomes maid in the high caste rich houses. This leads to occupational distribution, which means the distribution of work force in different occupations of the country in different places. This leads to forced migration of the Dalits and Adivasis from their places, seeking for different job opportunities for their survival of them and families depended.

Education

Education seems to have a negative effect on the practice of untouchability. Study shows the incidence of the practice by the highest level of adult education in the household. The percentage of households practicing untouchability is seen to fall with a rise in the level of adult education. We observe a 6 percentage point drop in the incidence of the practice of untouchability between households with no education and those with an adult who has acquired education up to the graduation level or above. Significantly, education seems to have much more of a negative impact on the practice of untouchability for the Brahmins and the OBCs, the two communities that report the highest incidence of untouchability. It shows a sharp fall in the percentage of households indulging in the practice with a rise in the level of education of adults in the household. Thus, we see a fall of 15 percent and 16 percent in the practice, among Brahmins and OBCs, respectively, between the illiterates and those with education up to the graduate level or above.

However, we also find that across all social groups, the incidence of untouchability seems to rise among households with graduation or higher level of adult education. The reports clearly highlights the idea of superiority (that is, the concept of a particular caste being purer than a lower caste group), as is inherent in caste hierarchies. At the same time, we find that beyond the graduate and higher level of education, the incidence of untouchability rises across all groups, except the Dalits and Adivasis.

Ecological Deviations

In the last 100 years, human managed to destroy most of what it took nature millions of years to create it on earth. At no point of time in the history of our

12 I. John Mohan Razu, *Dalits-Tribals as Victims of Asymmetries* (Bangalore: BTESSC/SATHRI, 2006), 58.

13 Prasanna Kumari Samuel, *Dalit Women's Experiences: A Theological Imperative for Indian Feminist Theology* (Chennai: GLTCRI, 2009), 85.

planet has no much damage been done to the nature. Humans have poisoned the river systems throughout the world and in this turn have upset the ecological balance of the rivers and oceans. Trees are indiscriminately being chopped down because of the greed of human.[14]

In the modern era, the development is more oriented towards industrialisation and technology. The environment and development has not been keeping pace with each other. Industrialisation and the technology adopted for the industrialisation has completely misbalanced the ecology and environment in the areas where industrialisation and development activities are taking place. The developed countries have gone for various aspects of development without bothering about environmental degradation. India chosen to adopt Nehruvian model of development, especially after the second plan, which emphasises rapid industrialisation for economic development. This has led to the growth of energy sector and industries. A multitude of environmental problem such as deforestation, desertification, soil erosion, silting of rivers, impoverishment of important flora and fauna and loss of biodiversity, depletion of non-renewable resources of energy, global warming and pollution of land, water and air have resulted from rapid industrialisation.[15] Industrialisation and concomitant global warming is threatening the very existence of human life.[16]

Religious Constitution

India is a nation of many religions and freedom of religion has been bestowed constitutional protection. Articles 25 to 28 constitute significant constitutional provisions on freedom of religion. Any discussion on religion in public sphere in India (as opposed to religion being a subliminal human experience) automatically brings the spotlight on secularism or more specifically Indian model of secularism. There can be no universal model of secularism as there is no universal religion.

Donald E. Smith explains that "To most Indians, secular means non-communal, or non-sectarian, but it does not mean non-religious. The basis of secular state is not a 'wall of separation' between state and religion but rather 'no preference doctrine' which requires that no special privilege be granted to any one religion. The secular state includes the principle that the function of the state must be non-religious."[17]

14 Jagbir Singh, ed., *Environment and Development, Challenges and Opportunities* (New Delhi: I K International Pvt. Ltd., 2005).

15 B. Suresh Lal, *Industrialisation and Environment in Tribal World* (Ambala: The Associated Publishers, 2016), 129.

16 Rajesh Roshan and P.K. Singh, "Ecological Imbalance in Bastar Region," in *Changing Tribal Society in India: Issues and Challenges*, edited by Pradip K. Bhowmick, Prabhat K. Singh and M.P. Rajak (New Delhi: Abhijeet Publications, 2016), 229.

17 Donald E. Smith, *India as a Secular State* (New Jersey: Princeton University Press, 1963), 381.

The Indian position on the freedom of religion entails non-interference of the state in religious matters and the only permissible interference is confined to matters incidental to religion. Though there are constitutions on the religious freedom, Dalits and Adivasis been restricted from worshiping the gods and goddess in the temples and take part in the public worship.

Caste discrimination still holds the sway in certain temples in this part of the State. In the latest incident, the ugly face of social menace came to fore when an engineering student of Dalit community was barred from entering a Shiva temple. Rojalini Sethy, pursuing engineering in a private college in Bhubaneswer, had come to her village Badgaon to celebrate New Year with her family. On Thursday morning, she went to Sankeshwar temple to offer puja. But, the priests refused to perform puja and prevented her from entering the temple as she belonged to Dalit community. Rojalini's father Basant Sethy said, "Since we are Harijans, my daughter was turned away from the temple by priest Narahari Panda. We have been deprived of basic social rights as Dalit families of the village continue to suffer from religious alienation."[18] Sources said there is a strict restriction on entry of 20 local Dalit families into the Shiva temple as per the tradition.

Following the incident, Basant sought the help of village chief and sarpanch to resolve the issue but local priests including Narahari and some upper caste persons refused to budge from their stand and vowed not to allow Dalits into the temple. On the same day, Narahari called a meeting of the villagers, most of whom were upper caste persons. The meeting decided to continue with the tradition and restrict entry of Dalits into the temple. Local priests argued that caste-based temple controversies are nothing new. Former Prime Minister Indira Gandhi was stopped at the gate of Puri Jagannath temple as she was deemed an outcast for marrying a non-Hindu.

After the meeting, tension flared up as the Dalits raised objection to the decision. Demanding justice, Basant sought intervention of the Collector and SP in the matter. The Dalits also threatened to intensify protest if steps were not taken to end the tradition and allow them inside the temple. Niharika Biswal admitted that Rojalini was barred from entering the temple. "There is a tradition of not allowing Dalits into the Shiva temple of the village. Steps are being taken to resolve the dispute," she said.

There are constitutions and laws related to the untouchability and freedom of religion, in reality it is not been followed by most of the high caste community. They continue to discriminate the Dalits and Adivasis and formulate and follow according to their own desire. The government authorities and police could not do anything against the powerful castist communities.

---

18 NA, "No Temple entry for Dalit Student", http://www.newindianexpress.com/states/odisha/2018/jan/12/no-temple-entry-for-dalit-student-1751606.html (accessed on 30 August, 2018).

Conversion

Caste has been a major factor of Indian society. It has determined politics here throughout history and continues to do so today. There are various claims and interpretations about the origin and prevalence of the caste system. While Ambedkar locates the origin of caste in the scriptures, the Hindutva ideology claims that all castes are equal in Hindu society and that other religious faiths wanted to proselytize and those who wanted to remain Hindus had to escape to remote places, leading to caste inequality. This interpretation reflects the upper-caste ideology rather than the events that actually took place. The simple reason to debunk this "aggressors and conversion" theory is the "holy books" like the Manusmriti, which show us the social impact of a full-fledged caste hierarchy by 2nd century AD, well before Islam came into being, well before Muslim traders arrived on the Malabar coast and well before Muslim kings' incursions took place. Contrary to this warped interpretation, Swami Vivekananda also tells us that major conversions to Islam took place due to tyranny of the caste system. It was this caste that remained in Indian society as an indelible scar despite the semi-modernization that Indian society underwent during colonial rule. It persists despite seventy years of independence and formal implementation of the Constitution, which promises us equality.[19]

Atrocities against Dalits and Adivasis have risen, as reflected in multiple incidents of violence in India. It is reported that close to 180 Dalit families from three western Uttar Pradesh villages have embraced Buddhism to protest against the atrocities that have increased after Adityanath became chief minister. In a few villages, the Thakur-Dalit animosity took an ugly turn. Thakurs had the local administration stop the installation of an Ambedkar statue. Later, Dalits objected to the Rajput procession to honour Maharana Pratap because the organizers hadn't obtained permission from the authorities."[20]

The most recent reaction from the Sangh Parivar though is the *ghar wapsi* campaign. Though this programme hit the headlines after Narendra Modi came to power, attempts by the Sangh to convert mainly Christian Adivasis and Dalits to Hinduism are decades old. Most of this consists of offering education and healthcare facilities, though in places like Kandhamal in Orissa and the Dangs in Gujarat, it has also resulted in mass violence. While it is generally assumed that *ghar wapsi* will adversely affect religious minorities, squeezing their freedom of religion, a major area of impact is forgotten: caste emancipation. The Ambedkarite strategy of using conversion as a stick to fight casteism has been

19 NA, "Dalit village in U.P. plans conversion after 'police atrocities," https://www.thehindu.com/news/national/dalit-village-in-up-plans-conversion-after-police-atrocities/article23483999.ece (accessed on 30 August, 2018).

20 Ram Puniyani, "Caste atrocities have hastened religious conversions," https://www.forwardpress.in/2017/05/dalits-atrocities-have-hastened-religious-conversions/ (accessed on 13th July, 2018).

quite successful, even without mass conversions taking place or the fact that caste, in varying degrees, still exists across all religions in India. The mere threat of Dalit conversions has resulted in significant reform within Hinduism (and the pace of reform since Ambedkar converted has not been insignificant).

By restricting the freedom to convert, however, the *ghar wapsi* issue undermines this Ambedarike strategy. In fact, for the Sangh Parivar, the final aim of ghar wapsi is quite clear: a national anti-conversion law. Rashtriya Swayamsevak Sangh chief, Mohan Bhagwat had suggested in December that "there be legislation in Parliament to stop this practice [conversion]". By removing the stick of conversion, the pace of reform within Hindu society will slow down. While administration accuses the outfit of precipitating violence, Dalits and Adivasis claim that it has often come to their aid and that the pro-upper-caste administration is targeting this outfit rather than nabbing the culprits. Dalits and Adivasis feel they have no option but to leave the fold of Hinduism, which is currently dominated by brahmanical norms or to leave their native places to go somewhere to live a peaceful and secured life.

Post condition of the Migrated Margins

Lourdusamy[21] argues that generally there are no striking differences between the Dalit migrants and other caste migrants, but in depth with various caste migrants' reveals differences on various levels. Dalit migrants still remain Dalit in manner worse than before. Because of cheap labour, lack of space for house to live, child labour, atrocities on women and men at living and work places, increasing criminality. Study compare pre migration and post migration situation of migrant Dalits on the basis of different levels such as spiritual, mental, psychological, social, economic, political and cultural. They found worse than non-migrated rural folk. Migrant Dalits became isolated due to cut off from home and relatives. They depend on fellow migrants to survive and get daily bread.

Major concern of the study is cultural factors which create space to carry their separate identity. It situation of Dalits in villages been clearly exposed. Forces of globalization bring changes in economic profit and condition of farmers and labourers in rural area. Most of labourers are belong to Dalits. This changes leads migration towards cities of labourers. Migrant Dalits lived in slums as they lived in ghetto in outside the village, but this urban way of life offers them avenues of mobility.[22] Prasad-Aleyamma, deals with working conditions and living conditions of the construction workers. And how these work opportunities,

21 S. Lourdusamy, "Migrant-Dalits and Mission: A Diagnosis of People's Perspective," in *Migration and Mission in India*, edited by L. Stanislaus and Jose Joseph (New Delhi: ISPCK, 2007), 85.

22 M.T. Joseph, "Migration and Identity Formation: A Case Study of Dalit Assertion in Augrangabad, Maharashtra," in *Migration and Mission in India*, edited by L. Stanislaus and Jose Joseph (New Delhi: ISPCK, 2007), 96.

process of recruitment, work condition and living condition shaping to the migration? There are supervisory hierarchies on the basis of caste identities and kinship of the worker. They get jobs according to their caste identity. Migrant workers are living in the very unhygienic condition at construction work site. Study finds wage discrimination on the basis of caste identities. Adivasi worker paid fewer wage than that of non-Adivasi workers. Company not provide any social security for these workers, because they work just for 52 days, and they were recruited through the contractor.[23] These were expressed by the migrated Dalit and Adivasi workers, contractors, and employers. The process of recruitment of migrant workers is having system of chain of some important characters, such as contractor, foreman and workers.

Conclusion

India attained independence 71 years ago in 1947. Three years later it became a republic nation with the self-confidence of having a government of the people, by the people and for the people. But in reality a large section of its citizens, the Dalits and Adivasis, have been neglected by successive governments and, therefore, were denied the full enjoyment of all the rights of citizenship assured by the Constitution. They still face subjugation, humiliation and exclusion on a daily basis from India's mainstream caste society. These prevent Dalits and Adivasis from accessing civil, political, economic and cultural rights in private and public spheres, state and religious institutions, labour and consumer markets as much as they are entitled to as per the laws and policies of the land.

Hindu nationalists have constructed a history that glorifies the ancient "values" of Hindu scriptures. Its attempt is to revive caste hierarchy, which can't have a place in a democratic society. There has been another stream of Hinduism, called Shramanism, (the Bhakti sect, for example), which rejected the hierarchical notions. But it has been eclipsed by the brahmanical versions, which form the core of Hindu nationalism being propagated for the past century. Landless and marginal workers and farmers from Dalits work on farms of upper castes people, or some migrate to towns. This migration is varying with the level of education of migrants.

The notions of 'purity and pollution' are ideas which, despite the spread of education and the advent of modern lifestyles, tend to stick and prey on our religious and social insecurities. Social change is invariably slow and necessitates a change in the political, economic, social and cultural environment. This, in turn, requires the social psychology of the masses to transform over time. The economic, social and cultural evolution of the Indian landscape has seen many of its traditions withering away or facing persistent resistance from modernity

23 Prasad-Aleyamma, Mythri, "Caste, Ethnicity and Migration: Linking Recruitment and Labour Process," in *Migration, Identity and Conflict: India Migration Report 2011*, edited by Irudaya Rajan (New Delhi: Routledge India, 2011), 87.

and rationality. For the entire nation, therefore, the need of the hour is to match words with action, Constitutional promises with compliance practices, thereby providing a safe and secure environment for Dalits and Adivasis. This is necessary for their advancement in life as citizens equal to all in rights and entitlements, and lesser to none in dignity. The Dalits and Adivasis are the children of the soil are still online to search for their identity in their own land.

Ours is a battle not for wealth or for power.
It is a battle for freedom.
It is a battle of reclamation of human personality.

- Dr. B. R. Ambedkar

9

Migration in Gender Perspective

W.S. Annie

Achama Varghese, 45, migrated to Kuwait from Kerala in September 2015. She had some debts to be cleared as she was working as a home nurse in a nearby town. "So, when I got an offer from an agent, I trusted him and migrated [to Kuwait] only to suffer", she complains. After seven months on the job, she was diagnosed with diabetes. As her health deteriorated, her employer refused to take her to the hospital for treatment. "I had to flee from there and take shelter in the Indian embassy," Achama explains. She was hospitalised in Kuwait for few months before she returned to India. "[My husband] cannot work because his right hand is paralysed. He is suffering from rheumatoid arthritis. That's why I migrated," she says. "Now, we both are sick and are struggling without any income," she adds.[1]

Nisha, originally from Mumbai, has lived in the U.K. since 2008, first as a student, then as a researcher on a 'Tier 1-Highly Skilled' visa. However, her hopes of making a life in the country were upended in 2016 when Britain's Home Office rejected her application for an indefinite leave to remain. The reason given related to errors in tax filing by her accountant. Many South Asian like Nisha face terrible hardship. They have no right to work, or to rent, they may have their driving license revoked. Most must go to reporting centres. Many from India and beyond who reluctantly decided to leave Britain because of the lack of options facing them and the lack of appeal routes. Nisha has pushed for a judicial review at great expense. Unable to work and facing financial hardship, she is horrified by the situation she and others have found themselves in. "I'm incredibly passionate about the work I've been doing. I've been here so many years and given my life to this country. This situation is just killing all of us from the inside."[2]

---

1 http://www.middleeasteye.net/in-depth/features/vanished-saudi-arabia-search-missing-indian-workers-gulf-1428918602 (accessed on 08.05.2018).

2 Vidya Ram, 'Victims of the U.K.'s 'hostile immigration' regime,' *The Hindu*, Chennai, 3 May 2018.

Why do the Nation States and its people come up with such rigid immigration policies, after welcoming or allowing immigrants to stay for such a long years? Is it xenophobia? Or are the Nation States concerned of their national security or population growth or scarcity of resources, which might lead to internal struggle? Many of the multi-cultural spaces in our times today are marked by such issues.

Migration leads women to different struggles and people who suffer most from issues related to migration are the women folk. They are most vulnerable ones. Even not only the migrant women in the host society, but also the women left behind in their native places undergo various physical and psychological struggles. Therefore, as 'Liberation Theology' talk about 'preferential option for the poor', while discoursing about 'Theology of Migration', we cannot, but talk about 'preferential option for women'. While looking at migration from gender perspective, this article attempts to feminize the whole issue of migration.

In order to arrive at this objective, the first section of the article deals with the different experiences women undergo because of migration. The second section discusses the Theology of Trinitarian sharing, sharing identity and sharing resources.

WOMEN AND MIGRATION

So far it is an established fact that migration is a complex phenomenon. But, even all the complex phenomenon is the Women's migration. Therefore, feminizing the whole issue of migration in general and looking at the women's migration from the gender dimensions is necessary theological task.[3] For almost half of the migrants in the world are women, which is one of the most significant migrant-pattern change in the last half century. Women migrate alone or with their family members and community. Even though, female migration is largely viewed as associations rather than independent migration, emerging studies argue complex and manifold reasons for female migration.

Vulnerable Experience of Women in Migration

Women migrate because of various factors and for different reasons. As men do, women also migrate in seeking job opportunities, better living and security in life. But in most cases, they migrate to escape from social, religious, cultural discrimination back at home. In fact they also migrate in large numbers as just as spouses of their husbands, but also many are left behind in their native places. Whatever the cases may be, the women are utterly vulnerable all sorts of struggles and suffering both physically and emotionally. It is therefore important to have a glance of vulnerable experiences women undergo when they migrate or migration take place due to various factors and reason.

3 G. Julie SSpS and M.A. Rani SSpS, Migration and Women: Ways of Empowerment, in L. Stanislaus SVD and Jose Joseph SVD (eds.) *Migration and Mission in India* ((Ishvani Kendra/ISPCK, New Delhi, 2007), 180.

First and foremost, let us see how women's life is migrant life and think of *marriage and migration*. Perhaps, women are susceptible to forced migration by the very tradition of marriage. Except the Nair women in Kerala, Khasi and Garo women in Meghalaya, women of all countries are to migrate to their husband's house after their marriage. As per patriarchal traditions and practice, first of all, a woman migrate to a man or a married woman migrate from her family to husband's family. And if any case of divorce, the migration continues. One can imagine what a struggle or vulnerable situation women undergo due to migration in marriage. For many perhaps it is a hell on earth: a new husband, new house, new people, new relatives and new responsibilities, and on the top, lot of expectations and demands. Often marriage fails when woman can't cope up with strange situations such as new role as a wife, daughter-in-law, sister-in-law, cook, home maker, mother, etc. A woman's life becomes more miserable if there is no support from her husband, husband's house as well as from her own house. In the process, if the case ends up in breaking the marriage, she is forced to marriage to yet another new situations of either her family/society or of another husband. In such situation, women are more susceptible to dehumanizing experience. All her name, identity and social status get changed. Often they are no more identified and called by name, but with divorcee as prefix or suffix to their name. Even they are not considered as normal woman, wife, daughter-in-law, etc. In short, marriage itself is a space where women undergo the vulnerable experience of migration both physically and psychologically.

Besides, migration for good reasons with legal procedures, one of the worrisome female migration in general, and India in particular, takes place through human trafficking. Large number of young girls, particularly from poor rural areas are brought to the towns and cities and sold for various domestic and commercial works in families, companies, brothels and even for organs implantation[4] where they undergo unreported physical exploitation, harassment and sexual abuses. The following case narratives may be help to understand this fact.

Ameena Case:

On 11 August 1992, the newspapers announced the dramatic 'rescue' of a 'child-bride'. On the flight from Hyderabad to Delhi (en route to Riyadh), Ameena, a ten or eleven years old child bride had been spotted crying bitterly by several passengers and the passengers had reported the matter to the flight attendant. Yahya Mohammed al-Sageih, a 60-year-old Saudi Arabian national had married Ameena and was taking Ameena to Saudi Arabia. Al-Sageih was arrested in Delhi.

4 http://www.rediff.com/news/report/rediff-labs-human-trafficking-in-india/20180308.htm (accessed on 02.05.2018).

The parents of the Child in Hyderabad were also arrested. After months of legal dispute the Delhi High Court ordered her restoration to her family.[5]

Sex Workers – Kamathipura:

India's second largest red light district houses a staggering number of sex workers, most of whom live in squalor. Many of the women who work in Kamathipura come from backgrounds of abject poverty. 80 percent of women are trafficked into the flesh trade by someone known to them. Girls, as young as 12 year old, are lured into the dragnet of traffickers, who convince their naïve families to send their daughters away for 'jobs' with a handsome income. The numbers of migrant women are also high. In 1992, the Bombay Municipal Corporation (BMC) recorded 50,000 sex workers in Kamathipura, a number that has gone down to 1,600 — as last recorded in 2009. The lowered numbers are a result of the increasing gentrification of Kamathipura — the flesh trade is now scattered over different areas.[6]

Surrogacy:

To reproduce is the strongest human desire, second only to survival itself.[7] Surrogacy is a thriving business in India. When India first banned surrogacy for gay couples in 2012, various infertility businesses in Delhi continued to sign on gay clients from all over the world. Clients shipped their frozen sperm to Delhi, which was used to fertilize eggs from Indian donors. The resulting embryos, legally belonging to the gay men, were implanted into Indian surrogate mothers. To avoid the ban, infertility clinics then moved surrogate mothers across international borders into Nepal. There they gave birth and clients arrived to pick up their children. This emerging trade route between Delhi and Kathmandu halted when an earthquake hit Nepal on 25 April 2015, killing 8,000 people and injuring more than 21,000. While various governments airlifted babies belonging to their citizens, the fate of the Indian mothers and how they got back home remains unclear.[8]

Organ Transplantation:

Villivakkam or "Kidney Village" is in South India, Tamil Nadu. Here, poor women (many migrants) are often convinced into selling their organs – a practice illegal in India. These vulnerable women are approached by middlemen who offer

---

5 Rajeswari Sundar Rajan, "The Ameena Case," Taisha Abraham, *Women and the Politics of Violence*..., 45.

6 Priti Patkar, Co-founder of Prerana, told Reuters. https://www.firstpost.com/living/mothers-day-in-kamathipura-women-here-want-their-children-to-be-protected-from-the-flesh-trade-3443146.html

7 http://www.surrogacyindia.com/about-surrogacyindia/ (accessed on 02.05.2018).

8 https://qz.com/1109531/surrogate-mothers-at-risk-in-india-after-the-commercial-surrogacy-ban-is-extended/ (accessed on 2.05.2018).

them between Rs.1,50,000.00 and Rs. 9,00,000.00 for a kidney. For most of the women, impoverished and desperate as they are, an offer of even a few thousand rupees is hard to resist. Many of them have never seen so much money in their lifetimes – it could allow them to buy a sheep or goat, expand their farming patch, and pay off all their debts. But the kidney harvesting procedure can be a dangerous one if not performed under the right conditions and with the proper equipment. Because trading in organs is illegal, the surgeons who perform this procedure are typically under-qualified and fail to take the necessary precautions. Not surprisingly, post-surgery complications – and even death are common. What is more injustice is that the middlemen often pay the women is only a fraction of what they promise them. After obtaining the kidney from the poor village women, the middlemen sell it on the organ trafficking black market, ultimately destined for a wealthy recipient.[9]

Ill Treatment of Domestic Women Labourers:

At least 146,000 female migrant domestic workers are employed in the United Arab Emirates (UAE). Migrating for work can certainly provide an opportunity, but only if the worker's human rights are respected. Some female domestic workers in the UAE have good and responsible employers, satisfactory working conditions, receive their wages in full and on time, and can remit money home to their families. But in many cases, their employers confiscated their passports. Migrant women accused their employers of having physically abused them and confined them to the homes, failed to pay the full wages due to them, had forced them to work excessively long hours without breaks or days off, or had denied them adequate food, living conditions, or medical treatment. Some couldn't sleep until their employers went to bed. Some workers were employed in circumstances that amounted to forced labour or trafficking. In the UAE, as elsewhere in the region, the *kafala* system ties migrant workers to individual employers who act as their visa sponsors and restrict migrant workers' abilities to change employers. The system gives employers great power over employees because it entitles them to revoke sponsorship at will. This automatically removes the right of a worker to remain in the UAE and triggers repatriation procedures.[10]

NAMING THE SIN

When we browse through the phenomenon and issue of migration, there pops up two grievous social sins against women – *Exclusion* and *Commodification*. An adequate reflection on exclusion must satisfy two conditions: First, it must help to name exclusion as evil with confidence because it enables us to imagine non-

9 https://www.oneworldeducation.org/kidney-village-truth-about-organ-trafficking (accessed on 03.05.2018).

10 https://www.hrw.org/report/2014/10/22/i-already-bought-you/abuse-and-exploitation-female-migrant-domestic-workers-united (accessed on 04.05.2018).

exclusionary boundaries that map non-exclusionary identities; at the same time; the second, it must not dull our ability to detect the exclusionary tendencies in our own judgements and practices.[11]

Migrants are populations who are socially, politically and geographically outside structures of power and who often do not have access to or control over processes of writing the stories and histories of which they are a part.[12] Especially, the migrant women are treated as 'other' and are excluded from the mainstream of society. Migrant speech, more so of migrant women is the unfiltered voice of people outside the ordinary structures of authority, policy construction and decision-making. The title of Spivak's essay, "Can the Subaltern speak?"[13] is a rhetorical question pointing out that whether migrants (subalterns), particularly women, are able to speak for themselves relates not simply to their capacity to utter words, but more importantly, to their access to mechanisms and sites of communication, to their freedom from retaliation, to the content of their speech being valued. Through the intersection of racialization[14] and gender discrimination across a wide range of institutional and cultural practices, migrant women's speech often is excluded, punished and trivialized. Consequently, often, they are invisible, their experiences are negated, and their agency is erased in narrative accounts of what has happened at local, regional, national and international levels. For migrants the reality is not absolute, nor are the challenges encountered faced by every one of them. However, negative racialization and gender discrimination frequently exclude or minimize speech about their unique experiences and, thereby, silence women migrants because what is voiced about their experiences often is not seen as important or valuable.[15]

Secondly, in the world where everything is commercialised, women too are treated as non-person and an object or commodity. They are *cheap bonded labourers* everywhere. Since, Asian women are 'docile' due to their socialisation, they are in great demand in the industry of migrant labour, and lot of menial, monotonous, low skilled jobs are assigned to them. Women are also used as mere *sex object*. Patriarchy as worst cruel form of society, women are used just for satisfying the erotic craving men. The most horrible crime against women is the institution of prostitution where women are used as mere objects. Women from

11 Miroslav Volf, *Exclusion and Embrace: A Theological Exploration of Identity, otherness and Reconciliation* (Nashville: Abingdon Press, 1996), 64.

12 Though the definition has that migrants are powerless, that need not be the reality all the time, everywhere.

13 Gayatri Chakravorty Spivak, "Can the Subaltern Speak?" in *Colonial Discourse and Post-Colonial Theory: A Reader*, edited by Patrick Williams and Laura Christian (New York: Columbia, 1994), 66-111.

14 Indians called as 'brown' in Western countries. North East Indians called as Chinese, in other parts of India. North Indians referring to all South Indians as 'Madrasis'.

15 Rosetta E. Ross, *God's Faithfulness on the Journey: Reflection by Rostered Women of Colour* (Chicago: ELCA, 2017).

poor and vulnerable conditions are the ones who are used and abused as non-persons.

CHALLENGES TO THEOLOGY

What is the task of theology and theologians in this context? Miroslav Volf suggests that theologians should concentrate less on social arrangement[16] and more on fostering the kind of social agents capable of envisioning and creating just, truthful, and peaceful societies, and on shaping a cultural climate in which such agents will thrive.[17] What kind of social agent should be fostered? Social agents should be able, strong enough to resist the temptation to dominate and should have the ability to arrest the tools of domination such as the ideology of entitlement on the part of the elite, stereotyping groups of people, scapegoating and blaming the victim. Regarding the issue of migration the "people of the land" claim identity and ownership as their entitlements. Migrants are stereotyped as robbers, inferior, refugees, uncivilised etc. They are blamed for all the misfortunes and made scapegoats.

Problematizing the 'Identity'

Poet Percy Bysshe Shelley in the following poem mocks at the King Ozymandias afflicted with Ozymandias syndrome[18] (named after him), absolutizing his identity and his power and ownership over 'others'[19]:

I met a traveller from an antique land
Who said: "'Two vast and trunkless legs of stone
Stand in the desert. Near them on the sand,
Half sunk, a shattered visage lies, whose frown
And wrinkled lip and sneer of cold command

16 Christian economist, political scientists, social philosophers, etc., in cooperation with theologians, rather than theologians themselves, that ought to address social arrangement because they are best equipped to do so.

17 Volf, *Exclusion and Embrace…*, 21.

18 A type of negative behaviour or mental state that is typical of a person in a particular situation.

19 Ozymandias refers to the ancient Egyptian pharaoh Ramesses II. It is believed that he was the pharaoh during the time of Moses, who used the 'Hebrews' as slaves for his building projects. He is well known, famous for the temples, statues and cities he built. He regarded himself as the 'King of Kings'. He considered himself as different and superior from all 'others". He believed that he owned and controlled all his creations and everything around him, "Look on my work". Here, Ozymandias is giving a warning to the other kings and rulers not to hope for much greatness, as they can never cross his achievements. That certainly gives an impression of his proud and commanding nature. But ironical enough, his own statue is now grounded by the great force of nature. 'The colossal Wreck' hints at how the gigantic statue and the high-flying passions attached to it are all dusted now. The 'boundless and bare' and the 'lone and level' sands stretching far away symbolizes the vastness of time. We the human beings are very little creatures in the vast passage of time. Our pride and might will eventually disappear.

Tell that its sculptor well those passions read
Which yet survive, stamped on these lifeless things,
The hand that mocked them and the heart that fed,
And on the pedestal these words appear;
'My name is Ozymandias, King of Kings;
Look on my works, ye mighty, and despair'
Nothing beside remains. Round the decay
Of that colossal wreck, boundless and bare,
The lone and level sands stretch far away."[20]

In the poem, the King claims his identity, 'My name is Ozymandias, King of Kings'. He doesn't want to share his identity. He claims to be the subject, that controls (tries to control the imagination of all) the objects. In our times today too, many are slaves or infected by the Ozymandias Syndrome. Rulers, national leaders, owners, many of us ordinary citizens, believe that we are different and greater than 'others'. People afflicted with Ozymandias Syndrome also believe that they are the ultimate owners of 'spaces under their control', on which 'others' don't have any say or claim.

Feminist thought rejects 'identity' because it rests on separation. Relational feminists, such as Nancy Chodorow have argued that separation always entails repression of existing relationships and therefore results in the domination of the 'other'. Postmodern feminists, such as Judith Butler and Luce Irigaray, have underscored that separation results in a 'unitary' and 'self-identical' self all that is non unitary and non-identical. What unites these two strands of feminist thought is an inability to conceive of "identity" in a way that does not repress either relationship to others or differences within the self. The above two feminist strands question, is a more complex notion of identity possible, a notion of identity that is not 'pure', but includes the other?[21]

In modernity, developing an integrated identity is increasingly difficult. Identity is formed and transformed continuously in relation to the ways we are represented or addressed in the cultural systems which surround us. Modern human beings are afflicted with permanent identity crisis, a condition conducive to considerable nervousness. This identity crisis is exploited by political, caste, leaders in India and many other countries throughout the world. They mobilize one group against the 'other', in their vote bank politics or for other ulterior gains.[22] As the characters and settings of our lives are multiple and become more diverse, weaving a coherent narrative that reconciles all of them seems impossible.

20 https://englicist.com/summary-analysis/ozymandias-shelley-summary (accessed on 30.04.2018).

21 Volf, *Exclusion and Embrace...*, 65-66.

22 http://faculty, Georgetown.edu/ivvinem/theory/hall.identity.modernity-1.pdf (accessed on 30.04.2018).

In the process, gradually we become second generation migrants as we are forced to straddle multiple cultures and locales.

No one can prioritise 'a single' – national or racial or gender or religious identity at the cost of our 'common human identity.' For a person has multiple identities. Some identities are permanent and others temporary. For example, a person is a son or a daughter of a parent- mother and father. Everyone has a birth place, sexual identity (male or female or transgender), caste or tribal or ethnic identity. These are few identities that are permanent, which are unchangeable. On the other hand, a person's religion, marital status, career identity, residential identity can be temporary and changing. Our parents and our nationality were never our choice. They were accidents that were never under our control. But the 'common identity' as 'human beings' is similar to both a citizen of a nation and the migrant.

Women identity is fluid and it floats from one to the other. They don't belong to any place permanently, but belong to multiple places. They belong to the father's land, religion, caste and denomination and then the husband's land, religion and denomination. Also, wherever they belong temporarily, neither they own anything nor expected to act on their own. Such reality of life moulds the consciousness of women. Their consciousness is moulded to accept change easily and accept contingencies gracefully. This fluid identity of women as a result has helped women in many cases not to accept anything as normative, standard and fixed. They are schooled in the school of contingencies. This experience has helped to foster love, respect for life to survive (poverty, communalism, and war). By and large the priority has been to foster life and women are more interested and involved in livelihood issues of the family and community at large.

Such identity chains and doom women to home for the business of hospitality and care giving. Women as home makers are segregated for hospitality. In fact, as custodians of hospitality they are open to strangers. They are also expected to be carriers of traditions. This explains why women are more casteist and patriarchal as they are held high and respected within their own caste groups for internalising and passing on their tradition. Entrusted with the business of hospitality they are more hospitable to the "strange", but as custodians of traditions they are averse to the 'strange'. As migration and its challenges overwhelm us, hospitality also requires that we not only understand the survival instinct of the 'migrant', the 'other', like all human beings but also help the 'other' to survive. Helping the 'other' to survive requires that the natural resources are shared.

Therefore, one of the most promising theologies that would serve as source for countering such tools of domination could be the Theology of Trinitarian Sharing.

Theology of Trinitarian Sharing

We often see Trinity in terms of equality, rather than seeing it in terms of terms of sharing. God, Jesus Christ and the Holy Spirit share power equally, share space equally, share the same personality, share their work, and share everything. So as we human beings created in the image of God, we are to share like the three persons in Trinity.

Sharing our Common Human Identity[23]

Very often xenophobic people who are against or oppose 'migrants' claim their identity and ownership of land, 'nation' as their entitlement. Here, these entitlements, such as identity and ownership or 'nationhood' are deconstructed. No one has a 'core identity'. All of us have 'fluid identity'. No human being is an absolute owner, God is the ultimate owner. There by, all human beings are strangers and migrants in an inclusive *oikos* - household, world community.

We see around the world different kinds of violence (active and passive) like communal violence, ethnic war, the reason is xenophobia triggered by 'Block thinking'.[24] Europe colonized and oppressed, destroyed cultures and imposed its religion, all in the name of its identity with itself – in the name of its own absolute religion and superior civilization. The identity of Europe with itself is totalitarian.[25] Brexit campaigners believe that British voters have taken an once-in-a-lifetime opportunity to restore Britain's sovereignty. Germany sought to conquer and exterminate in the name of its purity, its identity with itself. Donald Trump wants to end emigration. Hindutva wants to oust the minorities out of India.

Sharing Trinitarian God's Creation or Sharing Earth's Natural Resources

It was at creation that Trinitarian God the Creator committed the world and its resources to humanity (Gen. 1:28–29). It was because the man and the woman were made in the image of God that they were commanded to be stewards of the created order. As a result, Trinitarian God granted stewardship to this first

---

23 Desire for survival is common to all human beings, all living creatures. Everybody, every creature wants to live, survive. Also, all of us are migrants. If not we, our parents or our grant parents or great grant parents or ancestors were migrants. This, understanding that we all desire to survive and we all are migrants, should help us to empathize with the migrants today, in our midst. By, understanding and respecting the survival need of the 'other' (like that of ours) and being conscious that we are migrants, as well, should motivate us to take efforts, to accept, to include, to arrange, to share provisions for the 'other', 'migrants', to live a dignified life. This is to share our common human identity.

24 According to Priestley, "Human beings belong to various blocks – racial, national, social, political, religious, etc. Their way of thinking and attitude are coloured and conditioned by the block they align themselves with. They feel comfortable and gain recognition by the outfit they wear. They get so inextricably entrenched in their respective blocks that they fail to appreciate the existence and validity of other blocks." J. B. Priestley, quoted by T.S. Ramaswamy, "Peace amidst Inter-Religious Violence: A Hindu Perspective," in *Taming the Violent: Narratives of Conflict Resolutions*, edited by A. Amaladoss (Chennai: IDCR Publications, 2010), 105.

25 Volf, *Exclusion and Embrace…*, 17.

human pair under God's law, but God did not grant God's sovereignty to them, for Trinitarian God alone is Lord and the only sovereign over all.

Along with creation, this stewardship was reinforced in the Decalogue's eighth commandment, "You shall not steal" (Ex. 20:15), which provided for property rights as well. With this command, not only was the principle of individual ownership recognized, but it also thereby regarded as criminal all attempts to take that property from a person in a fraudulent way and to then regard it as one's own. However, in an ultimate sense, in world all property belonged to the Lord, as Leviticus 25:23 made clear: "the land is mine and you are but aliens and my tenants." The biblical picture is one in which absolute sovereignty is attributed to Trinitarian God alone, while stewardship responsibilities are attributed to human beings who are accountable to God for the fulfilment of these responsibilities.

Capitalism has made us to believe that few nations or humans are the ultimate owners of land and its resources. The way each country and people group perceive about the land and its resource is a mockery of themselves. They are modern Ozymandias. Ozymandias used Hebrew slaves to build his empire. Today, women's body and the bodies of the 'poor' are used by capitalist patriarchy for its vain pomp and show.

Female Body as Resource

Much changes in the status of women has helped women to own assets. Women do own property, business, production fames, farm lands, house, gold, silver vessels, vehicles and many other assets, though patriarchy never allows women to own assets. Women owning assets is mostly, grudgingly accepted. Capitalist, casteist, imperial patriarchy sees women's body, yet another resource to be exploited for labour and sex. For the poor and vulnerable migrant women their body is their only asset. Poor migrant women's body is exploited for labour and sex.

Resource is something that can be used to help achieve an aim (work done). Female body, docile Asian women are indispensable resource for the International cheap labour market. Women are ill-treated, unpaid, underpaid, over worked starved, locked in dark rooms without contact with the outer world. No holiday is given; even one day in a week, is a holiday. No rest is given; in some cases, they are treated just like machines (with human body and life) meant for labour 24 x 7. In surrogacy business women's wombs are incubators for some 34-36 weeks.

Resource is a stock or supply of materials or assets. In military bases, red light areas, brothels migrant women are stocks for sex. In surrogacy centres and organ transplantation clinics, the female body is a stock. Poor migrant women who have no relatives, parents, husband, sons to claim or search for them or to file a case in the police station when they disappear are the main targets of human traffickers.

What is the purpose of female body? The Bible speaks of celebrating sexuality. There are instances, where men were punished for sexually abusing women. King

Abimelech was afflicted for taking Abrahams wife Sarah (Gene 20:1-18). God questions and accuses the rapist.[26] Song of Solomon celebrates sexuality for the sake of love. The man and the woman are not even married. It is celebration of love for love sake. But what happens in brothels and prostitution centres today is crude violation of the dignity of a person. The migrant women's body, will, her dreams and her hopes are trampled and crushed. God has intended human beings to labour. But human life is not just for labour. Women are to enjoy life, have leisure, have time to worship God. She should be in control of her life. Women should also be co-stewards of God's resource.

Need for Collaboration

Life is a struggle and struggle is another word for hope. The Canaanite woman in Matthew's Gospel (and the Syrophoenician woman in Mark's Gospel) presents an example of perseverance by a woman "outsider" and gives one answer to the question "Can the subaltern speak?" Matthew presents this woman as "excluded" from the House of Israel and without rights to call upon Jesus. But the woman understands herself as "included" and boldly speaks inclusion by shouting out to Jesus, "Have mercy on me, Lord, Son of David!" Certainly, Spivak affirms that women can speak. The significance of her essay lies in its recognition and analysis of reasons for the absence of subaltern voices within the ordinary thinking and planning of so-called "insiders."

This points to the need for collaboration. So-called migrants, "subalterns" sometimes have entry points on the inside and are themselves "insiders" of communities with rich resources, rich traditions and wisdom. In the case of the host country, collaboration may occur, on the one hand, as those who have "host country-insider" power speak on behalf of migrants, subalterns but also, and more importantly, make room for full inclusion, so those viewed as "host country-migrants," migrants, for example, may speak inside the host country for themselves. On the other hand, migrants are insiders with knowledge of and access to experiences and communities that the host country needs.

Let us see the case of migrant Esther who was exalted as queen. Esther is seen as a tool, instrument, and providence of God to liberate the people of Israel. But the 'Book of Esther' silently, factually narrates sexual slavery of women. For neither the sexual slavery practiced by King Ahasuerus is critiqued, nor the banishment of queen Vashti for not displaying her beauty in an immodest way (King's wish), is questioned.

In fact, a paradoxical identity or image of Esther can be seen in the narratives. On the one hand she is a vulnerable *abused migrant,* but on the other, wise and courageous Liberator migrant. When events took a turn for the worst and Esther learned that Prime Minister Haman planned to kill all Jews in the Persian Empire,

26 Don't covet your neighbour's wife (Exo 20). Jesus said, if a man sees a woman with lust, he has committed adultery in his heart.

she decided to act quickly to prevent the genocide. She ordered her uncle: "Go, gather together all the Jews and fast for me, and neither eat nor drink for three days, night or day." Mordecai argued three days of fast. She invited both Haman and Ahasuerus to a private banquet. That day, Esther told the king about Haman's plan to massacre all Jews in his kingdom, and she acknowledged her own Jewish ethnicity. The enraged King ordered Haman's hanging, elevated Mordecai to prime minister and gave Jews the right to defend themselves against any enemy. Esther thus saved her people from death and becomes the liberator of the Jews.

The story of Ruth is yet another example where Moab allowed Elimelech's family to settle in Moab and marry Moabite women to Elimelech's sons. When the three men in the family passed away, Naomi wanted to return to Bethlehem. She requested both of her daughters-in-law to return to their people, marry and settle. Orpha returns. But Ruth clings to Naomi and journeys to Bethlehem. In Bethlehem Ruth is well received and Ruth finds her name in the genealogy of Jesus. The bond and love between Ruth and Naomi, women of different warring races is marvellous, which can be followed.

Conclusion

Migration in a way has become a way of life today for our claim of entitlements such as identity and ownership that excludes the stranger. Often we turn a blind eye to our own fluid identity and the reality that there is Trinitarian sharing and God's sovereignty over all creation. We always tend to dehumanises the excluded 'other'. It calls for a challenge that all human beings should be cured of our 'Ozymandias syndrome'. So, what is the way out? Perhaps, women's experience of having fluid identity and never being 'real' owners which help them to migrate easily as well as accept strangers and migrants easily, and also the culture of sharing may be the alternatives. For Exodus 22:21 speaks of a stranger (migrant) must not be abused, wronged in judgment by the magistrates, should not be imposed upon in contracts, nor any advantage be taken of their ignorance or necessity, nor must they be taunted or upbraided for being a stranger, for all these were vexatious. For they were strangers in Egypt and knew what it was to be vexed and oppressed there. Those who have themselves been in poverty and distress, if Providence enrich and enlarge them, they must show a tenderness toward those who are now in such circumstances as they were in earlier, now doing to them as they then wished to be done to.[27] This is the imperative Church and society of our times need in order to create an inclusive community where everyone wishes the welfare of everybody and form an inclusive multi-cultural *oikos*, the inclusive world community.

27 http://biblehub.com/commentaries/exodus/22-21.htm (accessed on 16.04.2018).

10

Migration from North East Indian Perspective

Walotemjen

The global phenomenon of human migration is not a new reality or a recent development. It has been a very part of human history and civilization and it still continues. The present-day world is witnessing the highest levels of displacement on record and people migrating from one place to the other or one country to the other in various forms and due to various factors. The number of international migrants worldwide has continued to grow rapidly over the past fifteenth years reaching 244 million in 2015 and India alone having largest 'Diaspora' in the world accounting to 16 million.[1] The total number of migrants around the globe today is reported to be over 3% of the total global population and if the current trend of push and pull factors continue, it is likely to increase in an unprecedented proportion in the near future.[2]

The phenomenon of migration - be it international or internal migration, North East India (NEI) is not in an exception. Great number of people from the region are migrating to other regions and cities due to various factors. Some of the factors of migration from the context of NEI basically are education, livelihood, job opportunities, and better life. Most of the migrants from the region particularly the uneducated or less educated or skilled ones voluntarily leave their place in search of better economic opportunities and work in various companies, building projects, shopping malls and hospitality industries. The issue of migration in general and lives migrants in particular do not go without challenges. Therefore, looking at the trend of migration in general and assessing the key issues and challenges of migrants from the perspective of NEI is unavoidable necessity.

---

1 *United Nations International Migration Report 2015* (New York: United Nations, 2016), 1.

2 Christine Lagarde, "Migration: A Global Issue in Need of a Global Solution," in *m.huffpost.com* (2017).

Dynamics of Migration

Migration which is a pragmatic and universal phenomenon has two major forms viz., international and intra-national. The internal migration may take place in the form of rural to urban, urban to urban, urban to rural and rural to rural and is related to the international migration either overseas or overland.[3] Migration is a complex process symptomatic of basic economic and social changes as it predominantly associated with complex economic, social and psychological problems. Since it also involves demographic, environment, anthropology, socio-cultural etc. and above all the dynamics of politics, reading it in multi-dimensional or in an inter-disciplinary approach is a must.

Migration is "a form of geographical or spatial mobility between one geographic unit and another, generally involving a change of residence from a place of origin or departure to a place of destination or arrival."[4] It implies a permanent or semi-permanent change in the place of residence. Legally speaking, migration involves crossing over administrative units or boundaries. When the national boundary of the country is involved it is called international migration and if the migration takes place within the national boundary, it is termed internal migration.[5] It is not merely a physical movement of people from one place to another, but a movement with multiple social, economic, cultural, religious and other dimensions as well.[6] Due to modernization and industrialization coupled with globalization, the cities are growing at a rapid pace in terms of infrastructure development, investment, job opportunities, high salaries, stable economy, etc. In the recent years, the information technology and digital system in industrialization and other fields have helped the growth faster than what people ordinarily expected.[7] Since most of the migrations take place due to economic factors, flow of migrants generally is from economically backward areas to economically advanced and prosperous areas. Most of the migrants move in search of better economic opportunities in those areas.[8] In short, the movement of people from one place in the world to another or one region to the other for the purpose of taking up permanent or semi-permanent residence, usually across a political boundary is called migration. People those choose to move with such objectives

3 A.K. Gupta, *Sociological Implications of Rural to Rural Migration: A Case Study of Rural Immigrants in Punjab* (Allahabad: Vohra Publishing & Distributors, 1988), 17.

4 M. Hassan, *Population Geography*. Jaipur: Rawat Publications, 2005, 281, quoted in Augustine Kanjamala, "Social Analysis of Migration in India," in *Migration and Mission in India*, edited by L. Stanislaus & Jose Joseph (Delhi: Ishvani/ISPCK, 2007), 1.

5 Augustine, *Social Analysis of Migration* ..., 1.

6 H.C. Upreti, *Social Organisation of a Migrant Group: A Sociological Study of Hill Migrants from Kumaon Region in the City of Jaipur* (Bombay: Himalaya Publishing House, 1981), 1.

7 L. Stanislaus & Jose Joseph, eds., *Migration and Mission in India* (Delhi: Ishvani/ISPCK, 2007), vii.

8 A. Datta, *Human Migration: A Social Phenomenon* (New Delhi: Mittal Publications, 2003), 16.

are called 'voluntary migration' and those who moves out or rather pushed out from their native place due to economic and livelihood pressures are known as 'involuntary migration.' Whatever the category is, apart from economic, there are also various other reasons behind the migration of people from NEI.

North East India: Overview of the Land and People

The NEI is a region comprising of the eight states, namely, Assam, Arunachal Pradesh, Meghalaya, Manipur, Mizoram, Nagaland and Tripura and the Himalayan State of Sikkim.[9] The region lies in the eastern corner of India and is bordered in the south and south-west by Bangladesh, in the east and south-east by Myanmar, and in the north by China, Tibet and Bhutan. It is linked to the rest of India by a narrow corridor in its Western corner. NEI displays a distinctive "geo-ethnic character."[10] About three quarters of the region is covered by hilly terrain and one quarter is made up of the four plains areas.[11] The States belonged to major races of the human family – the Tibeto-Burman, Austro-Asiatic and Indo-Aryan. 40% of the populations in NEI are tribals. Though the tribal people of NEI differ among themselves in many ways linguistically, ethnically and culturally they also have in common many structural and cultural characteristics.[12] For centuries the tribal people of NEI lived in isolation from the outside world and had or little inter-tribal contact.

The region is rich in natural resources covered with dense forests, has the highest rainfall in the country, with large and small river systems nesting the land and is a treasure house of flora and fauna. Marked by diversity in customs, culture, traditions and languages, it is a home to multifarious social, ethnic and linguistic groups.[13] NEI occupies a distinctive place due to its social, cultural, political, geographical and historical features resulting in lack of uniformity, integration and assimilation. As unified it is in conflict ridden issues like ethnic unrest, insurgency, and illegal immigration; there exist wide intra-regional disparities in socio-economic issues.

9 Sometimes, Sikkim is also included in the region but due to the geographical detachment by West Bengal in between, generally NEI is referred to as the seven states.

10 Annanda C. Bhagabati, "Emergent Tribal Identity in North-East India," in *Tribal Developments in India: Problems and Prospects*, edited by B. Chaudhuri (Delhi: Inter-India Publications, 1982), 218.

11 N.K. Das, *Ethnic Identity, Ethnicity and Social Stratification in North-East India* (New Delhi: Inter-India Publications, 1989), 28. The four plains are: the Brahmaputra valley and Barak (Surma) valley of Assam, the Tripura plains and the Manipur plateau.

12 S. Fuchs, "The Races of North East India," in *Indian Missiological Review*, vol. 12 (1990): 160-172.

13 Surajit Kumar Bhagowati, "Human Development in India's North Eastern States: A Study," *A Paper Presented at the Annual International Conference on Global Turbulence: Challenges and Opportunities* (Bangkok: May 5-6, 2012), 6.

According to the 2011 census, the geographical area of NEI in total covers approximately 2,61km, with a total population of 4,55,87,982. Geographical area and population of NEI are as follows:[14]

State	Area (sq.km)	Population	Density of Population
Arunachal Pradesh	83,743	13,82,611	17
Assam	78,550	3,11,69,272	397
Manipur	22,347	27,21,756	122
Meghalaya	22,720	29,64,007	132
Mizoram	21,081	10,91,014	52
Nagaland	16,579	19,80,602	119
Sikkim	7,096	6,07,688	86
Tripura	10,491.69	36,71,032	350
Total	**2,62,607.69**	**4,55,87,982**	**1275**

Ethnic and Language Diversity of NEI

The NEI is a region that has within its fold an ethnic composition of an extremely complex population who have been migrated into the region at different stages and waves. It may be called as 'mini India' due to its diversity of culture, language, religion and historical backgrounds.[15] Some scholars have classified the various groups according to language families. Thus, B.B. Goswami divides them into three families: The Mon Khmer to which the Khasi and Synteng belong; the Tibeto-Burman which includes people distributed over the hills and plains of Assam – The Nagas, the Kuki-Chin and the Bodo; and the Siamese-Chinese family which comprises the Phakials, the Khamtis and Ahoms. Diversity of origin and the absence of a common language have, therefore, kept the hill tribes of the NEI confined to their own geographical boundaries and made them zealous to their culture and dialect.[16] Speaking of the social groups with diverse ethnic origins of North East, Das says, "With her diverse population, speaking different languages and professing divergent faiths, it may be regarded as an epitome of India. It is the land where waves of immigrants from Tibeto-Burman and the Mongoloid stock have met and woven with aboriginals a pattern of common

14 *Census of India,* 2011.

15 Songram Basumatary, *Ethnicity and Tribal Theology: Problems and Prospects for Peaceful Co-existence in Northeast India.* (Bern, Switzerland: Peter Lang, 2014), 39. For further information on the Land and People, see 33-62.

16 Patricia Mukhim, "Christian Impact on North East India and National Integration," in *Impact of Christianity on North East India*, edited by J. Puthenpurakal (Shillong: Vendrame Institute Publications, 1996), 63-64.

condition and tradition."[17] Ethnologically, large portion of population comprised of tribals mainly of Tibeto-Mongoloid stock both in hills and plains. Thus NEI displays a distinctive "geo-ethnic character."[18] The linguistic composition of the region is also extremely diverse. The languages of the North-East region are classified into Tibeto-Burman, Indo-Aryan, and Austro-Asiatic families.[19]

Socio-Economic and Political Context of NEI

The social location of the people varies from region to region. There are differences in social organization, racial strands and ethnic, language, religious groups and cultural patterns and identities.[20] The social life of NEI is marked by festivals and feasts. All the communities have a rich cultural heritage and it is intrinsically linked with festivals and religious significance. Most of these festivals are celebrated in the presence of whole community. Thus the social life of the people is marked by communitarian life.

The region is endowed with huge untapped natural resources and is acknowledged as the eastern gate of India's 'Look-East Policy.' Nonetheless, the region is cited as a conflict-stricken remote corner of India, witnessing a series of insurgencies and illustrating the alienation of the locals from the mainstream. Although, the causes of insurgency in the region have been primarily political, the ambiguity related to the economic potential has added fuel to the turmoil.[21] The exploration of mineral resources has become a contentious issue and has fueled conflict in the region (e.g., in Assam for oil and Meghalaya – the extraction of uranium and coal has been a problem). The huge oil reserve spotted in Nagaland, reported to contain oil reserve worth billions, is also a major contention. Besides, ethnic conflicts among the tribes in the region are also sparked by competitive claims over the limited economic assets, which are an outcome of scarce economic development and limited opportunities. In Manipur, violent ethnic conflict broke out in the Moreh border area of Chandel among the Meitei, Nagas and Kuki and others because of their struggle to dominate the Moreh market. The most serious dispute was the Naga-Kuki conflict of 1992. The Kuki-Paite conflict of 1997-

---

17 S.T. Das, *Tribal Life of North East India* (Delhi: Gyan Publishing House, 1986), vi, quoted in Anati K. Yeptho & Vincent Rajkumar, *The Social Reality of the North East Migrants: A Case Study in Bangalore* (Bangalore: CISRS, 2014), 10.

18 N.K. Das, *Ethnic Identity, Ethnicity and Social Stratification in North-East India* (New Delhi: Inter-India Publications, 1989), 28.

19 T.B. Subba, ed., *North-East India: A Handbook of Anthropology* (New Delhi: Orient Blackswan Private Limited, 2012), xvi. For further information on the Land and People of the North East region, see Songram Basumatary, *Ethnicity and Tribal Theology...*, 33-62.

20 Aijazuddin Ahmad, *Social Geography* (Jaipur/New Delhi: Rawat Publications, 2006), 15.

21 H. Shivananda, "Economic Potential of Northeast India: An Asset or Threat?" Institute for Defence Studies and Analyses (May, 2011) (idsa.im/idsacomments/EconomicPotentialofNotheastindiaAnAssestorThreat_shivanandah_120511 (accessed on 30th March 2018).

1998 in Churachandpur district resulted in 1000 people killed, 4600 houses torched to ashes rendering many homeless and compelling to flee to other areas in the state.[22]

Industrialization in the region has not developed successfully and even small-scale industries have not been feasible due to lack of adequate economic infrastructure like transportation, communications and market accessibility. The region's economy remains primarily agricultural. Primitive farm practices of slash and burn (*jhum*) and shifting cultivation are still practiced in many hill areas, while traditional single crop farming in the plains continues. As a result, the region is not able to produce adequate food grain to feed its own population.[23] Most of the states in the region import food items from other parts of the country. While neither agriculture nor industry had developed, the service sector has expanded disproportionately though it is less productive and limited. In due course of time, while the national economy is growing at a swift rate, the economies of the region are slowing down creating economic gap between the northeast region and the mainland.[24] Moreover, the region remains isolated from the rest of the country and has not been able to attract investors or produce skilled labour and entrepreneurial resources. It has failed to transform even the primitive agricultural practices of the region into modern commercial agriculture. In addition, the region has not received the attention of the Central government in building the required essential infrastructure for progress. All this has alienated the northeast from the mainland.[25]

Conundrum of NEI: A Perspective

Troubled by history and geo-politics, the NEI has remained one of the most backward regions of the country. The poor infrastructure and governance combined with low productivity and market access keeps the region at backward. Inability of governments to control floods and river bank erosion causes unmitigated damage to properties and lives of millions of people every year in the region. If the quest for ethnic and cultural identities has sowed the seeds, frustration and dissatisfaction from seclusion, backwardness, remoteness and problems of governance have

22 "Manipur Backgrounder," *South Asia Terrorism Portal, Institute for Conflict Management* (http//www.satp.org/satporgtp/countries/india/states/Manipur/backgrounder, accessed on 30th March, 2018). See also Songram Basumatary, *Ethnicity and Tribal Theology* ..., 128-131.

23 A.K. Mishra and J.P. Mishra, "Sustainable Development of Agriculture in Northeastern India: A Quest for More Economical and Resourceful Sustainable Alternatives," *ENVIS Bulletin, Himalaya Ecology*, 14/2 (2006).

24 "Manipur Backgrounder," *South Asia Terrorism Portal, Institute for Conflict Management* (http// www.satp.org/satporgtp/countries/india/states/Manipur/backgrounder (accessed on 30th March, 2018).

25 "Manipur Backgrounder," *South Asia Terrorism Portal, Institute for Conflict Management* (http//www.satp.org/satporgtp/countries/india/states/Manipur/backgrounder (accessed on 30th March, 2018).

provided fertile ground for breeding armed insurgencies groups.[26] The region has a population of 45.5 million (as per 2011 census) comprising 3.77 percent of India's population and geographically covers 8.05 percent of the country's total geographical area. The region is also the abode of approximately 225 tribes out of 450 in the country, the culture and customs of which have an important role in understanding biodiversity conservation and management issue groups.

NEI by and large is hilly region characterized by curves and terrains; rivers and streams. Lack of developed transport (i.e., road and bridges), communication facilities therefore makes the region inaccessible and intensifies its geographical isolation. Provisions for economic and infrastructure overheads are poor. None of these states has been able to generate adequate funds to meet the budgetary requirement for their respective governments, and thus to a great extent, depends on the flow of financial resources from the central government under the provisions of 'Special Category States' in which out of total central assistance to the state 90 percent accounts for grants and remaining 10 percent are loans groups.[27] Insurgency or terrorism is a political weapon and it is often the result of accumulated anger due to political, economic and social causes. The states within NEI have witnessed a rise of insurgent activities and regional movements in the recent pasts. These movements derive their roots from difference of language and ethnicity, human rights, tribal rivalry and ethnic resentment, migration, underdevelopment, control over local resources, access to markets and a widespread feeling of exploitation and alienation from the Indian state.[28]

As stated, NEI has been deeply affected by political unrest. Due to several problems and issues armed insurgency has plagued the region.[29] Historically, insurgency took place in Nagaland and Manipur in the early fifties, immediately after the establishment of the republic (of India), those in Mizoram, in the sixties, in Tripura in the seventies, while in the case of Assam it has arrived in the eighties. Meghalaya and Arunachal Pradesh are just menacing militant, not yet insurgent though, Karbi Anglong, district of Assam too is equally poised.[30] S. Shimary expresses that, "Northeast India is known for its insurgency movements. The region is, on one hand, home to different indigenous groups and, on the other, to different insurgency groups. Various indigenous groups and tribal people's

---

26 Surajit Kumar Bhagowati, *Human Development…*, 6-7.

27 Surajit Kumar Bhagowati, *Human Development…*, 6-7.

28 *Economic Problems of Northeast India*, www.ukessays.com, 23rd March 2015 (accessed on 31st March, 2018).

29 For a brief overview of the ethno-politics in the North East region, see Lalsangkima Pachuau, *Ethnic Identity and Christianity in North East India: A Socio-Historical and Missiological Study with Special Reference to Mizoram* (New York: Peter Lang, 2002), 46-58.

30 Nibaran Bora, "Insurgency in the North-East," in *Political Development of the North-East*, vol. 2, edited by B.C. Bhuyan (New Delhi: Omsons Publications, 1992), 1, quoted in Lalsangkima Pachuau, *Ethnic Identity and Christianity …*, 46.

movements are engaged in defining the concept of rights and self-determination in different ways. Some want autonomy within the existing state system, while others want a separate state within the Union of India. There is a third group for whom right to self-determination means complete independence from India."[31] Most of the states are crippled by ethnic and communal clashes,[32] tensions between people and army, insurgency and so on. All these problems generally affect the normal life of the region. Until the 1970s the Indian government used collective punishment, forcible relocation and military occupation in an attempt to end insurgency in the NEI. In addition to creating a severe sense of grievance among some groups, this strategy rendered civil and political institutions virtually meaningless by concentrating power over local affairs with the security forces. Even today, the military remains the only Indian institution with any significant presence in the parts of this region, which has given rise to anti central government sentiments.[33] This is the stark reality of NEI as a whole.

Literacy Rate

Education is the most effective instrument for socio-economic empowerment and there has been a visible increase in the literary rates of NEI. As per Census on Literacy rate in India,[34] Mizoram has the highest literacy rate of 91.6%, followed by Tripura with 87.8%. Literary rate of NEI are as follows: Arunachal Pradesh 67.7%; Assam 73.2%; Manipur 79.8%; Meghalaya 75.5%; Mizoram 91.6%; Nagaland 80.1%; Tripura 87.8% and Sikkim 82.8%. In fact, literacy rate in NEI is high when being compared to other states in India. Unfortunately, the system and the situation in the region do not create significant space for employment opportunities. The unemployment rate in the region is high and this is why people from the region migrates to other regions of the country for better employment opportunities. It is also crystal clear that despite a high literacy rate, the region is characterized by a visible lack of sufficient opportunity for higher or

---

31 Shim Shimary, "Human Rights Violation in Northeast India with Reference to Armed Forces (Special Powers) Act, 1985," *God's Image: Journal of Asian Women's Resource Center for Cultural and Theology*, 19/4 (December 2000): 5-11.

32 See Songram Basumatary, *Ethnicity and Tribal Theology …*, 147-182. Songram deals with the *Major Inter-Ethnic Conflicts in North East India since the 1990s along with Three Test Cases* to base his argument to the consequent rise of inter-ethnic tension in NEI. An attempt is made to underscore the grave issue of ethnic trends in the region and highlight some of the innate factors behind the inter-ethnic conflicts and the self-deprivative consequences of them by considering three test cases: the Naga-Kuki conflict in Manipur, the Boro-Santhal riot in western Assam and the Hmar-Dimasa clash in the North Cachar Hills, Assam. The author opined that tribal loyalties, religion, language, sharing of political power and economic opportunities have all been utilized systematically for ethnic mobilization.

33 *Economic Problems of Northeast India* (www.ukessays.com, 23rd March 2015, accessed on 31st March, 2018).

34 *Literacy Rate in India, Census 2011* (www.mapsofindia.com (accessed on 29th March, 2018).

technical education or vocational training. Therefore, in general the NEI states are less developed than other states of India. This under-development has in turn greatly impacted on employment and other opportunities in the region.[35] For this very reasons people of the region are migrating in great number every year to other regions particularly in the metro cities in search of better education and job opportunities.

Migration: North East Indian Perspective

Migrations from NEI to metro cities like Delhi, Mumbai, Kolkata, Bangalore, Hyderabad and Chennai, etc., has increased rapidly in the recent years. This movement of migration as described above may be attributed to poverty, unemployment, ethnic and political conflict, poor developmental infrastructures, poor higher and technical educational facilities, etc. When people land in other regions or cities they often face problems and difficulties like abuses, harassment, exploitation, racial discrimination, etc., because of socio-cultural and environmental setting and differences. In fact, they are even more marginalized for the fact that they fall outside the shared imaginary of what counts as having a 'typically' 'Indian face.' People from the region with few exceptions of plains tribes are often confused for foreigners and are often pejoratively referred to as 'Chinkies.'[36] As a result of this complex unfolding of identity politics, the migrants from NEI are negatively conceptualized by the majority population in the cities as the quintessential 'Other' and are placed in a marginal and vulnerable position facing various forms of discriminations and abuses. This perhaps raises serious questions of reflection as to why then people of the region migrate? Do they any way fulfill their aspirations? What are the positive and negative treatment they receive? Contrary what are the positive and negative impacts the migrants make in the host region or cities?

In fact, as noted above, people chose to migrate into other regions and metro cities for various reasons. In general they migrate due to both "Push" and "Pull" factors. As explicated by the scholars, particularly, Evert Lee, the phenomenon of internal migration is due to 'push-pull'. Both factors are at play in the migration of people from NEI. Mostly the lack of livelihood and job opportunities push them out and the prospective livelihood means and job opportunities in the other places pull them in. Besides, there are also 'intervening obstacles' and 'personal decisions' that play a decisive role in the process of migration. For example, in the less developed countries or regions rural-urban migration occurs primarily not because of 'pull' factors in the urban areas but because of strong 'push' factor in

35 Anati K. Yeptho & Vincent Rajkumar, *The Social Reality* ..., 18.

36 From the British English slang term 'Chink.' See footnote no 39 bellow for some detail on this term.

the form of appalling poverty, acute unemployment and insecurity.[37] Other push factors like high population pressure on land, unsettled political condition, and economic insecurity of the people[38] are also at play. In short, though the both the factors are at play, the 'Push' factors seem greater force than 'Pull' factors in terms of migration scenario in NEI. This is why though they are not treated well in the destiny regions and cities, they choose to migrate.

Challenges and Issues Faced by North East Migrants

In order to understand the seriousness of challenges and issues facing migrants of NEI, it is necessary that some of the important areas like Racial Profiling and Discrimination, Unequal Treatment at Work Place, Violence, and Insecurity are highlighted.

Racial Profiling and Discrimination

Many are still ignorant about the identity of NEI people and are looked and treated as strangers or foreigners. Reason is their appearance more than anything else. They are being mistaken as people from Asian countries as most of their racial origin is from Mongoloid stock completely different from the appearance of the rest of Indian population. Of course, there are a good number of populations in the mainland India who are aware of the diversity of the region and the people there in, but still their mind-sets and attitudes are mostly the same. They often look them down as the 'other' or strangers. Many North East Indian people especially women living in different parts of Indian metropolitan cities undergo the experiences of stereotyping as outsiders, vulnerability of abuses and insecurity of life. Often they are mismatched as Chinese, Japanese, Korean, Nepalese and so on, and at times called as 'chinky'/'chinkies' with derogatory intent.[39] The migrant workers all the more encounter various serious forms of racism and treated as second-rate citizens.

---

37 For elaborate list of "Push and Pull Factors", see Augustine Kanjamala, *Social Analysis of Migration* ...; A.K. Gupta, *Sociological Implications* ...; G.S. Aurora, *The New Frontier Man: A Sociological Study of Immigrants in United Kingdom* (Bombay: Popular Prakashan, 1967); S.C. Joshi, *Migration to a Metropolis* (Jaipur: RBSA Publishers, 1994); Anati K. Yeptho & Vincent Rajkumar, *The Social Reality.*

38 G.S. Aurora, *The New Frontier Man: A Sociological Study of Immigrants in United Kingdom* (Bombay: Popular Prakashan, 1967), 11, quoted in Anati K. Yeptho & Vincent Rajkumar, *The Social Reality* ..., 40.

39 Anati K. Yeptho & Vincent Rajkumar, *The Social Reality* ..., 65. The term 'chinky' is a racist and offensive term, derived from the word "chink" which is used to describe anyone that is oriental or Eastern Asian descent, particularly ethnic slur usually referring to a person of Chinese ethnicity. Of course, it is used to describe the eyes of those of East Asian descent. Interestingly, the word usually doesn't have the same racial effect when used by two Asians. But the term is indiscriminately used against people of East Asians in racist and offensive sense such as odd look, inferior, stranger etc.

It is true that India contains many communities earmarked as 'others' base on religion, caste, and even ethnicity and yet the nationality and origin of these communities are not questioned at every turn. They can blend into the heartland in ways. But it not in the case of migrants from NEI. In fact, this is not to argue that these 'others' do not face discrimination and violence. The fact is that the North-East Indian migrants face racism different from those 'others' and they feel their experience of racism distinct from others. To put it in simple, because of their strange look, they are not viewed and accepted as one among vast Indian population. They are still subjected to different perceptions and treatment than other groups.[40] For this reason the migrants from the region in their own country work and live in vulnerable situations.

Unequal Treatment at Work Place

The people from NEI in most cases feel that are not treated on equal footing with the local population. In some cases unskilled migrants' living condition in the work places are unimaginably unhygienic, unequally and untimely paid, and at times easily alleged of crimes. For instance, NEI Welfare Association Chennai (NEIWAC)[41] in number occasions helped trace and rescue workers who were forced in bonded labourers with the support and help from nodal officers; helped in negotiating the non-release of salaries and wages in massage parlours and restaurants.[42] They are respected and treated well because of language barrier, cultural difference and most importantly because they are from NEI and know them from their documents as tribal.[43]

Insecure and Unprotected

Due to large number of migrants, there is an increase flow of undocumented migrants. Many of them come even through human trafficking, particularly the women. They come to the cities in search of jobs but end up in trafficking and various other vulnerable situations. Women are perhaps the easy target and the most vulnerable to abuse, exploitation of all sorts. Generally, the migrants are an ignored lot by the government. Young girls are more frequently becoming victims of such situation. Their state of affairs are not even studied or highlighted. The laws and regulations governing the conditions of the migrants are largely not implemented or in most cases ineffective. They are unnoticed, ignored, uncared,

40 Duncan Mcduie-Ra, "The North-East Map of Delhi," *Economic and Political Weekly*, 47/30 (July, 2012): 71.

41 North East India Welfare Association Chennai (NEIWAC) came into being on 21st June 214 following the recommendation of Bezbaruah Committee. NEIWAC is being supported by two nodal officers from the Govt., of Tamil Nadu.

42 *NEIWAC Voice: Co-Existence, Souvenir 2016*, "Secretary Report," 8-9.

43 Anati K. Yeptho & Vincent Rajkumar, *The Social Reality* ..., 69.

unprotected, undefended, vulnerable and lost.[44] So, their life is insecure in many ways. Often there are open threat, physical assault, verbal abuse, sexual harassment, etc. Even the mode of job for them is concern for insecurity especially those working in call center/BPO sectors. They are also unsecured and unprotected in their places of stay because of racial differences.[45]

The people from the region feel all the more insecure an unprotected because the way the law and order authorities particularly the police force functions. On any dispute or incidents of violence their conclusion often is to blame and accuse them of inviting violent encounter themselves. For instance, in the infamous pamphlet Security Tips for North East Students/Visitors in Delhi issued by Delhi Police, north-east women are advised to act and dress more conservatively.[46] And often in the case of sexual harassment and violence, women themselves are held responsible for the victimization while the perpetrators are largely ignored.

Challenges of/to the Migrants from NEI

While talking about the migration from the perspective of NEI, there numerous challenges that calls for both critical analysis and academic reflection as well as practical action by concerned authorities. On the one hand it requires multi-dimensional approach and analysis, and on the other multi-level practical steps to address the issue. Perhaps, first and foremost, is an objective reading of the whole scenario of migration. There are multiple challenges here in terms of factors of migration, direction of migration, benefits of migration, consequence of migration and the very types and forms of migration. In relation to these number of questions arises: Who migrate for what and where? How do people consider migration and migrants? Who are benefitted or affected by the migration? What about the history of migration and the situation migrants within in NEI? How do the natives treat the migrants today? What is position of Church on the issue of illegal migrants in NEI?

Secondly, a concrete strategy for practical action to address the issue of migration. Here, question arises as to who is responsible for those vulnerable migrants? Is it home state, society and the church or the host state, society or the church? How are to response the issue? Is it preventing the flow of migration from the home state or place? or it is addressing the situation of migrant in destiny region or cities?

There is no easy or readymade answers to these questions. There are open challenge to all for holistic and retrospective reflections and come up with

44 Pushpa Anbu, "Mission among the Migrants in Bhopal," in *Migration and Mission in India*, edited by L. Stanislaus & Jose Joseph (Delhi: Ishvani/ISPCK, 2007), 149-150.

45 Anati K. Yeptho & Vincent Rajkumar, *The Social Reality* ..., 69.

46 The Pamphlet Reads: "Revealing dress to be avoided. Avoid lonely road/by-lane when dress scantily. Dress according to sensitivity of the local populace," (Delhi Police, 2005), See Duncan Mcduie-Ra, *The North-East Map*..., 72.

practical suggestions on how the complex phenomenon of migration of/in NEI is to be addressed by all concerned institutions such as academia, state, civil society, church and communities as a whole.

Conclusion

Even though a thorough survey of the NEI population in metro cities in India is not available and perhaps it is impossible to make, as many people arrive and leave unregistered, it is still plausible to suggest that many thousands come to stay in cities. Due to the unfavourable economic environment, the unstable political situation and the lack of diversified college education, many North East people migrate to cities in search of education and employment opportunities. Therefore, assuaged by a mixture of necessity and opportunity, the North East people migrate to cities. They inhabit the social space of the cities and benefit from the economic and opportunities it offers, but they remain socially excluded from the main stream. They do not fit into the shared imaginary of what represents Indian-ness in terms of culture, religion or even facial features, and they are often stereotypically perceived as foreigners of morally questionable character. Daily Newspapers are interspersed with news about molestation, abuse by landlords and employers and various forms of sexual assaults committed against the North East people. Caught between the extremes of economic inclusion and social exclusion, the NEI migrants are to navigate their way in the strange lands. The great challenge remains, "What is the way out?" and "Who should help whom?"

III

TOWARDS THEOLOGY OF MIGRATION

11

Migration
Exploring a 'We Communion Theology'

J. Daniel Kirubaraj

Migration is universal phenomenon which theologically speaking is within the scheme of God's creation itself. It is the natural and common experience of an individual and corporate human and other creatures' in time and space. The human experience of migration involves personal, social, political, technological, religious, and economic realms of life. Birds and animals migrate during specific seasons and procreate their species wherever sources of life are available sufficiently. It is also natural and seasonal network in which all lives live in support of sustenance of life everywhere and in all times. In this way, migration is one of the ways of living life in communion universally.

Unfortunately, migration seems to have become a humanly induced threat for lives in recent times. The human polity has distressed the process of natural-seasonal cycles of migration. Almost all species experience threat for life due to the endangered eco-human environments. This may be the result of irresponsible and inadequate human management of the nature related systems of life. Anything that endangers the cycle of natural, seasonal and universal mobility of life, distresses not only the course of life but the very core of life.

People manage to cross boundaries of space and time besides socio-religious and political boundaries creating new orders of life.[1] Eventually, this challenges the theological scheme of migration, negating the 'Image of God' being lived in the universal communion of lives. Such non-theological intrusions perhaps create

---

1 According to the highlights of the International Migration Report published on 18th December 2017, by United Nations Department of Economic and Social Affairs, "There are now an estimated 258 million people living in a country other than their country of birth... This reflects a modest increase from a 2.8% in 2000. By contrast, the number of migrants as a fraction of the population residing in high-income countries rose from 9.6% in 2000 to 14% in 2017. This reflects a modest increase from a value of 2.8% in 2000." www.un.org/development/desa/publications/international-migration-report-2017.html (accessed on 22.08.2018).

a vacuum in the theologically comprehended world order of life; practiced from within the community of individuals' plurality.

The theological essence of migrating with liberty is to live the life in its fullness in the world of God. It can be experienced with dignity of life from within the God-shared Self Community both individually as well as collectively. This is claimed because the individual lives the community and form a community; from within and without. Hence, a migrant who lacks this dignity of life is in search of it from any community of individuals. Unfortunately, this seems to be not only impossible, but also in real turns into a death trap in the process of search for live. Neither in their own contexts nor in any other community contexts, could the migrants in our present world live individually or as a community. Millions of migrants are losing not only their self-dignity but their very lives.[2] Yet, evidently, thousands of migrants die in the oceans, deserts, so-called refugee camps and anywhere on their way to a place where they hope to live their lives with certain dignity. Among the many million migrants who survive their fatal journey, hardly a considerable number of migrants find their lives easy and comfortable.

To larger extent, it is a shameful reality that migrants as our contemporaries die desperately and could not live their lives neither in their natives and nor elsewhere in this world of God. That is, all people in general and migrants in particular, in this our world of developments, constantly seek for a definite cultured life. In all these, it is clear to us that migration is not only a matter of living the lives somewhere and somehow in the vast time and space of God. It is also seeking for a possible theological experience of maintaining a culture of 'We Communion.'

The above discussed phenomenon and challenges of migration demand answers to following basic questions: Is migration a suffering of the humankind? If migration a demand for a new and meaningful communication. How the 'We Communion Theology' can be a 'way of life' in the present scenario of migration?

In making attempt to answer these questions, the author employs the explorative method.[3] This method is preferred here because it gives certain liberty

2 For example, the Berlin based International Organization for Migration's Missing Migrants Project (MMP) Report published on 23 February claims, "…6,142 deaths and disappearances were recorded during migration globally last year (2016), the third consecutive year that more than 6,000 fatalities were recorded by the project. Since IOM began tracking migrant deaths in 2014, nearly 26,000 fatalities have been recorded – but this is likely only a fraction of the real number of deaths on migratory routes worldwide… on the continent of Africa, MMP recorded more than 1,700 migrant deaths, with over 690 reported in the Sahara Desert." These are only two examples among the numerous statistics given on migrants' death from other parts of the world.
https://reliefweb.int/report/world/6000-migrant-deaths-recorded-2017-only-fraction-real-number-worldwide-gmdac (accessed on 22.08.2018).

3 Explorative method is receptive to new ideas and unusual thoughts which change the course of research to get new ideas and change the focus of attention simply because they are keen to learn about the new possibilities in the given field of study. In the absence of any formal design,

to seek new avenues of views other than already established ones. And it is assumed possible through asking questions.[4] Summoning the benefit of searching for new and feasible theological and communication scheme of migration, it is hoped that we could leap from the massively known and technically powered mass and cyber communication into a practically enriched 'We Communion' by critically looking into certain scholarly defined and traditionally dominant ideas of living the life with dignity. It is aimed here to go beyond the academic study about migration, to reveal, to realise and to propose 'We Communion Theology' for a wider practical and theological relationship, especially from the perspective of migrants who are pushed to the point of death. However, it is just an exploration in a way to lay the ground work for further reflection.

Migration and Migrants

In the process of promoting a 'We Communion Theology' as a way of life to answer questions raised earlier, migration is deliberated here as 'a daring and desperate search for life, in and through the ways of death of those migrants, who for sure do not see any other way to live their lives and survive in this world'. This meaning of migration is preferred here to distinctively identify the migrants, from those immigrants who with certain job guarantee stay in a foreign lands legally or illegally.[5] Further, migrants meant in our exploration here is not those who migrate to other places stay as refugees and come back home after some time. Migrants we mean here are those who leave their natives in search for a life affirming community, not knowing their destiny; but their undue death.

The cases of migrants whose predicament of life is as described above, obviously, are on the rise. Surprisingly, migration as it might be shocking but yet in real, can be easily attributed to the on-growing global free market economy systems.[6] In our globalised world of economy, migrants are welcomed or rejected on the basis of one's economic affluence. This is also nationally legitimised and internationally implemented with political and religious impulses. Yest, it is perhaps a reality that to millions of people around the world today, migration is the only option to continue their lives even at the cost of emptiness or death. Logically, this reality can be claimed as a forced social misery. Hence, migration

---

the imagination of the researcher posits the vital crux. Paul Kumar, http://preservearticles.com/2012022523768/what-is-exploratory-research-method.html, (accessed on 04.04.2018).

4 Patricia Shields and Rangarajan, N, *A Playbook for Research Methods: Integrating Conceptual Frameworks and Project Management* (Still Water. OK: New Forums Press, 2013).

5 Emigration means to leave one's country to live in another. Immigration is to come into another country to live permanently. Migration is to move, like birds in the winter. The choice between emigrate, immigrate, and migrate depends on the sentence's point of view. https://www.vocabulary.com/articles/chooseyourwords/emigrate-immigrate-migrate/ (accessed on 28.08.2018).

6 For proper understanding of this, see the previous article – "Manipulation of Migrant Labour Flow and Capital Accumulation by Free Market Economy" by Livingstone Arputharaj.

of migrants is seen as a theological arena and expedition for exploring for a 'We Communion'.

Migration and Theology

Theology is *the field of study that treats God and God's attributes and relations to the universe; study of divine things or religious truth; divinity.*[7] Theology could also be redefined from the perspective of communication as "God being in Communion within God's Self Community and with God's-self extended world community, which is the fullness of Creation." Apparently, in the very act of creation, God extends God's Self-Communion in and through the very Nature and the Human individual's selves (Gen. Chaps 2-3). This theologically is the *Theos* and *Logos* mutually migrating one into the other. This perhaps could be the possible model of moving around everywhere and at all times to live the God-shared life, in communion with God and the entire creation of God.

One may question how migration can be theological. As described above, basically migration itself is seeking communion within one's self and it culminates only when it gets communed with other individual selves. Migration is therefore theological and a continuous theological event seeking to be in communion within the God-extended God-world-community.[8] Any individual lacking this becomes a non-theological, a selfish individual self and the one who does not care for same God's-Self lived by others. This theological dynamics of migration identifies the majority sophisticated settlers who do not welcome strangers as non-theological; and the very minority migrants who are in search for communion and those accept them, indeed are theological.[9]

The 'We Communion Theology' proposed here refers to such theological identity of oneness shared by humankind. It is an individually lived community model, derived from within the Trinitarian Community of God. In this divinely shared human identity with self-esteem of life, no one is lesser than the other. In terms of living this God shared 'We Communion Theology', the dignity of life is extended to the whole creation and is communicated practically into the reality of life in the world.

How do we connect or apply the conceived 'We Communion Theology' practically in the calamitous lives of migrants? A theological concept proposed here is 'We-ness' as way of life. This calls our attention to live one's 'I' subjectively in one's self and live the same 'I' theologically in the other 'I' individuals. This

7 www.dictionary.com/browse/theology?s=t, 04.04.2018, 15:35 p.m.

8 As such the Trinitarian Community God conceives within God's Self, i.e. the intrapersonal communication; delivers the world and humans through the Word-in Action, i.e. communi-action; Communes continually with the creation through incarnation i.e., migration (Matt.28:18-20); and awaits for the fulfilment or complete communion, i.e., eschatological judgement.

9 As defined in Luke 13: 22-30.

way of living one's 'I' in the others' 'I' is a theologically dignified and embracive way of living the God Community. On this basis, each 'I' member of the 'We' Community individually live one's own 'I' without discriminating the collectively lived many 'I' individuals. Thus, anyone is everyone's individual. These individuals collectively are the integrated 'We' community of God. As such the communion and the oneness shared by all is the 'We Communion Theology.' In that sense, all individuals are equally part of the other individual selves. With this conceptual understanding, question of whether migration is a suffering to the humankind is focussed and reflected here.

Migration and Suffering

Dictionaries define Migration as seasonal movement of birds, fishes, group of people from one part to another to find work or better living conditions.[10] Looking at the migration of birds and animals, one can therefore perceive how natural migration is a part of God's plan for lives to be lived universally. However, migration in the present times seems to be rooted deeply in the complexities of communion[11] than a mere attempt to 'find a work' or 'seek better living conditions.'[12] It is apparent that the natural, universal, eco-friendly migration which once was a life facilitating cultural communion has now become a hazard in the recent past. Moreover, 'Migration has become death-trap to all living species including humankind'. For example, millions of birds on migration are killed each year by communication towers and tall buildings.[13] Perhaps, the suffering of many who migrate seems to be their last step before their death. For people migrates risking their lives. It seems that migrants suffer voluntarily and conscientiously.

10 The two primary resources being sought are food and nesting locations. www.allaboutbirds.org/the-basics-how-why-and where-of-bird-migration/ (accessed on 04.04.2018).

11 Non realisation of the equal self-values and the possibility of accepting to live other selves in one's own-self theologically, because of the pressing socio-economic and political constraints of the divided world. With reference to Lev.19:13-18; Luke 10:27; Mark 12:30-31; Luke 15:32; John 15:13; 17:20-23.

12 We need a total human development approach, even if our immediate goal might be economic development. The latter, of course, is not the end in itself, but only a means to enable human beings to live more humanly. *For a man may be rich and still live like a pig.* Economic development doesn't help him. V. Genaro Ong, Jr. *From the Village to the Medium* (Manila: Communication Foundation for Asia, 1976).

13 www.allaboutbirds.org/the-basics-how-why-and where-of-bird-migration/ (accessed on 04.04.2018).

Humans migrate on their own choice[14] or even forced[15] into a 'modern slave trade', especially the women and children. Since legal migration is costly, some opt internationally schemed illegal smuggling or trafficking. They let themselves to get exploited with forced labour or sex slavery and be 'reduced to a mere instrument of another's will.'[16] Within the international law, trafficking is an exploitative slavery forced on migrants and such migration is illegal. In the words of Julia with reference to Quintana, "Though the factors that underpin migration in the contemporary world are many and varied international debt and the neoliberal policy measures with which it is associated forms part of the background context against which many people make the decision to migrate."[17]

The migrants also suffer new[18] and dynamic[19] contexts of cultural decline. On arrival, they undergo severe debt obligations. Therefore, they are made as contract workers, controlled, supervised, intimidated and threatened[20] to be or to become 'willing slaves'. They suffer and obligate themselves as 'commodities on terms favourable to their buyers.'[21]

All the more, when people decide to migrate, they convey a definite message to others that they are prepared to suffer from outside of their own community.[22] It is unusual and a strange for people to opt to suffer; to being determined to explore their selves from yet other stranger-selves to whom they can hardly belong to; seeking acceptance mostly from a cold-blooded mob-communities. If there

14 As seen in the case of Adam and Eve (Gen. 3:1-7) and in the parable of Lost Son (Luke. 15:11-13); in the interest of extravagant life. Making a choice to move away from a responsible community communion and opting an irresponsible, ungodly selfish and divided community life.

15 As in the case of Joseph (Gen.37:12-28).

16 B. Anderson and J. O'Connell Davidson, *Is Trafficking in Human Beings Demand Driven? A Multi-Country Pilot Study. IOM Migration Research Series, No.15* (Geneva: IOM, 2003).

17 V. Quintana, G. Gonzalez *et al.* as quoted in B. Anderson and J. O'Connell Davidson, "Troubling Freedom: Migration, debt, and modern slavery" in *Migration Studies*, vol.1, issue 2, (1 July, 2013): 176-195.

18 In the context of new flora and Fauna: plants and animals besides all inanimate beings. Casey E.S, "How to Get from Place to Space in a fairly short of Time: Phenomenological Prolegomena", in *Senses of Place*, edited by Stephen Feld and Keith H. Basso (New Mexico: School of American Research Press, 1996), 26-38.

19 *The self does not know itself immediately by the detour of the cultural signs of all sorts which are articulated on the symbolic mediations which always already articulate action and, among them, narratives of everyday life.* P. Ricoeur, "Narrative Identity," in *On Paul Ricoeur: Narrative and Interpretation*, edited by D. Wood (London: Routledge, 1991), 188-199.

20 J. Cole and S. Booth, *Dirty Work: Immigrants in Domestic Service, Agriculture and Prostitution in Sicily* (New York: Lexington, 2007).

21 Anderson and Davidson, "Troubling Freedom....," 176-195.

22 As in the case of Ruth, when she decided to follow Naomi, her mother-in-law when she returned to Israel from Moab (Ruth 1:15-18).

is liberation for migrants from such suffering, it could be only within the will of God and at the cost of their wilful surrender to certain theological scheme.

Based on the above argument, migration as defined earlier refers to the migrants' journey leaving their own community contexts desperately, in search for a better community context for livelihood.[23] In doing so, all migrants lose their self-identities and the very dignity of their lives both in their own and other communities. It also relates to their preparedness to suffer and to live an unknown and undignified life without any community values. In this manner of migration, migrants suffer their lives practically and yet with a desperate hope against every hopeless situation. In doing so, migrants practice and preserve their faith and readily offer their services to those others in the given affluent supportive or oppressive or manipulative community contexts.[24] Such suffering is the theological fact that migrations imply to our world. Thus, the migration of the present times, calls the whole humankind to a feasible and better theological way of life to be shared with the migrants. This theological way of life necessitates for a 'We Communion', which is community communication different from the present media influenced, profit and popular oriented world of virtual communication.

Migration and Communication

Migration like communication makes all efforts to live the lives in an accepted community context. Basically, this human-urge to be in communion with others from within and without one's self has now become an on-going struggle. The struggle is about how to share one's self-dignity with others in the world of know-how.

In the process of seeking communion, basically it is the 'Intrapersonal Communication' which becomes the ground for people to communicate *from* within and *to* one's own-self. As such, one needs to maintain a balance between *self* and *selfish* as well as *rational* and *emotional* dividedness. In doing so, it is hoped that this helps one to experience a flawless interactive communion and community experiences from within one's self. Also, only with this individually balanced self-communion one can own another self through the next level of one to one 'Interpersonal Communication'. Eventually, this communion of selves can also be practically experienced in small and big 'Group Communication'. This self-identity valued human-dignity could practically be shared at large through the media channelled Mass Communication and thereby communication transformed into *communi-action* with 'We Communion' theological values.

23 T. Bastia and S. McGrath, *Temporality, Migration and Unfree Labour: Migrant Garments Workers, Working paper no. 6, Manchester Papers in Political Economy* (Manchester University of Manchester, 2011).

24 As in the case of Joseph in the Old Testament (Gen. chaps. 37-50) and Jesus, the Christ in the New Testament (Phil. 2:1-11).

In contrary, communication today seems to fail to unite people in real life.[25] As Hena Fisk observes, mass media today, 'are bias in spreading news about migration or human trafficking issues related to India or other Asian countries; but are ignorant and silent about migration in the USA'.[26] Genaro V. Ong also argues that "*...one of the banes of modern mass production techniques - despite their obvious benefits - is that they tend to dehumanize people and turn them into masses.*[27] It is also said, "*...too much preoccupation with style and technique can be a hindrance to communication, not to call attention to itself.*[28] Thus, mass communication although claimed to develop human life, it can be far from helping people to be socially democratic and participatory. Nevertheless, they can be better used to change people's socio-cultural environments than shaping them to be masses. As B.R. Ambedkar, the Indian jurist suggests, 'Primarily a model of life associated to conjoint communication experience promotes an attitude of due respect and reverence towards other fellow-beings.'[29]

Mass media in their mass communication, in fact, are not totally hostile to the migrants. They also play vital roles in the making of the life of migrants. For example, Communication strategies of the International Organization for Migration (IOM) represent their perspectives specific to communication about migration and with migratory peoples. The television documentaries present the plight of migrants in the prime time broadcast, help to clarify migration issues, to convey strong, simple, practical and persuasive messages of campaigns organised by humanitarian and relief organisations, returnees and migrant's first-hand information.

Migration magazines too function as effective tools to bring migration related information to a wide audience; brochures, handbooks are distributed through NGOs or schools and inform details of migration to people. Simple printed materials with issues of major migrant and public interest presented on a country-by-country include sections on family reunification. Networking and seminar tours provide people concrete legal information about realities of migrants.[30]

---

25 'Media colonize young minds with false promises and attractions. Entertainment media penetrate into home and individualise members through internet and mobile devices. Mobiles with internet are inevitable and irreversible, they rule or ruin home communities and affect individual's personality, psychology and cognition'. Wenisch, S. "New Wine in New Skin: Modernising Youth Movement" in *Rally*, vol. 92, no: 3 (August 2014): 09-10.

26 Hena Fisk, "Media bias on Human Trafficking", in *Rally*, vol. 92, no: 3 (August 2014): 15.

27 Genaro V. Ong, Jr. *From the Village to the Medium* (Manila: Communication Foundation for Asia, 1976).

28 Genaro V. Ong, Jr. *From the Village to the Medium* (Manila: Communication Foundation for Asia, 1976).

29 Durgam Subbarao, "Some notes on Quintessence of Ambedkarism" in *Rally*, vol. 92, no: 3 (August 2014): 16-23.

30 www.comminit.com/global/content/developing-communicationstrategies-international-organization- migration-iom (accessed on 27.03.2018).

Yet, what is positively done to migrants in these ways remain at minimum level compared to those millions of migrants who are left to suffer. Rather surprisingly they seem to have very little room for humans. As such, communication has superseded human concerns. For example, migration in Information Technology (IT) refers to the process of ...*upgrading to new hardware, new software or both.*[31] In that process, the new environment's features are exploited, old settings do not require changing and that current applications continue to work. Similarly, data migration in communication means transfer of data between data storage systems, data formats or computer systems.[32] More and above, there are Software migration, System migration, and Digital migration and so on.[33]

As a result of these technological migrations, the human community communication had shrunken its frontiers due to world of reasons. In the history of communication, humans have experienced migration from cave drawings to the internet based web blogs. This history proves to us, beyond any doubt that communication possibilities have minimised self-values and relatedly the self-dignity of the humankind. This is made clear to us as Margaret Rouse writes: "The social lives of many (young) people today revolve around social media and blogging, and this isn't necessarily healthy. You lose sense of reality when all of your communication is conducted electronically."[34] Though the scientific inventions have made our world a 'Global Village', information as communication with less relationship among people dominantly is Virtual and is *Cybernetic*. The worst possible level in this regard is, humans migrating into Cyber-world. Against such communication Catherine Steiner-Adair while referring to Mary Aiken alarmingly warns that "Increase in the use of internet communication dominates human life, changes fundamental human behaviour, compiles people to be more secretive, more cruel and disconnected from becoming better selves and responsible for others."[35]

To add more, humanity had already begun to migrate from 'man-machine interactive' communication into a fully Robot co-lived and Robot ruled world. A news in the *India Times* on November 27, 2017 gives a detail reports that "The era of intelligent machines is well and truly upon us. After Sophia was confirmed as the first robot citizen in Saudi Arabia last month, it's time for us to gape in awe

31 Margaret Rouse, WhatIs.com Contributor(s): ... (accessed on 27.03.2018).

32 Margaret Rouse, WhatIs.com Contributor(s): ... (accessed on 27.03.2018).

33 The digital business triggers 'physical to virtual' migration of data, the massage from computer main disk to a virtual machine or a disk partition. The 'virtual to virtual' is migration of data from a virtual machine to another virtual machine. 'Virtual to Physical' means migration of data from a virtual machine to computer's main hard disk. Margaret Rouse, WhatIs.com (accessed on Contributor(s): ... (accessed on 27.03.2018).

34 www.creativedisplaysnow.com/articles/history-of-communication-from-cave-drawings-to-the-web/ (accessed on 13.04.2018).

35 Catherine Steiner-Adair, www.washingtonpost.com/opinions/who-are-we-and -who-are-we-becoming--in the cyber-world (accessed on 14.04.2018).

at SAM, who's become the world's first Al-powered virtual politician from New Zealand.[36]

It is claimed for serious consideration 'who and why in the world of Robots bothers about human migration?' Sarcastic it may be, yet this question raises serious concerns that the communion and community centred theological values seem to be of no more a concern of human communication. Yet, theologically it is pertinent to those who want to be more human in the God intended way of living their lives; preserving the communion of selves with God and with the whole of creation.

The above discussions reveal to us that in the world today, people communicate with others superficially and miss rationale of fully involving their inner selves in the making of the We Communion of the immediate and extended communities. Communication is now possible without communion with one another and community values. Evidently, now communication is primarily a science and so it neither has room for God values nor for We Communion Community values. Also, it is evident that while people communicate with others, they do it superficially without a rationale for maintaining relationship and so do not fully involve their inner selves. This seems to have made communication possible without people's communion which declines the community values. When a common person involves communication as a social science s/he may not have God values in it. Thus such communication will lack the We Communion values. Whereas, when people in the theological community communicate they will continue to strive to live one's self in the every other self. If it is done so, there will not be a migrant suffering to death in our God world for want of communing community.

Sufficient is discussed on how communication is the very in-built human activity. Unfortunately, evacuating the very humanness from human communication will minimise the dignified relational communion and curtail certain community responsibility. With this understanding, migration is posited within certain theological concerns so as to propose a 'We Communion Theology' as a new way of life, in the contexts of increasing number of migrant deaths in the world today.

We Communion Theology

Etymologically, the meaning of the English word 'We' refers to two or more individuals. For a better understanding, let us equate 'We' with *YAM* in *Tamil* language.[37] In Tamil, though the word *Yam* generally refers to any one individual, it also carries the plural value of many individuals and thus convey inclusiveness.

---

36 Jayesh Shinde, "Meet SAM, World's 1st Al-Powered Virtual Politician Hoping to Contest Elections by 2020," India Times.com (accessed on 27.03.2018).

37 Tamil is a very ancient and rich language spoken in the state of *Tamilnadu* in the Southern part of India.

It may, hence, be concluded that *YAM* is the 'I' with the We-ness of other individuals.

To explain it in another way, in English, just as we suffix *s* to a singular noun to make its plural form, such as pen***s***, pencil***s***, tree***s***[38] and so on, the word 'we' can be otherwise understood as '**I*s***'. It is suggested so because, theologically, the God's 'I' signifies God's 'We' meaning, proposing a theological value with reference to the grammar of God language.

This change in the very meaning of how the 'I' is being the 'We' as purposed here because, it is believed useful and practical to establish the God-intended value/s of being oneself and at the same time, being an equal partner responsibly with every other individual I*s*. It is in this way of living the lives anyone can help everyone/migrant as the universal partner of the theological personhood. It is in this shared personhood the full theological meaning of communion and community is claimed. It is believed that the 'We Communion Theology' will help every individual to being and becoming one and the many within the God's theological scheme of living the We Communion, Community and Communication.

Interestingly, the above claimed theological 'We Communion' with a plural expression of I*s* is also found in *Hebrew* language. Theologically, God the *Theos* Self, reveals God's Self in the *Logos* inherent in God and incarnated in the world, who is Jesus, the very God-Word, who is spoken and lived in God-Spirit; who also is within God's Self; and is the God-shared God's Breath in every part of the whole creation; especially to the humankind. Thus, the only I-God, who is also lived in the three I*s* Trinitarian Communion shares the very God's We/I*s* community which is the theological and practical *Communi-action*. This *communi-action* is the theological and holistic communication. It is to experience the theologically inherent communion of God in individuals and simultaneously experiencing the same God-shared self from other individuals; and altogether being part of God Community. As God lives in this way, God also helps God's people to live so in God's world, theologically.

Also one needs to know the relatedness between the words Communion, Community and *Communi-action* here. The noun form of the word 'Communion' here is claimed theologically as a verb *communi-action*. It means, to God what is said is also done in the same way as of the Word; and at once. Thus, to God and all God's people, communication truly is *communi-action*. It is a God shared Community I/We experience of being one and the same in the Communion of God.

Summarily, the 'We Communion Theology' proposed here affirms the theologically interwoven cultural relationship between God, Nature and Humans. In this God initiated, God shared theologically cultured communion, the commonly shared and lived cultural essence is, the very *God-Breath*. Thus, the very Breath of God enables all living beings to be part of the We Communion

38 Bold for highlighting and italicised for emphasis.

and provides the theological precept of communi-acting. That is, migrating to any place at any time and to celebrate this universal cultural community life with a liberty to live. This theological cultural communion is perhaps practical both globally and locally, and it can be the norm to experience the highest decree of the fullness of life. For the fullness of life, theologically, cannot be any other thing but the commonly shared oneness, and is the very inclusive Community of God where communication practically turns into *Communi-action*.

The challenge here we have is to change the mere scientifically upheld and technologically globalised mere information sharing mass, digital and cyber kinds of communication into a complete *Communi-action* where the migrant have-nots will have a lot to be shared equally and rightfully in the world of the haves.

In real life, on the one hand, our scientifically prompted hi-tech communication world seems to dismay migrants miserably. On the other hand, the church as a theological community struggles to promote the 'God-Cultured We Communion'[39] for the people to live together in harmony and address the on-going misery of migrants. The irony is neither the philosophical religious majority[40] nor the theological minorities in India cease to communicate God-matters with certain hidden political agenda, locally and globally. In doing so, it only increases distress on individual and collective migrants.

To address this challenge, an effort is made here to posit migration as people being in search for a meaningful 'We Communion Theology'. Thereby, an appeal is made to the church at large, in being and becoming a responsible theological community involving *Communi-action*. In doing so, it is hoped to maintain the individuals' self-dignity reflecting God shared God's Self-Image in the We Communion. This is believed to being the very theologically cultured way of living the life locally and globally.

Theologically, to be in communion with others, one has to empty one's selfish self to the benefit of others. The emptying process of one's selfish self could happen all at once or gradually. In this process of emptying of oneself, others get helped to gain their lost self-value.

God emptied God's-self for the first time at creation and made the world complete and filled it with the sources of living the life. When the creation had to get apart from God and God set values of life, the need for meaningful communion arose. Whenever, defective and greedy systems and structures gripped the human community, communication too became the tool of confusion. It resulted with severe constrains in the way of living the communion of God, Nature and Humans.

---

39 The Kingdom of God, as envisioned at the creation event, established in and through Jesus and his Ministry and continued through the ministry of Holy Spirit; within and outside the church. As mentioned in Isaiah 11:4-9.

40 For example, the *Hindus* in India and their astounding philosophical (knowledge based) religious justification of human sufferings and lesser connectedness to cultural commitment for the preservation of the nature.

When such confusion struck the individuals' ways of life, humans became selfish. This non-theological way of life severely affects the selfless minority leading to lose their identity from among their own community and to become isolated. It is this ex-communication makes one to move elsewhere as a migrant.

The human migrants migrate mainly because of people's unwillingness to share their life and life-resources with one another. In such worldly, accumulative selfish and greedy world, God, within God's scheme of salvation becomes the companion of the migrant 'wanderers' and reunites God's Self with them in and through their suffering. In this way of the incarnation of God in this world and the Reign of God becomes the very theological community of God; who maintain the relational centred communication. Communication otherwise is a communion denied non-theological community activity. It claims to create community but not the communion. Migration thus is theological and it is a search for the way of living life within the culture of God Communion. Thus, migration in the context of Nature and through responsible self-sharing individuals and with the guidance of the Holy Spirit turns into the wandering and powerful presence of God Communion Theology in real.

Unfortunately (?) members of the church today seem to miss this theologically cultured life in their community. God present communion, community and *communi-action* values seem to be missing in our churches. Therefore, we see an endless migration of its members from one church to the other; and wherever possible migrate to adopt certain philosophical community values of other religions.

In this context, it is crucial to ask, what is the ultimatum of such wanderings? What could be the way out to being the united communion and community of God at local, national and global scenario? Are the Ecumenical ways of Christian life an answer to the wandering theological community? What goes wrong with our so-called church structures and systems? Is there a difference between the theologically cultured polity of the church community and the non-theological or other secular ones? Ultimately, the theological question that reflects all concerns mentioned above is 'should the church be on migration or not?'

A theological answer to this pertinent question brings in the hope for eschatological events in the minds and hearts of migrants. In and through migration, the migrants keep their hope alive in God. One can realise, this could be the true living of migrant's hope theologically, even if it is not possible with the others who confess it in the church regularly. One needs to wait for the second coming of Jesus Christ, to make things clear as to if the migrants are part of true theological communion and community. Till then, the 'Grace of God' will let the theologically cultured minority migrants and majority civilised powerful settlers to go on living their lives in their own ways.

The above discussion show us that migration in the plan of God, is a possible theological journey that all could experience in the world of God. However, some within the theological purposes pursue it. Many with their non-theological way of living their life make it a curse on the minority migrants. The church however, is seems to be at the cross roads of being theological or not being theological. With this understanding, the study further moves on to suggest how the We Communion Theology posit the issue of migration culturally.

At this juncture, to understand the newly comprehended 'We Communion Theology', a new theoretical proposal is made on basis of communication process.[41] In the We Communion Theology, the Creator God is the **Sender.** God as the **Sender** shares God-Property which is God Communion, is Theology.[42] God communes with the creation through the spoken, written and incarnated *God-Word Jesus, the Truth* who becomes the **Message.**[43] This God shared, 'God Word' Jesus is the message and is being lived in and through *the Holy Spirit*, who is the **Channel**. Of this God shared Jesus and the Holy Spirit, the creation and humans are the **Receivers**. In this manner of God becoming one with the creation and the humankind is the We Communion Theology, the **Effect.**

In such effective, contextual, practical and ethical viable We Communion Theology is the possibility for all to celebrate the 'We-ness', in our individual **Experience**. This experience, in fact, is the We Communion, lived theologically and culturally. That is, every living being and individuals are theologically living one in the other.

Migration as a theological journey in search of living one's life in the other would also mean the process of pro-creation, with which one's life be survived and lived in one's offspring in this world of God; vertically over time and horizontally in the space. As this cultural sequence goes on without break, life is preserved with community values; without losing God Community identity; and it will be lived continually for ever generation after generation. Indeed, this responsible sharing of God shared God Self as the community of God is the 'We Communion Theology'; and which is also the God set cultural way of life.

Essentially, the We Communion is highly theological and wholly practical in its nature. Why because, this is the Trinity-God's way of life. Where in, the God-Communion, God-Community and God-Communi-action become its cultural bases for all that exist and live. It means, culturally, every being has originated and have come to exist independently forever from within God. From such God's cultural extension, since creation, the Nature had become the context

41 Parallel to H.D. Lasswell's Model of Communication (1948) in which the Sender, Message, Channel, Receiver and the Effect are the basic elements of Communication. In addition, from Wilbur Schramm's Model of Communication (1954), the Field of Experience is also is adopted here.

42 The Greek term *Theos* refers to God and *Logia* refers to 'communication of divine origin', which also in Jewish and Christian traditions means 'the divinely inspired Scriptures'.

43 Both absolutely relative and relatively absolute – solving the theological and philosophical constraints related to the Truth.

to live this theological We Communion. This We Communion Theology, while being continued in history, practically becomes a God + Nature + Human Culture (GNH Culture); and a complete and continued migration of theological selves both individually and collectively.

Thus, the GNH Culture[44] is indeed, the 'We-ness' God Community and in that community, theologically, there could not be any difference among the 'I – individual selves'. This being the strength and fullness of the We Communion Theology, it is claimed that Migration is a desperate search for recognition of an individual self, from the other individual selves from one's own and other's contexts, for a We Communion.

Conclusion

Migration theologically is, 'a search of individuals for a feasible, holistic *We Communion* livelihood, allowing to suffer their God-Shared and divinely dignified *Self-Image*; from among the divided community of selfish-selves who prioritize their 'me' and 'my' agenda. Members of such selfish communities, see migrants with a tag of 'other-ness' and unwanted ones'. Probably, they think so because of their non-theological or wrong theological or philosophical values.

Obviously, migration in the increasing life eliminating contexts, challenges the migrants to live in their own space and time with cultural dignity; be it with humans or other living creatures. Ecologically, celebrating life's plurality in this world is at grave levels. The threats for such 'We Communion', in the present time are also justified and quickened through greedy, selfish, hard-hearted, intolerable, life-killing, war-thirst, global-market-economy based, Techno-Robot-Cyber Communication cultured and irresponsible human polity.

Such subtle but a sure life negating culture of human polity has become the platform not only for the increase of global migration; but also for its innumerable sufferings of humans, the nature and the very values of universal communion. In that process, Migration for many migrants has become a theological journey. Wherein, theology challenges every God Community members to accommodate and accompany those migrants could live their lives with the God shared dignity of life. Since the creation event and throughout its process till now, sharing one's life with the others is still practical and real because, horizontally it occurs in the geographical 'Landscape,'[45] and vertically in the historical 'Here and Now'[46]

44 See also Daniel Kirubaraj, 'Dalit Theology as Communication Theology: Prospect and Problem' in *Gurukul Journal of Theological Studies*, vol. XXIV, Nos. 1&2 (January & June 2013): 139-146.

45 Landscape as spatial 'foreground' of here and potential 'background' space where people, birds, animals meet to share their livelihood. Hirsch, Eric, "Introduction- Landscape Between Place and Space," in E. Hirsch and M. O'Hanlon, eds., *The Anthropology of Landscape: Perspectives on lace and Space* (Oxford: Clarendon Press, 1995), 1-30.

46 With the temporal everyday experiences of the members within the local community and those of other communities who can become part of the community through certain practices

time contexts; in spite of the humanly made life eliminating contexts. As such Migration remains an exploration of this God gifted We Communion Theology.

and at some special times. Julieta Elizaga, "Us and Them: The Landscape Dialogue", in www.academia.edu/1705779/_Oneness_and_Otherness_Self_and_Identity_in_relation_to_material_and_animal_worlds (accessed on 02.04.2018).

12

Discerning the Signs of the Times
Towards a Theology of Migration

N. G. Prasuna

The term migration continues to emerge as a focal subject of media interest in the current times. Migration-related issues are regular features in the headlines. Migration has been an integral part of human history and it contributes to the world economy, to the global societies and to the enrichment of multi-cultural civilization all over the world. At the same time, migration poses a number of challenges. Modern day migration is highly complex. As it is mentioned in previous articles, people migrate for multiple reasons: in search of job, in order to earn better income, to find new avenues in life, for further education, to join families, sometimes due to natural disasters, to take refuge, and so on. Migration may be temporary or permanent; internal or international. The discourse on migration has grown significantly in different disciplines, such as sociology, anthropology, politics, law, communication and economics and of course in the discipline of theology recently.

The purpose of this article is to offer a relevant theology of migration and to stimulate further reflections on how Christian churches can meet the challenges of migration. The theme 'migration' is not a new thing to the Bible.. "The Bible can be read as a book of immigration testimonies" says Miguel A. De La Torres in his "forward" to *Church on the Way: Hospitality and Migration.* The task of formulating theological articulations to the subject migration remains a difficult task. And it requires a serious attention, time and efforts in the coming years. This article takes the concept of identity as a tool to develop the theology of migration. The hypothesis of this article is that migrants undergo identity crisis when they migrate to a different place either internal or international. It acknowledges that there are number of cases where migrants can resolve their identity crisis and achieve identity that carries dignity. At the same time, it also asserts that migrants suffer identity crisis due to multiple factors. The article has its own limitations; it does not deal with either internal or external migration deeply, rather it articulates theology of migration while using some of the experiences of migrants both internal and international with regard to their identity crisis. As we have become part and parcel of migration, the article emphasizes the need to articulate a relevant theology of migration as we discern migration as a sign of the times.

Current Age is an Age of Migration

We live in an age of migration. People are on the move constantly. The IOM guesses that the figure of international migrants could rise to as much as 405 million by 2050.[1] Indian migrants topped the list of international migrants in 2017. A report published by the United Nations said 17 million Indian-born people are international migrants.[2] In the scope of international migration,[3] xenophobia and anti-migrant sentiment[4] is growing day by day.[5] People within India migrate constantly. Chinmay Thumbe argues that India has been a witness to a 'culture of migration' for over a century and around 200 million people are affected.[6] Migrants, either internal or international, feel uncertainties and identity crisis. Their identity is at stake. Migrants suffer identity crisis due to many challenges such as leaving home, family, friendships, country, culture and an encounter with a new culture, new language, a sense of no belongingness, sense of uprooting from the homeland and replanting in the foreign land and the list goes on.

The causes and effects of migration are many and wide-ranging. The phenomenon of migration sees a strong dichotomy between "the West and the

---

1 Marlene Laruelle, "Introduction" in *Migration and Social Upheaval as the Face of Globalization in Central Asia,* edited by Marlene Laruelle (Boston: BRILL: 2013), 5.

2 Of these, at least 5 million live in the United Arab Emirates and Saudi Arabia and 2 million in the United States of America. "India had the most number of People Living abroad in 2017: UN Report" in *https://scroll.in › India › Indians Abroad* (accessed on 19.3.2018).

3 For International Organization for Migration (IOM) international migration is a "movement of persons who leave their country of origin, or the country of habitual residence, to establish themselves either permanently or temporarily in another country." International Organization of Migration, *World Migration 2008,* 495.

4 Jamie Bordeau, *Xenophobia: The Violence of Fear and Hate* (New York: Rosen Publishing Group. Inc.: 2010), 17.

5 Recent international events such as the global financial crisis, the Arab Spring, Syrian Civil War, the Ebola crisis, terrorism, natural disasters and the rise of the Islamic State of Iraq and the Levant (ISIL), nationalism, global warming and ethnic conflicts, etc., have led to an anti-migrant sentiment in most of the countries.

6 Meenakshi Thapan, Anshu Singh and Nidhitha Sreekumar, "Women's Mobility and Migration: An Exploratory Study of Muslim Women Migrants in Jamia Nagar, Delhi" in *Internal Migration in Contemporary India,* edited by Deepak K. Mishra (New Delhi: Sage Publications: 2016), 47- 48.

rest," "rich and poor," "privileged and underprivileged," and between migrants and locals. The more people migrate, the more hostile public opinion against foreigners turns up. This leads to deadly consequences.[7] The *Times of India* reports the hostile attitude towards internal migrants in Chennai:

> 55-year-old Syed Ahamed, a bed sheet vendor from UP, who was also staying in one of Periamet lodges with his six children, died of cardiac arrest after he was allegedly beaten up by some residents of Anna Nagar who mistook him for a burglar. According to the officials at the Thirumangalam police station where a case has been filed under Section 174 of the IPC, Ahamed in the afternoon of November 15 tried to enter a construction firm in an apartment complex in Anna Nagar to sell his wares. Unable to explain his presence to the residents in a language they understood, Ahamed was roughed up, say police.[8]

Number of similar stories are reported repeatedly. International migrants face violence too. Human Rights Watch (HRW) reports that women and children detained by US Customs and Border Protection (CBP) along the US-Mexico border where about 350 million people cross it each year are regularly held in freezing cells and suffer other harsh treatment.[9] According to reports, hundreds of refugees living in Paris claim that they have been subject to physical abuse and sexual violence from French nationals.[10]

Migration often becomes a religious disaster too particularly in gulf countries. In my personal interview with Isai Priya from Chennai, who is currently a nursing superintendent in Saudi, I learn that it was a cultural shock to her when she entered into the new land, especially when she was asked to wear burka all the time. She further stated that, "foreigners are treated as less spiritual beings, Saudi Arabians don't eat anything given by the foreigners on the grounds of purity. Christians cannot worship on Sunday as it is a working day." This experience put her into her identity crisis.

A migrant student of theology from North India (name is avoided for a few personal reasons) shares her experience, which is a painful experience. Her two years of study in one of the seminaries in South India left her with bad and sad memories. At the end of the two years of training, she said as her tears were

---

7 Judith Gruber, "Remembering Borders; Notes Toward a Theology of Migration," in *Migration as a Sign of the Times: Towards a Theology of Migration*, edited by Judith Gruber & Sigrid Rettenbacher (Leiden: Brill Rodopi: 2015), 80-81.

8 "Tamil Nadu's dark side: Bigotry towards poor migrants," *The Times of India* reports on Dec 1, 2016.

9 Creede Newton, "Women and children detained in 'freezing cells' on US border: HRW" in *https://www.aljazeera.com/topics/people/migrants.html* (accessed on 17.3.2018).

10 "Migrants tell of abuse and violence on the streets of Paris" in https://www.theguardian.com/world/migration (accessed on 17.3.2018).

rolling down, "people mocked at me and they made fun of me when I could not communicate in English." She further says that though she has learnt a lot in the seminary, the unresolved sad memories made her feel vulnerable even after completing her studies. In her new place she encountered language issues and she was shamed by native students. This is a serious psychological identity crisis many people undergo in India. Thus, the issue of migration is not "their" issue alone but also "our" issue. Poverty, powerlessness, language barriers, alien status, lack of identity, discrimination, lack of access to education, health, livelihood, food security, poor living conditions, unsafe, hazardous working conditions, less or no legal protection, lack of information about the rights and application of laws and so on are the salient features of migration. These features lead migrants to identity crisis.

Yet, as on now, theology has made no or very little impact in India on the complex situation of migration. In a modern theological discourse in India, an experience of migration has not been given much importance. Nevertheless, migration is a profound theological theme in the Bible and an extreme sensitivity towards a stranger has been commanded and demanded in Jewish-Christian tradition. Re-visiting the Jewish-Christian theme of migration will provide new insights to a modern theological discourse on Migration. This article tries to develop a theological approach to migration by conceptualizing migration as a sign of the times.

Migration as a Sign of the Times

Biblical theme of migration as an integral part of Jewish-Christian identity calls for a preferential option for the stranger in the current times. Reinhold Niebuhr took his title "Discerning the signs of the time: Sermons for Today and Tomorrow" from Matthew 16:1-3, which is published in 1945. In Matthew 16: 1-3, the Pharisees and Sadducees came to test Jesus and demanded him to show them a sign from heaven. Jesus answered them condemning them for their faithlessness: "O ye, hypocrites.... Can you not discern the signs of the times?" (Mt. 16:1-3).[11] Niebuhr draws his strength from the teachings of Jesus and says that to discern the signs of the time mean to interpret historical events and values in the present context.[12] Niebuhr explains his theme as the "special relevance" of the Christian faith to an "age confronted with so many possibilities...but also confronting

11 Reinhold Niebuhr, *Reinhold Niebuhr: Major Works on Religion and Politics: Leaves from the Notebook of a Tamed Cynic* (This volume is a compilation, notes and chronology) (New York, The Library of America: 2015), 9. Niebuhr focused his address on the United States and specifically on how the Christian faith could help illuminate the country's responsibilities in the new world order, in his context of Nazism, Second World War, American growth as Nuclear weapon, etc.

12 Scott R. Erwin, *The Theological Vision of Reinhold Niebuhr's "The Irony of American History": "In the Battle and above it"* (Oxford: OUP, 2013), 50.

so many frustrations."[13] For Niebuhr Christian interpretation of history should be made directly relevant to the modern age. The age of the Messiah is the age in which the doubts of history are clarified; its frustrations are overcome and human life would flower in a community of perfect peace and harmony.[14] Hence, migration as a sign of the time provides room for articulating theology which is an urgent need of the hour.

For Judith Gruber, "a theological reading of the signs of the times fosters a mutual process of interpretation: borders are interpreted in such a way that life-giving God-talk becomes possible, and simultaneously, borders offer a new language for talking about the life-giving God."[15] Borders are the margins where the migrants are marginalized in fear of security, protecting once identity, stranger mindset, xenophobia, and so on. For Gruber, migration as a sign of the times informs us that a clear fundamental border is drawn today between "us" and "migrants." These borders disclose the dangerous and unstable border drawings of our identities.[16] Judith Gruber gives an example how borders are drawn in migrant context, in his "Notes toward a Theology of Migration":

> Christian theology offers a new language where security might mean giving up everything to follow the Lord. It might mean obeying the law in such a way that it serves the fellow human being. Security for a society might even mean providing resources for widow, orphans and strangers and foreigners.[17]

A theological reading of migration as sign of the times in this article raises the questions: What is the identity of migrants in their new places? Do they face an identity crisis? How do they perceive God's community when they encounter a serious identity crisis? What is the identity of God that migrants can recover and embrace as the image of God? Can God become life-recovering God to their context? To construct theology of migration, this article takes the concept of "identity" as a theoretical tool to investigate migrant context.

Concept Identity

Identities are formed by what people are socialized into. Identity formation is an ongoing process. Identities are derived from a person's one's own self-conceptions, and from the perceptions and declarations of others. Social structures play major role in identity formation of an individual.[18] According to Erik H. Erikson,

13 Erwin, *The Theological Vision…*, 50.

14 Erwin, *The Theological Vision…*, 50.

15 Gruber, "Remembering Borders…," 84.

16 Gruber, "Remembering Borders…," 84.

17 Gruber, "Remembering Borders…," 84.

18 Jenny McGill, *Religious Identity and Cultural Negation: Toward a Theology of Christian Identity in Migration* (Eugene, PICKWICK Publications: 2016), 17.

identity formation focuses on three things: the self (Who am I?), acculturation (With whom do I fit in?), and social identity (What does it mean to be part of the group?).[19] Identity can be tested at personal, social and collective ranks. Personal identities relate to one's individual perception of oneself and this perception is certainly impacted by one's social location. Social identities reflect one's individual identity based on group membership. Collective identities together form group identity.[20]

Erikson was one of the earliest psychologists who were extremely interested in the concept of identity. His theoretical framework rests upon a distinction and a process between the ego identity or the personal identity and social identity or the cultural identity. He spoke of identity as a both conscious and unconscious motivation for continuity of individual personality. He used the term 'identity' to refer to that which results from the 'silent doings of ego syntheses and 'that sense of inner solidarity which deals with values of a significant social group.'[21] He affirmed that the development of a strong ego identity leads a person to a stronger sense of identity in general. That also means that the inferior complex leads a person to a weaker sense of identity. The concept of identity portrays a number of issues such as the conceptualization of race, sex, caste, class, ethnicity, culture and how one articulates beliefs in psychology, sociology, religion, theology and other social sciences. Annie Sophie Roalt defines identity as 'those factors of a person's or a group's belief-system, nationality, ethnicity and class, educational background, rural or urban back-ground, gender or sexuality which are highlighted at certain periods of time and in certain places....[22] So, each human being has multiple identities in multiple contexts based on ethnicity, education, employment, caste, class, race, gender, religion and so on. The identity of migrants is complex, based on the experiences of homeland and host land. Having said that human being has multiple identities in multiple contexts, the section below briefly explores the identity of migrants.

Identities of Migrants

Identities of Migrants are shaped by their own status of homeland, employment status, ownership and social network. These factors are interwoven, leading to

19 William Gaudelli, *World Class: Teaching and Learning in Global Times* (London: Routledge, 2003), 101.

20 McGill, *Religious Identity*..., 17.

21 Jane Kroger, *Identity Development: Adolescence through Adulthood* (New York: Sage Publications, 2005), 7-8.

22 Annie Sofie Roald, "Who are the Muslims? Questions of Identity, Gender and Culture in Research Methodologies" in *Gender, Religion and Diversity: Cross-Cultural Perspectives*, edited by Ursula King and Tina Beattie (London: Continuum: 2005), 184-185.

more than one identity in migrants' narratives.[23] Being a 'migrant' is often a negative identity imposed by the dominant culture on those who migrate. In response to this complex situation, identity is critically analyzed as constructed, multi-faceted, negotiated, situational, or according to some, fragmented.[24] On the one hand, social movements of marginalized people are placing a wide range of identity issues related to class, caste, race, gender inequalities, ethnic and religious persecution on the public. Through these movements, people constitute themselves as social subjects, reasserting and redefining their identity and struggle to achieve an identity that they desire.[25] On the other hand, Amartya Sen, in his work, *Identity and Violence: The Illusion of Destiny* argues that identities are multiple and violence happens when this multiplicity is denied or forcibly removed for the sake of a single identity. Violence also takes place when people hold on to otherness either by excluding or by not including oneself.[26]

According to Amartya Sen, "many of the conflicts and barbarities in the world are sustained through the illusion of a unique and choice less identity."[27] A sense of identity can be a source not merely of pride and joy, but also of strength and confidence. And yet identity can also kill. A strong and exclusive sense of belonging to one group can in many cases exclude from other groups.[28] For Sen, the sense of identity contributes strongly to the strength and the warmth of our relations with others, such as neighbors, or members of the same community, or fellow citizens, or followers of the same religion. Our focus on particular identities makes us do many things for each other and takes us beyond our self-centered lives.[29] At the same time, Sen strongly asserts that, "a sense of identity can firmly exclude people."[30] This exclusion leads to migrant identity crisis in one way or the other.

Identity Crisis of Migrants

Each human being experiences identity crisis at some time in life. Erik Erikson has coined the term 'identity crisis' to describe generally the crisis that brings about identity problems and specially the shell-shocked condition of the war victims that he treated during the Second World War. He says that the patients experienced dilemma that 'they had lost their sense of themselves as having past

23 Rina Benmayor and Andor Skotnes, "Some Reflections on Migration and Identity" in *Migration and Identity*, edited by Rina Benmayor & Andor Skotnes (New Brunswick: Transaction Publishers: 2005), 9-10.

24 *Ibid.*

25 *Ibid.*

26 *Ibid.*

27 Amartya Sen, *Identity and Violence: The Illusion of Destiny* (London: Penguin: 2015), XV.

28 *Ibid.* 1-2.

29 *Ibid.* 2.

30 *Ibid. 3.*

and future.' Their sense of ego identity was severely impaired. Erikson came to an understanding that identity confusion associated with ego identity impairment among young people during the war.[31]According to Erikson, identity confusion is manifested in terms of 'contradictory self-images, or aspirations, roles or opportunities or as split of self-images, a loss of center and a dispersion.'[32]

This is what exactly happens in migration. According to psychologists, the events of leaving one's own homeland and adjusting to the host land bring identity crises into the lives of migrant.[33] The social identity that is integral part of life of seems to be in danger in the context of migrants. Therefore Michael Pavlasek, says that:

> It is justifiable to say that migration is a crisis situation because the migrants have to cope with a range of obstacles such as unfamiliarity with the new environment and the local language, preserving the dominant culture and facing the uncertainty of the future. Migration can thus be a cause of crisis, an identity crisis.[34]

Migrants are vulnerable and face identity crisis at various levels. Erikson elaborated the idea that the identity crisis leads to reformulation and a gaining of a sense of personal stability. The process of identity formation is always associated with feelings of insecurity and risk. Identity crisis, which is created by migration, is closely related to the phenomenon of cultural shock and an adaptation stress. It is a natural psychological reaction to a strange environment. "Migration, which is the process of leaving the homeland and adapting to a new environment, meant that each migrant was faced with his/her identity crisis."[35]

James E. Marcia's work on identity status addresses the role of ideological exploration in human maturity and development.[36] From his research, Marcia has come to a conclusion that four identity statuses, such as Identity Diffusion which characterizes low commitment and low exploration, Identity Foreclosure that contains high commitment and low exploration, Identity Moratorium which portrays low commitment and high exploration, and Identity Achievement

---

31 Erik Erikson, *Identity: Youth and Crisis* (1968). Cited by Cote James E, Charles G. Levine, *Identity Formation, Agency, and Culture: A Social Psychological Synthesis* (Lawrence Erlbaum Associates, Inc. Publishers. 2002), 91-99.

32 *Ibid.* 95.

33 Michal Pavlasek, Brno, "In a New Homeland: Adaptation Strategy and Overcoming Discontinuity of Czech Migrants in Banat" in *Cultures of Crisis in Southeast Europe*, edited by Kalua Roth & Asker Kartari (Berlin, LIT: 2016). 127.

34 *Ibid.*

35 *Ibid.* 122-123.

36 James E. Marcia, "Theory and Measure: The Identity Status Interview" in *Capturing I: Quantitative and Qualitative Methods*, edited by Meike Watzlawik & Aristi Born (Lanham: University Press of America: 2007), 4.

which characterizes high commitment and high exploration. Every individual is a combination of these four statuses.[37]

Memories of exclusion, alienation and marginalization and discrimination play strong role in the identity formation processes.[38] The rhetorical questions 'Who am I' and 'Where am I' and "With whom I am connected to" lead to 'Identity Achievement' as proposed by Marcia.[39] Rooted in Marcia's theory, J Phinney, who has focused her study on ethnic identity identifies three stages: identity diffuse/foreclosed, in which the issue of ethnic identity is unexplored or still to be addressed; identity moratorium in which there is active searching for but not a clear acceptance of ethnic identity; and identity achieved, in which an ethnic identity has been embraced. Acceptance, clear understanding, and a deep sense of belonging to the group characterize the final stage.[40]

Phinney's explanation has strong implications for migrants in their search for identity. Identity diffusion/foreclosure of migrants minimizes themselves from making choices about their future, without questioning them or investigating the alternatives and remain arrested in compromising in their lives. For example, Raphael Hembrom, a 35 years old indigenous Santal Catholic who works at a textile factory in Zirani in Bangladesh, shares his experience as a Christian migrant. He says Lenten season spells gloom every year. He recollects his experience back at his home country, India, "I can still recall my days back home in my village during Lent. I used to join my friends in celebrating the Way of the Cross on Fridays. I found the Lenten songs of sorrow and Jesus' suffering very moving... Since coming to Dhaka, I've been unable to attend the Way of the Cross, Sunday Mass or any religious practice," he told UCANnews.com. He says that he can't even fast on Fridays as he had to work on Fridays. He regrets for being there but he says, "there's nothing I can do."[41] Raphael compromises with the given condition although he is in identity crisis.

The second status Identity moratorium is where individuals in contrast, struggle to accept the given fixed situation and get into a crisis. Migrants in general suffer identity crisis, in spite of being immigrants for several years and have achieved much in terms of their social status. Isai Priya (mentioned in the second section of this article) says that she underwent serious religious identity crisis when she is forced to wear Burka, when she could not worship on Sunday.

37 David Moshman, *Adolescent Psychological Development: Rationality, Morality and Identity* (second Edition) (Mahwah: Lawrence Erlbaum Associates, Inc., Publishers), 83-84.

38 *Ibid.* 87.

39 Marcia, "Theory and Measure...," 4.

40 Jean S. Phinney, "A Three-Stage Model of Ethnic Identity Development in Adolescence" in *Ethnic Identity: Formation and Transmission among Hispanics and other Minorities*, edited by Martha E. Bernal and George P. Night (Albany: New York Press, 1993), 61-80.

41 "Catholic workers in Bangladesh labor over Lent" in *ucannews.com,* Posted on March 18, 2018.

She felt identity crisis when she was treated less human being based on purity aspect. However, she found place in the community of believers, where she finds her religious and social identity is strengthened.

The third status is identity achieved. People with an achieved ego identity have resolved uncertainties about their future direction and have made commitments that will guide future action. For instance, in my conversations with my sister Surekha Nelavala, who moved to the USA almost two decades ago, had many experiences of discrimination of being a woman of color from India, in spite of her achieved identity as a highly educated pastor and scholar both in church and society. And it is common for migrants to face the circumstances of rejection, whether in the progressive societies or in conservative societies. Even though, Surekha has faced many obstacles as a first generation migrant, in many ways, she has overcome the hurdles. She is now a pastor at Evangelical Lutheran Church in America and has started a multicultural congregation, Global Peace Lutheran Fellowship, which she claims as a welcoming space for all cultures. She also sees this as a ministry that is intentional in being multicultural to those who come together to worship and celebrate one another. The ideal outcome of the identity process is an achieved identity, characterized by a clear, confident sense of one's own identity. However, in some countries which are conservative in nature, migrants have no choice but to compromise with the life insecurities.

Migration as a sign of the times sends us indications that migrants are vulnerable and their identity is in crisis when they move to a new land. Here it is argued that the theology needs to be worked out from the perspective of the migrants in order for them to come to an achieved identity status. As Surekha and Isai Priya stated, they could search for their lost identity in the community of believers. The Bible narrates number of stories where Jewish-Christian community was involved in treating the strangers or foreigners and including them into their community. Hospitality towards strangers and solidarity with them is commanded and demanded in the Bible. Biblical history helps us to draw new theological insights to articulate theology of migration which is the need of the hour.

Towards a Theology of Migration

The stories of God's identity as a stranger are visible in the Bible. Abraham and Sarah receive stranger with kind hospitality and discover those strangers came with good news from God. God is depicted as a God on the move. Immigration is a common theme in the Bible and it refers to both God and people. God is a migrant in the Incarnation of Jesus. The Holy Spirit that proceeds from God and Jesus is on the move constantly. Immigrants and refugees play major roles in the biblical stories. God used migrants to accomplish greater purposes. The power of the Holy Spirit pushes and pulls people to migrate in order for them to establish Kingdom of God where there is peace and joy.

God reminds Israelites to remember that they were aliens in a foreign land and commands them that they should welcome the immigrant among them: "When an alien lives with you in your land, do not mistreat him (her). The alien living with you must be treated as one your native born. Love him (her) as yourself, for you were aliens in Egypt. I am the Lord your God" (Leviticus 19: 33-34).[42] It has to be noted with high appreciation that, "The same law applies to the native born and to the alien living among you" (Ex 12:49) and this verdict is repeated throughout the Pentateuch.[43] At the same time, immigrants are treated as vulnerable. Therefore, God commands Israelites to have special concern for them. God commands Israelites to make special provisions for immigrants as well as for orphans and widows (Deut. 24). Many of these biblical imperatives also warn that those who disregard God's instructions, particularly care for the alien and other who are vulnerable, will face God's judgement. The Prophet Malachi compares those who deny justice to immigrants with sorcerers and adulterers (Mal 3:5).[44]

New Testament is rich in dealing with the stories of migration. God the migrant chose to dwell among people through Incarnation. Donald Senior asserts that Jesus begins his earthly journey as a migrant and a displaced person. It has to be noted that when hospitality is not given, Mary and Joseph are unable to find a place to stay and found a place in the manger. They had to leave their own homeland Bethlehem with baby Jesus and arrived in foreign land Egypt as international migrants. There were refugees in Egypt. When the Jesus' family returned from Egypt to their homeland, found that Herod's son was ruling over Judea, the family "withdrew to the district of Galilee, and lived in a town called Nazareth" as internal migrant (2.21-23).[45] Jesus' expression of hospitality to the stranger is a standard principle of judgment. For Matthew, hospitality becomes the customary of salvation: "I was a stranger" unrecognized, "and you welcomed me" (Mt. 25.35). Jesus who lived both as international and internal migrant teaches the importance of hospitality. Paul urges believers to welcome one another just as Christ has welcomed those (Romans 15:7). Love of the stranger remains a fundamental motif of New Testament discipleship.[46] The first group of people who witnessed to the power of the Holy Spirit in Acts were migrants from different parts of the world. The power of the Holy Spirit binds multi-lingual and multi-cultural communities on the day of Pentecost and they were

---

42 *Ibid.*

43 *Ibid.* 86-87.

44 Matthew Soerens & Jenny Hwang, *Welcoming the stranger: Justice, Compassion & Truth in the Immigration Debate* (Downers Grove, Intervarsity Press: 2009), 88.

45 Paul Hertig, "Jesus' Migrations and Liminal Withdrawals in Matthew" in *God's People on the Move: Biblical and Global Perspectives on Migration and Mission* Eds. vanThanh Nguyen & John M. Prior (Eugene: Pickwick Publications: 2014), 49.

46 Donal Kerwin & Jill Marie Gerschutz, *And you Welcomed Me: Migration and Catholic Social Teaching* (Lanham, Lexington Books: 2009), 149.

filled by the Holy Spirit in unity. The sign of the coming of the Holy Spirit (Acts 2) is that the message of Jesus as Messiah is given in the languages of all those migrants assembled in Jerusalem for the feast of Pentecost. Pentecost was a multi-cultural and cross-cultural and multi-lingual gathering. God's mission through the Holy Spirit is always about breaking down barriers erected by human beings and human systems. Succeeding Pentecost, the Book of Acts gives details about the cross-cultural journey undertaken by the Jewish believers to proclaim the message of Jesus. This was not an easy journey at all, there were struggles, conflict and hurdles in this journey.[47]

G. Cruz mentions that theology is a reflection on the transcendent significance of all aspects of human experience, but especially of those aspects in which human dignity and solidarity at stake.[48] Migration plays a major role in relocating human geography in current times and it redefines cultures and religions. Migration is also contributing in reshaping identities and subjectivities. This leads to both new forms of oppression and creating new avenues to human survival and liberation. This dialectic context of migration provides gifts and challenges for theology on main fronts, making migration a valuable sign in articulating contemporary theology of migration. Migrant context discloses that there is a continuous quest for human dignity, identity and life in fullness. Theology is no longer considered as an advocate to a set of doctrines whose meaning is unchangeably fixed. Rather, theology is an adventure of renegotiating and redefining the meaning of these doctrines in each of their new contexts.[49] Against this framework, it is theology's main task to mediate between the normatively defined Christian doctrines and the world today.

God-talk of Migration in the Old Testament: Towards Hermeneutics of Hospitality

The Old Testament portrays God as Migrant from the beginning. Genesis 18 depicts one of the first divine epiphanies of YHWH entering human world in the appearance of a stranger, mysterious appearance in the form of three guests (Gn 18: 1-8). Exodus pictures YHWH where God reveals God's identity to Moses: "I Am Who I Am" at the burning bush (Ex 3:14), which is interlinked with God's activity of liberating and restoring the identity of the strangers in Egypt. Following Exodus event Israel received "covenant identity" with a community endorsed that "there shall be one law for citizen and sojourner alike" (Ex 12.49). And of course,

47 See for further details. T Aechtner, *Health, Wealth, and Power in an African Diaspora Church in Canada* (New York: Palgrave Macmillan, 2015).

48 *Ibid.*

49 Gruber, "Remembering Borders...," 84.

when Israelites broke this covenant they were punished to be under Babylonian captivity.[50]

Hospitality towards stranger is a major biblical theme that provides a paradigm for theology of migration. YHWH the migrant God migrates to humanity in order to receive hospitality and to provide hospitality as well. Hospitality is a sacred duty of Jewish community, consequently, a visitor or a foreigner or a stranger had a right to expect hospitality. Jewish hosts were expected to address the needs of their guests such as food, lodging, protection and escort, and even the defense of the guest with one's life[51] and even rests needed to be provided on the Sabbath day. Hospitality is highly exalted throughout the Old Testament. Israel must ever cherish "the heart of a stranger" (Ex: 23.9). Two prominent stories of women's hospitality needs a mention here: The Prophet Elijah, traveling to a foreign town, asks a widow for hospitality (I Kings 17: 7-24) in the midst of the drought. At the edge of starvation, the widow of Zaraphath shares the last of her resources with Elijah, and receives abundant blessings in return. Another foreigner, a wealthy Sunammite woman provides hospitality to the prophet Elisha (2 Kings 4:9), went to the extent of building a guest chamber for him. And for that she was rewarded with the blessing of a son. Hospitality to the foreigner is commanded by God and it was also rewarded greatly in the Old Testament. Hospitality is considered a virtue (Job 31:32), and referred as poof of true faith in God (Isa. 58: 6-7).[52]

Migration as a sign of the times is a key to our understanding of hospitality. When immigration policies are not human oriented, people are trafficked, they are sexually abused, slaved, and face all kinds of violence. When human communities lose the heart of welcoming the foreigners, migrants become vulnerable. Their identity as God's creation is at stake. Migrants face identity crisis when the community of faith doesn't come forward to uphold them and welcome them. Migration offers a new language for articulating theology. Hospitality towards the stranger is the major theme in the Old Testament. God-talk of migration in the times of Old Testament offers a new hermeneutics of hospitality towards the migrants in the current age. Hospitality and solidarity towards the stranger remains a fundamental motif of New Testament discipleship too.[53] Faith community in various parts of the world needs to re-visit the theme "hospitality towards stranger" as it is a command and demand of God from God's community.

---

50 Ched Myers and Matthew Colwell, *Our God is Undocumented: Biblical Faith and Immigrant Justice* (Maryknoll, Orbis Books: 2012), 57-58.

51 Kathleen Philipps, "Hospitality and Emerging Populations: Toward a Theology of Migration in the Context of the Catholic Church in the United States" *Doctoral Thesis* (Toronto, University of St. Michael's College of Theology: 2015), 130.

52 *Ibid.* 131-132.

53 Donal Kerwin & Jill Marie Gerschutz, *And you Welcomed Me: Migration and Catholic Social Teaching* (Lanham: Lexington Books: 2009), 149.

Jesus' Identity as the Migrant Messiah: Towards the Hermeneutics of Solidarity

The term "solidarity" has its roots in the Roman law of obligations. *Solidum* in Latin is an obligation to an unlimited responsibility of each individual member within a family or other community to pay common debts.[54] The concept, "solidarity" is used by different people in different ways in different contexts and it has manifold meanings. The broadest of these meanings, is that of "connection" or "cohesion." It also corresponds to the etymological source of the word, which is the Latin "solidus." Indeed, "solidarity" or "social solidarity" is often understood, particularly by sociologists, in the general sense of "social cohesion."[55] "Solidarity" is often used in social psychology in the sense of a "feeling of belonging together," "good relations," "sympathy," or "altruism."[56] Leroux calls "True love" and "harmony and identity of (hu)mankind with (hu)man are "solidarite."[57] Karl Barth, a reformed theologian, in a section of the *Church Dogmatics* entitled *Die Nahen und die Femen*, translated a "Near and Distant Neighbors," gives a bold exploration of the Word of God that transformed his life. Barth asserts that the command of God directs people towards their fellow human beings, to "affirm, honor, and enjoy" them.[58] Barth suggests, that the alien members of other people are only relatively alien because they are fellow human beings, partnering human beings before God the Creator. Christ reaches out to all those considered, "alien life." Christ did not move away from alienation, difference, and otherness but towards it. God's identification with humanity is so total that in Christ, God not only reaches out to the stranger but becomes the stranger. Karl Barth recognizes the Incarnation as "the way of a Son of God into the far country."[59]

Daniel Groody states that no aspect of a theology of migration is more fundamental and more challenging in its implication than the Incarnation. Groody adds like Karl Barth, "God migrates into a world that is poor and divided, not because God finds something good about poverty and estrangement, but because it is precisely in history's darkest place that God can reveal hope to all who experience pain, rejection and alienation."[60]

Latino Christians and theologians confess that Jesus Christ is a migrant in two ways: the resurrected Christ can be called migrant because of his presence and

54 Kurt Bayertz, "Four Uses of "Solidarity" in *Solidarity,* edited by Kurt Bayertz (Boston: Kluwer Academic Publishers: 1999), 3.

55 *Ibid.* 216.

56 *Ibid.*

57 *Ibid.* 212.

58 Robert W. Heimburger, *God and the Illegal Alien: United States Immigration Law and a Theology of Politics* (Cambridge: Cambridge University Press: 2018), 46.

59 Karl Barth, *Church Dogmatics*, Vol. 4.1 (Edinburgh: T&T Clark International: 1956), 157.

60 Daniel G. Groody, "Crossing the Divide: Foundations of a Theology of Migration and Refugees," *Theological Studies,* vol. 70, no. 3 (2009), 649-50.

solidarity with migrants in their search for hospitality and justice. The other way is to articulate on "migratory and hospitality paradigm" as key in understanding Jesus' identity and work as the Christ.[61]

God becomes migrant in the form of Messiah. Donald Senior asserts that, Jesus begins his earthly journey as a migrant and a displaced person. It has to be noted that when Joseph and Mary were not welcomed, they were unable to find a place to stay and manger becomes Jesus' birth place. They had to leave their own homeland Bethlehem with baby Jesus and arrived in foreign land Egypt as international migrants. There were refugees in Egypt. When Jesus' family returned from Egypt to their homeland, found that Herod's son was ruling over Judea, the family "withdrew to the district of Galilee, and lived in a town called Nazareth" as internal migrant (2.21-23).[62]

While Christians were to regard hospitality as a fundamental expression of the gospel, they were also asked by Jesus to become strangers. Jesus instructs disciples to go without money, extra clothes, or even any shoes and proclaim his arrival to those in the surrounding towns. Jesus did not stop there. He told them to stay in the homes of those who receive them as longs as they will have them. It is very clear in Jesus' instruction that his people should go as strangers in need of hospitality as they proclaim the good news of the kingdom. The disciples are in a state of dependence on the hospitality of those they are visiting. Jesus wants them to stay with the hosts, eat what they provide and enter into the lives of everyday people in a way that would foster true relationship. This is the Shalom of God which Jesus wants his people to proclaim. (Lk. 10:1-12).[63]

Welcoming the stranger shows that taking the person into one's commonality. Jesus who lived both as international and internal migrant teaches the importance of solidarity in other words "true love." When people suffer identity crisis, the faith community needs come forward to welcome them and allow them to feel belonging to the group that in turn would help migrants to recover their sense of belongingness.

God the Holy Spirit: The Push and the Pull of Migration: Towards the Hermeneutics of Hope

God chose to dwell among us through the Incarnation of Jesus Christ and God continuous to dwell among us through God's Spirit. The Bible depicts Holy Spirit

61 Luis R. Rivera, "El Cristo Migrant/The Migrant Christ" in *Jesus in the Hispanic Community: Images of Christ from Theology to Popular Religion*, edited by Harold J. Recinos & Hugo Magallanes (Louisville, Westminster: John Knox Press: 2009), 144.

62 Paul Hertig, "Jesus' Migrations and Liminal Withdrawals in Matthew" in *God's People on the Move: Biblical and Global Perspectives on Migration and Mission*, edited by Harold J. Recinos & Hugo Magallanes (Eugene: Pickwick Publications: 2014), 49.

63 Craig S. Hendrickson, "Displacement: A Missional Theology of Place for the North American Church," *In God's People on the Move*..., 113.

in various images, such as fire, wind, breath, life, power, energy, spirit, gift, grace and love. All these images are on the move, they don't belong to one particular person or place. Consequently, on the one hand, Christian theology of the Holy Spirit highlights the Spirit's activities on the move constantly within the Trinity and within the doctrine of salvation. On the other the Holy Spirit pushes people to move to save lives and establish Kingdom of God and pulls people to receive liberation in the Kingdom of God. "In this sense the Holy Spirit may be said to be the "push" and "pull" of the kingdom of God."[64]

The low wages and the high rate of the unemployment in the sending countries "push" their people to migrate, while the countries, normally the developed ones "pull" people with better pay and providing employment opportunities. From the Christian perspective, the Holy Spirit plays a role in on the one hand to "push" the migrants out of their poverty and inhuman living conditions and inspiring them with courage and power to find a better life for themselves and their families. On the other hand, the Holy Spirit acts to "pull" the migrants toward its final goal in search of life in fullness with dignity.[65] To be a migrant is to be on the move, and one of the most fundamental virtues required of people on the move is either to provide better life or to receive better life. Missionary movements all over the world witness to this "push" and "pull" power of the Holy Spirit.

This is a faith journey. In this faith journey of migration, T. Aechtner says, that the power of the Holy Spirit bonded Africans together in Canada, and he says, congregants professed that the church operated as spiritual family, which provided new brothers, sister, mothers, and fathers for those in the diaspora.[66] By the push and pull power of the Holy Spirit, people carried the vision of Jesus and migrated to India from different parts of the world and proclaimed Gospel of equality and dignity.

Implications

The UN General Assembly held at New York in 2006 has focused on high level dialogue on International Migration and Development. And the following year Global Forum on Migration and Development was held in Brussel.[67] In these Conferences, participants, in general, agreed that migration holds considerable

64 Peter C. Phan, "Embracing, Protecting, and Loving the Stranger" in *Theology of Migration in the Abrahamic Religions,* edited by E. Padilla and P. Phan (Palgrave Macmillan, 2014), 103.

65 *Ibid.*

66 *Ibid.*

67 See High Level Dialogue on International Migration and Development, United Nations Assembly, 14-15 September, 2006 in the website, *www.un.org* › ... › Population Division › International Migration and Development; See Belgium, GFMD 2007, First Meeting of the Global Forum on Migration and Development, *https://gfmd.org/meetings/belgium2007* (accessed on April 4.2018).

potential for economic and social development.[68] Migration is a global phenomenon. Together the migrants would constitute roughly the equivalent of the population of Brazil, the fifth largest country on earth.[69] People migrate for various reasons. Whatever may be the reasons, migrants face death, identity crisis, uncertainties, violence, and harsh treatment at some time in their new areas of settlement. However, a few migrants withstand the hurdles, and try to resolve the identity crisis in the given space and they move towards an identity that is achieved and recognized and respected. But this is not the case with the majority.

The first implication here is for the church in India: From the very beginning church has been the multi-cultural and multi-lingual. The church has been established on the command, "Therefore go and make disciples of all nations, baptizing them in the name of the Father and of the Son and of the Holy Spirit" (Matt 28:19), is a clear indication that Church is a migrant church and has embraced diversity. Theology of migration reflects in way of searching for insights into questions of their identity and what God means to them. Internal migrants in India need a platform to deal with these questions. It is the church that can provide platform for the migrants to come together and search for their identity in God who prefers migrants and who identifies with them; Church needs to engage with this developing migratory context in depth as the biblical mandate is to look after the foreigners and aliens.

The second implication of this study is for the theological institutions in India: More research on the theology of migration is needed. Theologians should begin to construct theological methodologies from the perspective of the migrants which a serious need in India today. It is highly essential to articulate relevant theology as migration becomes a valuable sign of the times which no longer theological institutions can ignore.

Recommendations

Indian church can establish a migration desk through which, the church can reach out to migrants in providing them a platform to be included in the Kingdom of God.

1. Theological institutions should include extensively migration studies in the curriculum. This would help people understand the intensity of the context of migration.
2. Church and the theological institutions should prepare liturgy that includes the struggles of migrants.

68 International Organization for Migration, *World Migration 2008*: 1.

69 Daniel G. Groody, "Crossing the Divide: Foundations of a Theology of Migration and Refugees," in *Theological Studies* 70 (2009): 637.

3. One Sunday can be set up as Migrant Sunday that would empower the congregations and individuals to understand their responsibility towards migrants.
4. Inclusive liturgy for Migrants can be prepared.

Conclusion

Migrants are people created by God with full potential. The time has come to listen to the voices of migrants and recognize the need for more serious theological engagement on migration. For migration as a sign of the times help us understand that migration is widespread and migrants are under identity crisis. There is a necessity to articulate the identity of the God of the Bible as a migrant God who expects hospitality, solidarity and provide a habitat for the strangers. God identifies Godself with the strangers. The Holy Spirit fills the people with her power to love and invite migrants into the Kingdom of God. Hence, there is a great challenge to ecclesiology and theology that calls the church to understand the significance of migration and provide space to migrants to deal with their identity crisis and to connect themselves to God and to God's community.

Contributors

Prof. Bernard D' Sami is a Senior Fellow at Loyola Institute of Social Science Training and Research (LISSTAR) in Loyola College (autonomous), Chennai. *bernarddsami@gmail.com*

Rev. Livingstone Arputharaj is Assistant Professor and Registrar of Gurukul Lutheran Theological College & Research Institute. He teach in the Department of Christian Ministry. *amlivingstone@gmail.com*

Rev. Nagaiyasamy N.S. Samuel is an ordained minister of TELC (Tranquebar Mission) and currently serving as an Assistant Professor in the Department of Old Testament, Gurukul Lutheran Theological College & Research Institute. He is also pursuing his Doctoral Studies at Pondicherry University. *nagaiya@gmail.com*

Fr. S. Jaganathan served Gurukul Lutheran Theological College & Research Institute as an Associate Professor in the Department of Old Testament until May 2018. *jaganathansusai@gmail.com*

Rev. Dr. K. Balakrishnan served Gurukul Lutheran Theological College & Research Institute as an Assistant Professor in the Department of New Testament until May 2018. *balan_8k@yahoo.co.in*

Rev. Dr. K. David Udayakumar served Gurukul Lutheran Theological College & Research Institute as a Professor and Head of the Department of Missiology as well as Principal until May 2018. Currently, he is serving as Principal at Master's College of Theology, Vishakhapatnam. *kdavidudayakumar@gmail.com*

Rev. J.M.P. Thomas Birla is Assistant Professor and Dean of the BCS Programme at Gurukul Lutheran Theological College & Research Institute. He teaches in the Department of Religion. *birla27@gmail.com*

Rev. Anthony Jeevaraj is Assistant Professor in the Department of Religion, Gurukul Lutheran Theological College & Research Institute. *mail2jeevaraj@gmail.com*

Dr. W.S. Annie serves as an Assistant Professor at Gurukul Lutheran Theological College & Research Institute, Chennai. She teach in the Department of Christian Theology and Women Studies. *anniews1@yahoo.co.in*

(Late) Dr. Walotemjen served as an Associate Professor and Head of the Department of History of Christianity in Gurukul Lutheran Theological College & Research Institute, Chennai. He passed away on 15th July 2018.

Rev. Dr. J. Daniel Kirubaraj is Professor and Head of the Department of Communication, Gurukul Lutheran Theological College & Research Institute. *daniel4uin@yahoo.co.in*

Rev. Dr. Nelavala Gnana Prasuna serves as an Assistant Professor at Gurukul Lutheran Theological College & Research Institute, Chennai. She teach in the Department of Christian Theology and Women Studies. *prasuna_gnana@yahoo.co.in*